DATE DUE

Wildlife Research and
Management in the National Parks

Wildlife Research and Management in the National Parks

R. Gerald Wright

University of Illinois Press
Urbana and Chicago

This book is printed on acid-free paper.

Library of Congress Cataloging-in-Publication Data

Wright, R. Gerald.
    Wildlife research and management in the national parks / R. Gerald
    Wright.
        p.   cm.
    Includes bibliographical references and index.
    ISBN 0-252-01824-9 (cl). — ISBN 0-252-06195-0 (pb)
    1. National parks and reserves—United States—Management.
2. Wildlife management—United States.   3. Wildlife conservation—
United States.   4. National parks and reserves—Government policy—
United States.   5. United States.   National Park Service.
6. Yellowstone National Park.   I. Title.
SB482.A4W75   1992
639.9'0973—dc20   91–28602
                                                            CIP

Contents

Illustrations follow page 110

Preface

National Parks occupy a special place in the hearts of most Americans. The policies governing the management of park natural resources, particularly animal life, are, however, unclear to most people. I long ago recognized that the "average" visitor typically does not make a distinction between native and nonnative animals, does not understand why animals should not be fed, even in times of great stress, often fails to believe that even benign animals can be dangerous, and clearly does not understand the concept that animal populations in parks should be, where possible, naturally regulated. Although these misunderstandings bespoke the need for greater efforts to educate park visitors, they did not trouble me.

However, when I transferred to the University of Idaho's Wildlife Resource Department as part of a National Park Service Cooperative Unit and became involved in undergraduate and graduate education, I soon found that lack of knowledge and misunderstanding of National Park Service animal-management policies was not limited to the average park visitor. I gradually realized that a major reason for this was that existing NPS management policies and the historical background for them was poorly documented, primarily in obscure government publications.

In response to students' pleas for more information on NPS policy and management actions, I began compiling the information contained in this book. Chances are, however, that it would have gone no further than an informal set of lecture notes were it not for the award of a 1985 Herbert E. Kahler Research Fellowship from the Eastern National Park and Monument Association. The funds provided the opportunity to travel to various parks and libraries and to interview several individuals. More than that, they provided the incentive to continue this project, and for that I am ever grateful. Without that support, this book would not have been completed.

Still, it was a struggle. Not endorsed by the NPS, travel was deferred to annual leave and writing was left to late nights and weekends, and despite the constant support of my wife, Harley, it seemed at times to be a never-ending task. A trip to Glenwood, New Mexico, in May 1987 to interview Lowell Sumner provided the incentive I needed. Lowell and his wife, Marietta, could not have been more gracious in allowing two strangers, my wife and myself, to visit with them. Lowell, from the unique perspective of a career ranging from the time of George Wright in the thirties to the renewed increases in research of the midsixties, provided many invaluable insights into the formation and development of the Park Service science program. However, beyond that, he convinced me that the endeavor was extremely worthwhile—the story needed telling. My wife and I left the Sumners' home with a unique feeling of warmth and I with a new sense of commitment, excitement, and devotion. Sadly, Lowell passed away in October 1989. It was a privilege to know him, however briefly, and to his memory I dedicate this book.

Many people have reviewed all or portions of the manuscript; their suggestions have been invaluable—correcting areas of fact and interpretation. Jim Larson, Richard Sellars, Paul Schullery, Lowell Sumner, Philip Tanimoto, and Harley Wright reviewed the entire manuscript. Walt Kittams, Bob Linn, Coleman Newman, Gorden Olsen, Bob Wasem, and Ro Wauer reviewed the first two chapters. Maurice Hornocker, Kathy Jope, Kate Kendall, Cliff Martinka, and John Dalle-Molle reviewed the chapter on bear management. Glen Cole, Neil Guse, Doug Houston, Mary Meagher, Dale Miquelle, and Jim Peek reviewed the chapter on wolf reintroduction and Chuck Stone the chapter on alien species. Becky Standard gave the manuscript the professional editing it badly needed and suggested many changes to contribute to its readability. Frances Cassirer, Norma Craig, Roger Hoffman, Doug Houston, Kathy Jope, Bob Krumenaker, Mary Meagher, Philip Tanimoto, and the Glacier Park Museum helped supply the photographs. Many, many other individuals, too numerous to mention, provided valuable insights and access to park records and libraries. To all I give my thanks.

Introduction

National parks are one of the most revered institutions in America and are a vacation destination for millions of people each year. There are numerous books describing the physical splendors or the enormous opportunities for visitors that national parks offer but few discussing their contributions to scientific study. This book, however, focuses on the important role they have played in the protection, management, and sometimes mismanagement of the wild animals that live in the parks. The history of animal management in national parks has been inexorably linked with the evolution of a program of scientific study in the agency that manages the parks, the National Park Service (NPS). Thus, in a true sense, this book is the story of science in the national parks.

National parks play an extremely important role in the preservation of many species of animals. It has been estimated that between one-third and one-half of the rare and endangered species in the United States live within the national park system. Because animal life is protected in parks, densities of most species are higher than on other public lands and it is easier to see them. National parks have thus become renowned for opportunities to view animals in a natural setting, and observing animal life is a major reason people visit parks.

The park visitor is the NPS's most important constituency, park resources its sacred trust. The dilemma of how to satisfy the often conflicting requirements of protecting the natural and cultural resources of parks while providing for the needs of the visitor has plagued the Park Service since its inception.[1] This task was made more difficult by the almost continuous and sometimes explosive growth in park visitation. Although the parks suffered at times from overly ambitious development plans and misguided resource-management strategies, and most of the time fiscal restrictions severely limited needed research and management, the resources of the parks have so far survived.

Today, the NPS still fights the battle of use versus preservation. Fiscal restraints still limit needed research, resource management, maintenance, and development. However, the national parks are also confronted with much larger concerns. Unlike problems of old, many of these new problems, such as air and water pollution, acid rain, and pesticide contamination, may originate far beyond park boundaries and are thus difficult to control and regulate. Parks are also no longer insulated from external harm by surrounding undeveloped lands since these lands are being altered through development and their resources extracted.[2]

Today more than ever, NPS needs the expertise and guidance provided by a strong science program to inventory and monitor park resources to help counter assaults on these resources. In undertaking this program, the NPS is hindered by the legacy of its past neglect of science. This has resulted in a paucity of knowledge about many park resources, in little continuity in past programs undertaken to monitor environmental conditions, and in an inadequate scientific infrastructure.

This book explores the role that science has played in the management of national parks, specifically of its animals. At times, neglect of scientific study has caused serious management problems. Likewise, there have been periods when science flourished and scientific thought had a significant influence on management policies. Throughout the history of the parks, scientists and resource managers have had to understand and cope with many unique aspects of animal behavior and activity for which little precedent existed, including the development of techniques to manage bear-visitor conflicts, to control alien species, and to manage ungulate populations, which are limited not by hunters but by environmental conditions. The successes and failures of these programs are an important part of the legacy NPS scientists have contributed to the scientific community.

However, one park clearly has had a dominate influence on that legacy—Yellowstone—the oldest and the largest park for many years. Even today Yellowstone remains in most people's minds the premier national park—the flagship of the system. Resource problems there have always assumed a greater importance, received greater scrutiny, and have had the potential for greater controversy. This fact was made undeniably clear in the national press coverage devoted to the fires that burned in the park in the summer of 1988. Events at Yellowstone helped to define many of the resource-management policies of the national parks and established the framework for the administrative structure of the NPS.

The Influence of Yellowstone

In the late 1800s many of the federal lands in the West were lost through theft or destroyed by overuse. These abuses spawned a small but powerful conservation movement. Within that community, there was general consensus over the urgent need to protect federal lands in the West, but there were also strong ideological divisions within the movement over how to manage these lands (Swain 1969). Not unlike today, advocates of strict protection of land resources faced arguments from those who believed that this tactic would lock up potentially valuable resources and would be detrimental to the economic growth of the country. Yellowstone was established in the midst of this controversy. Primary support for the establishment of the park came from prominent eastern sports enthusiasts, such as George Grinnell, editor of the conservation-oriented magazine *Forest and Stream* in the 1880s. Detractors ranged from those who saw potential mineral wealth in the region to those who maintained no one would ever go there.

At the time Yellowstone was established there was no model for what a national park should be. The concept most supporters had in mind was probably similar to English and American game preserves that, while designed to conserve wildlife, allowed for "gentlemanly hunting" and for management activities that met this objective (Haines 1977). At the turn of the century, there were some five hundred of these wildlife preserves in the United States. Most were maintained as private sport-hunting clubs, although on others wildlife was strictly protected, and the preserves provided a means of replenishing depleted game stocks on adjacent areas (Palmer 1912). Grinnell's appeal to western sports enthusiasts to support national parks because they would provide a reservoir of game animals that would disperse outside the park and therefore be available to hunters indicates he supported this concept (Grinnell and Storer 1916).

This idea combined with the fact that wildlife preservation had little public support was probably the main reason animal protection was not an issue in the debates over the establishment of the park or in the 1872 Yellowstone Park Act itself. Yellowstone was established primarily to preserve the unique scenic wonders of the region, including the great geyser basins and the Grand Canyon of the Yellowstone River. The act provided only for the preservation "of all timber, mineral deposits, natural curiosities, or wonders within said park" (72).

The general lack of concern for the welfare of animal life at the time was commonplace. It was a utilitarian age, and there was no precedent for the absolute protection of animals. The harvest of animals was seen as necessary for food, clothing, or marketable goods. The Yellowstone Act prohibited only the wanton destruction of fish and game or their capture for profit. Hunting, trapping, and fishing in the park was otherwise permitted for recreation or to supply food for visitors or park residents.[3] The Senate gave the secretary of the interior the authority but not the legal power to regulate all unreasonable destruction of fish and game (Ise 1961). Whether this action was simply an oversight or a purposeful curtailment of authority is hard to determine. The fact remained, however, that authorities in Yellowstone had no means to control the killing of animals in the park. The harvest of big-game animals in the park by commercial hunters, particularly elk and bison,[4] soon turned into an outright slaughter (Reiger 1975). In the winter of 1875, over four thousand elk were reportedly killed solely for their hides in the Mammoth Hot Springs Basin alone (Strong 1875). Hundreds of bighorn sheep, mule deer, antelope, moose, and bison were also reported to have been killed. During this time, game animals were also routinely killed to feed hotel guests (Hampton 1971).

For the first twenty-two years of the existence of Yellowstone, park and national authorities, such as the secretary of the interior and concerned senators, fought a continuous and unsuccessful battle to stop the killing of game animals in the park. In many respects the situation at Yellowstone paralleled events in other parts of the nation. For example, the lack of effective game laws was also driving the white-tailed deer close to extinction in the East. What set Yellowstone apart was only that game animals were more concentrated and more numerous.

Events reached such a critical stage in 1879 that Yellowstone superintendent Norris proposed saving animals from harvest by turning part of the Lamar Valley into a game preserve where livestock managers could protect and gradually domesticate them (Haines 1977). This proposal resulted in the employment of Harry Yount as a park gamekeeper for one year in 1880, after which he resigned in frustration over the impossibility of his task.

Secretary of the Interior Carl Schurz finally issued regulations in 1883 prohibiting all hunting and killing of game in the park. However, like other regulations in the park, there was no punishment for breaking the rules. Legally, poachers caught in the act faced only confiscation of equipment and expulsion from the park.

An 1883 law gave the secretary of the interior the authority, if needed, to ask the secretary of war to provide troops to police Yellowstone. In 1884, Congress failed to make an appropriation for the park. It has been speculated that Congress did this to force the military to take control of Yellowstone, thus assuring better protection (Kasten 1966). Secretary of the Interior Lamar therefore requested that army troops be stationed to protect the resources and to administer the park. The first detachment of cavalry arrived in August 1886, and Captain Moses Harris assumed the duties of acting park superintendent. The army remained in control of the park until 1918.[5]

The military had the regimentation and personnel needed to bring order to the chaos that characterized the existing park administration. The military superintendents in general had a strong commitment to animal protection, although their allegiances to different species varied considerably, and as a result policies were often inconsistent.[6] The insights they brought to the management of the park helped set the groundwork for future policies. For example, in 1886 Acting Superintendent Harris foresaw the concept of natural regulation when he advocated that "it is not the policy of the government to endeavor to make this park attractive by making it a collection of domesticated animals, but rather to preserve the reservation in its natural condition and to protect the existing game animals so that they may breed in security" (Hampton 1971:91).

More specifically, the military set policies limiting the cutting of green timber and the removal or displacement of any mineral deposits, prohibited hunting and trapping or the discharge of firearms, set regulations for fishing, set up a system to fight fires, limited stock use, and established programs for feeding certain species of wildlife and for eliminating predators. Military orders directed camping parties to build fires only when actually necessary; prohibited visitors from throwing rocks, sticks, etc. into springs or geysers; and sought to assure that employees of the park did not maltreat visitors (Haines 1977). Use and resource protection enacted during its early years subsequently laid the foundation for future policies of all parks.

The military used a number of methods to protect park animals. Rifles were sealed whenever they were brought into the park and checked again when they were taken out. No Hunting signs were posted along the park roads. A system of outposts and patrols were extended over the most heavily used roads and best game ranges. Still, deterrent punishment for game-law violators was lacking. Six times between 1883 and 1890 Senator Vest of Missouri unsuccessfully introduced bills in Congress that would have made hunting in the park illegal and violators subject to punishment.

The continued slaughter of the dwindling numbers of bison in Yellowstone finally provided a catalyst for congressional action. By the mid-1890s the bison in Yellowstone were essentially the only animals of this species living in a wild state, and they numbered less that one hundred (Hague 1893). Emerson Hough, a writer, and F. J. Haynes, a photographer for *Forest and Stream,* happened to be in the park when Ed Howell, a major buffalo poacher, was arrested. Hough's account so inflamed the public that a bill protecting Yellowstone wildlife was introduced in Congress only thirteen days after the poacher had been caught.[7] In 1894, Congress passed HR 6442 "to protect the birds and animals in Yellowstone National Park, and to punish crimes in said park, and for other purposes" (78). This legislation, known as the Lacey Act, was revolutionary for its time, and made it illegal to carry firearms in the park and prohibited, subject to fine and imprisonment, "all hunting or the killing, wounding, or capturing at any time of any bird or wild animal except dangerous animals when it is necessary to prevent them from destroying human life or inflicting an injury" (78). Providing for a maximum of two years' imprisonment and a $1,000 fine for the killing of game, the law gave the army the necessary legal power to curb poaching activity. Acting Superintendent Anderson called Howell's action the most fortunate thing that ever happened to the park, while Howell told Anderson, "I have done more for the good of the park than you ever have" (Joffe 1941:9).

With the passage of the Lacey Act, the harvest of wildlife in Yellowstone greatly declined. Poaching continued, however, for there still remained old-time hunters in the surrounding communities who disdained game laws and there were occasional soldiers who also killed game (Kasten 1966). Because taxidermists were paying $300-$500 each for bison head and $5 for a pair of elk tusks and because the risk of capture was low, the incentive to poach wildlife remained high. Over time, however, even these incentives began to lessen as local communities began to support game protection, partly because of the growing economic benefits from the increasing influx of visitors to Yellowstone after 1900.

Military occupation and the active interest the military commanders took in resource management played key roles in protecting Yellowstone and assuring its status as a great game refuge. It most certainly prevented the extinction of the bison (Hampton 1971), and the reestablishment of bison in Yellowstone was probably one of the greatest conservation achievements of the military occupation. A 1902 census of the Yellowstone bison herd counted only twenty-three animals,[8] a decrease from an estimated one thousand that inhabited the park when it was established. Shocked by this census, Congress appropriated $15,000 to help reestablish a Yellowstone bison herd. Twenty-one animals were purchased from herds in Texas and Montana and placed in fenced pastures in the park, where they were managed for many years as domestic livestock (see chapter 5). These animals along with the remaining wild stock formed the basis for the bison herds that inhabit the park today.

The advancements and policies initiated by the military led to the development of the national park system and the National Park Service. The military brought in a proven command structure based on line authority. The acting military superintendent was the boss in the park and ultimately responsible for all decisions and actions. This administrative structure was very effective in enforcing the rules and regulations of the secretary of the interior and the provisions of the Yellowstone Park Act (Henneberger 1965), so it was natural for the NPS to adopt it. In addition, the new NPS inherited a number of individuals who were very familiar with that system. For example, when the military left Yellowstone in 1918, twenty-two soldiers were discharged from the army to form the basis of the permanent ranger force. These early rangers can be generally characterized as an extremely dedicated and competent group. In subsequent years, many of these former soldiers spread throughout the expanding park system, carrying with them the philosophy and training acquired at Yellowstone.

NOTES

1. The origin of this dilemma is the Organic Act, which established the National Park Service. It mandates the NPS to preserve the resources of the parks while at the same time making them available for public use and enjoyment.

2. Although this situation is commonly perceived as only being a problem in major parks such as Olympic, which is surrounded by timber clear-cuts, it is nowhere more apparent than around eastern Civil War parks, which are being encroached on by housing developments, shopping malls, and the like.

3. There were debates in the Senate over this provision in the bill and whether there instead should be a clause to prohibit all game killing in the park. These provisions did not pass in part because it was believed that visitors and residents would require fish and game for sustenance.

4. The scientific names for all species are found in the Appendix.

5. Between 1887 and 1901 the army had complete charge of the park; between 1902 and 1917 it was under the supervision of the secretary of the interior. The severity of resource protection problems in the Sierra parks also became so acute that they, like Yellowstone, used military troops to protect the resources.

6. Acting Superintendent Harris, for example, advocated the protection of all animals, even predators, stating that "more injury would result to the game from the use of firearms or traps in the park than from any ravages which may be feared from carnivorous animals" (Haines 1977:80). Later superintendents reversed this policy and initiated large-scale predator control programs. The inconsistencies were not unique to Yellowstone. For example, in Sequoia Acting Military Superintendent Dorst sought to enlarge the park to protect game, while Acting Military Superintendent Hughes concluded that animals such as the bear were not essential and should be exterminated.

7. Hough's account of the capture was accompanied by Haynes's photos (Hough 1874) and was reprinted in Schullery (1979).

8. Considering bison habits, behavior, and the difficulties in counting them, Meagher (1973) estimated that perhaps forty to fifty animals survived in the park at that time.

1

The Early Years of the National Park Service

In 1900 there were fourteen national parks, monuments, and military parks in the United States administered by the Departments of Interior, Agriculture, and War. Each agency had its own idea of how to manage a park. Some areas were neglected because of isolation and budget restrictions. Others were managed in a utilitarian manner, e.g., for timber and grazing. Still others received intense, and by present standards, enlightened management. For example, a very detailed reforestation plan was developed and carried out at Gettysburg to recreate the scene as it existed during the battle (Kempton 1903). The lack of uniform management policies in parks and monuments spurred efforts to create a central bureau to manage all areas. An active campaign for a national park bureau was begun in 1910, led by Horace McFarland of the American Civic Association. This campaign gathered added momentum with the establishment of thirty-five additional parks and monuments (ranging from 17-acre Tumacacori in Arizona to 1.01-million-acre Glacier between 1902 and 1916. This increase was enhanced by the passage of the Antiquities Act in 1906, which provided protection to archaeological and scientific objects and granted authority to the president to establish national monuments by executive order.

Congress finally passed the National Park Service Act creating NPS in 1916. The 1916 act stipulated that the role of the new agency was "to conserve the scenery and the natural and historic objects and the *wildlife* therein and to provide for the enjoyment of the same in such manner and by such means as will leave them unimpaired for the enjoyment of future generations" (NPS 1988:1). All of the parks and monuments in the Department of the Interior were placed under the NPS, while monuments in the Department of Agriculture were gradually transferred to the NPS.

In the early years, the limited NPS personnel was kept preoccupied with efforts to keep the seventeen national parks and twenty-eight national monuments intact and to fend off the continual demands of special interests to eliminate or exploit them. Park protection was made more difficult by the U.S. entry into World War I only eight months after the Park Service was formed. Many individuals, both in disguised attempts to exploit the parks and in patriotic support of the country, felt that the resources in the parks should be used for the war effort. There were demands for grazing permits by western cattle and sheep owners ostensibly to increase food production for the army (Sherfy 1978). Ranchers requested the right to graze fifty thousand sheep in Yosemite; the Oregon wool growers applied for permits at Crater Lake, and there were similar proposals for Glacier and Mt. Rainier.[1] World War I was an encouragement not just to ranchers but to all who sought to exploit parks. There were demands on parks to harvest fish and game for food, and in general it was considered to be a time "not to worry about the flowers and wild animals" in the parks (Shankland 1970:205). Though the NPS could effectively counter all of these demands, the parks were threatened because of insufficient wartime staffing.

In retrospect, that the NPS with its relatively inexperienced leaders survived the financial and political pressures of its initial years was a testament to the combination of political skill, ability to compromise, and adherence to principle displayed by its first director and assistant director, Stephen Mather and Horace Albright. Their actions helped establish the character of the agency (Sherfy 1978). The early assaults convinced Mather of the need to put the parks on a more solid footing secure against future threats. He quickly recognized that one of the best ways to bring national parks into the public consciousness was to increase park visitation. This became his principal goal throughout his tenure as director, and he was brilliantly successful at it. He worked with tour companies, the railroads, and park concessionaires in an effort to publicize the beauty of parks and thus attract visitors. Mather also recognized that park animals were important in luring visitors. Unfortunately, many species of animals in the major parks had been depleted due to excessive harvests prior to park establishment or were difficult to see because of poor access into remote sections of the parks. He encouraged parks to set up fenced animal viewing areas where species typical of the park could be seen at close range. The Park Service's efforts to secure a broad base of support were largely successful because of these changes.[2]

To administer the parks, the NPS adopted the hierarchical structure successfully used by the military in Yellowstone and Sequoia. In a given park the superintendent, like the military commander, was the boss, whose interpretation of policies was accepted without question. Mather quickly asserted his authority over the Park Service by establishing a small and efficient agency. His goal was to maximize the use of personnel in other federal agencies, such as the Biological Survey and Bureau of Fisheries, for technical assistance (Shankland 1970). Many of the existing park managers, who were political appointees, were replaced. Horace Albright was transferred to run Yellowstone in 1919, Arno Cammerer was hired as assistant director, and a small but efficient Washington office was developed. Mather set the tone for the NPS administration in his belief that the Park Service could operate best with minimal interference from the Washington office (Shankland 1970). Rangers held a prominent role in the administrative structure of the new park service. Haines (1977) characterized the early park rangers as practical men with less education and more experience than their present-day counterparts. They showed an esprit de corps that became an NPS trait and pride in their ability to do whatever was required.

The legacy of this trait has dominated park administration even to the present era of specialization. The ranger corps has created a powerful positive image that has always produced much public support for the agency, though some rangers believe that only they represent the true values of the NPS. Most superintendents came from the ranger corps and continued this feeling of superiority.

During the first two decades, park managers concentrated on preserving and protecting spectacular resources and on developing visitor accommodations. Natural resources received little management or scientific attention in most parks.[3] Although Mather encouraged the general use of parks as fields for scientific study, no individuals were employed for this purpose, and historical records indicate that little natural-resource research was conducted. This is not surprising, for few individuals in the agency had any biological training. For help in dealing with resource-management problems, Mather, in keeping with his philosophy, turned to nationally prominent conservation organizations such as the Campfire Club of America, the Boone and Crockett Club, and the American Game Protective Association. Mather also used the services of the Bureau of the Biological Survey to direct predator control programs in various parks.

The first explicit attempt to begin to gain an understanding of wildlife in the parks came during the early twenties when Albright requested parks to begin conducting spring and fall game counts and to document the habits of animals. These counts continued for several years, and summaries of this work for each park were contained in the regular superintendent reports to the director. These reports were generally nontechnical, often proclaiming the abundance of wildlife in the parks and listing the numbers of predators killed. Considering the techniques employed and the training of the investigators, the accuracy of most of these accounts is questionable.

Yellowstone was an exception in its ability to maintain a program of scientific research. For several years, trained biologists working through the Roosevelt Wild Life Experiment Station, established in 1921 under the direction of C. C. Adams and based out of Syracuse University, conducted and published scientific studies. These papers were among the earliest publications offering ideas and policies on wildlife management in the national parks. Reasonable prices placed on the books and brochures resulted in their wide distribution to park visitors. The station also attempted to institute a summer school for field biologists in the park that failed due to funding problems. The experiment station itself lasted for about a decade before it too was closed because of funding problems and personnel changes. Although it provided a good model for the organization of scientific study in a park, it would be many years before a similar program would be undertaken.

The Development of Science Administration in the Park Service

When Albright assumed the directorship following Mather's retirement in 1929, he philosophically held many of the same opinions as his predecessor and therefore made few initial organizational changes. However, he did effect a more subtle change in his administration by depending less on personal relationships and more on structure. As a result, more authority was delegated to staff, something Mather had been unable or unwilling to do (Unrau and Williss 1983).

The stability that came from having a secure and recognized place in American society allowed the Park Service by 1930 to turn inward and begin to develop and strengthen visitor-use programs and learn more about park resources. Although limited campfire programs for visitors had been in existence for several years, their content was generally superficial and often limited by the lack of in-depth information about park resources. Even by 1930 there were few positions in the

Park Service devoted to the collection of resource data. NPS had only one research scientist (William Rush, who was appointed in 1928 to study large mammals in Yellowstone) and only nine wildlife rangers and six naturalists for seventy-four parks and monuments. The wildlife rangers were assigned many duties, and none (except for the Yellowstone bison keeper) were able to spend more than a small amount of time on wildlife projects (Cahalane, Presnall, and Beard 1940). The role of the existing staff of naturalists was primarily to educate visitors. Though many of them were trained in the biological sciences, they were generally considered neither "real rangers" nor scientists, and were often ignored by park managers. This status embittered many naturalists, particularly those with extensive biological training. Skinner, a naturalist at Yellowstone and the author of several monographs on the park's wildlife, was one who was particularly critical about the lack of wildlife research (Skinner 1927). His arguments foretold what was to become a long and often frustrating battle between those who supported more research and those who did not.

Demands for individuals within the agency[4] and from influential academic scientists such as Joseph B. Grinnell urged parks to pay more attention to natural-resource research. One result was the convening of the first naturalists' conference in November 1929 at the Educational Division office in Berkeley, California. Four days of this conference were devoted to natural-resource-management subjects, including balances, predator problems, research, wildlife problems, and the protection of scientific assets from development. This conference was one of the first times natural-resource-management concerns were addressed by field personnel from throughout the NPS. An outgrowth of this conference was the reorganization of the Division of Education into the Branch of Research and Education in 1930 under the direction of Harold Bryant. This was the start of the Park Service natural-history research program. Bryant summarized the role of this branch as follows: "The intention of the Park Service in launching a research program is not to duplicate work done elsewhere nor to trespass upon fields amply covered by other Government bureaus, but solely to gather the scientific information necessary to the development of the museum, educational and wild-life administration programs of the national parks" (Bryant and Atwood 1932:40).

This viewpoint coincided with Albright's goals of limiting NPS scientific expertise and relying on other agencies for assistance. It sanctioned scientific investigation in support of park management needs but negated the role of basic research. The narrow scope of this mission was quickly criticized by the same groups that had initially pressured for the program. They argued that a broader research mission was needed to deal with the unique resource-management programs facing the parks, such as the reintroduction of animals in Yellowstone and Grand Canyon and defining the role of predators (Albright 1933). Their plea was answered, albeit indirectly, by the studies initiated by George M. Wright.

Creation of the Wildlife Division

NPS support of scientific research would probably have changed little had not George Wright, a ranger naturalist at Yosemite, taken a two-year absence without pay from his position and initiated the first program to survey the fauna of the national parks.[5] A former student of Grinnell at Berkeley, Wright hired Joseph Dixon, a noted field biologist from the university, and Ben Thompson, a recent graduate, and set up an office in Berkeley. His initial surveys took almost three years to complete. Wright was ideally suited to this role. In addition to his scientific ability he had a warm, relaxed, friendly, and persuasive personality and was on a first name basis with rangers in the backcountry as well as high officials in the administration (Sumner 1967).

Wright had little trouble justifying his program, arguing that animal life was one of the most important assets of parks, that animals were more sensitive to the threats of civilization than any other park feature, that many species were in danger, and that NPS lacked trained personnel to deal with these problems. He concluded that protection alone was not enough to preserve wildlife and that direct intervention was sometimes needed to counteract the factors threatening it. Equally important, he suggested that the prevailing practice of using non-NPS scientists from other agencies and academia had not helped solve the animal-management problems confronting park administrators. He was convinced that the only way progress could be made was if the studies were undertaken by NPS employees who were conversant with agency policies and "imbued with a devotion to its ideals" (Wright, Dixon, and Thompson 1933:5). Wright set a precedent for having scientific studies in parks conducted by NPS scientists.

In large part because of Wright's enthusiasm and ability, the fauna surveys met with wide acceptance in the parks in which they were conducted. This caused NPS to gradually integrate them into its own program and to finance them. In 1932, Congress allocated $22,500 to continue the surveys, and Wright's Berkeley office was formally established as the Wildlife Division within the Branch of Research and Education. The division was the first organizational unit in NPS responsible for planning, reviewing, and conducting biological research. It also assisted in policy development. The surveys of the Wildlife Division helped develop a concern for the welfare and well-being of wildlife within NPS (Russell 1937), and many long-term biologists have judged the division to be one of the most successful mission-oriented units ever to have existed in the organization (Smathers and Sumner 1975).

Throughout the early thirties surveys by the Wildlife Division proceeded at a rapid pace and were published in 1933 in what became known as Fauna 1 (Wright, Dixon, and Thompson 1933). Several studies of winter range conditions in western parks concluded that they were seriously depleted and that herds of deer and elk were above carrying capacity. Fauna 1 discussed at length the range conditions at Rocky Mountain and Yellowstone. While most of the management philosophies espoused in the report have proven to be wise well beyond their time, some of the specific conclusions, such as interpretations of range conditions, need cautious evaluation. The judgments of the investigators on this subject were probably unduly influenced by prevailing range-management dogma, the views of local managers, and the investigators' relative unfamiliarity with the areas in question. At the time, heavily browsed or grazed ranges were universally considered to be a sign of excess use by overabundant animal populations. Some of these judgments were probably true, but it is equally possible, as some contemporary investigators have concluded, that conditions were also the natural consequence of long-term ungulate use or were not representative of the range as a whole.

Fauna 1 essentially formulated the first park wildlife-management policies. The broader implication of the report was that it made science a necessary ingredient to proper park management. Each NPS resource technician was given a copy of Fauna 1 for use in applying the policies to problems in their respective areas, and it became "the working 'bible' for all park biologists until after World War II when it went out of print" (Sumner 1967:8). In 1935, Fauna 2 (Wright and Thompson 1935) was published and the research for Fauna 3 (Dixon 1938) was completed. Fauna 2 was divided into two parts; the first section reprinted several articles or presentations published elsewhere by George Wright and Ben Thompson. These articles discussed a land-use ethic for parks and the role that animal life should play in the scheme. The second part focused extensively on plans or actions needed in various parks to reintroduce formerly extirpated species. These ranged from bighorn sheep and Merriam's turkey in Mesa

Verde to bison in Glacier and white-tailed deer in Shenandoah. Fauna 3 described the birds and mammals of Mount McKinley, and was the first report since Skinner's at Yellowstone to detail the natural history of animals in a specific park.

The thirties was an active time for field studies and publications. During the first six years, several hundred articles and internal reports were published on wildlife in the parks. There was support for research at the highest levels.[6] Interest in natural resources during the period was also reflected in the type of new parks added to the system. For the first time several major parks were created primarily because they contained unique biological resources. Among them were Olympic (Roosevelt elk), Isle Royale (moose), and Great Smoky Mountains (climax deciduous forest), and plans were begun to preserve the Everglades (colonial nesting birds).

The growing interest in wildlife management in the national parks during this period was reflected throughout the federal government. Between 1933 and 1939 there was unprecedented federal involvement and expenditures for wildlife restoration (Cart 1973). Federal employment programs to counteract the depression, such as the Emergency Conservation Work Program through the Civilian Conservation Corps (CCC) made needed labor and expertise available to the parks. Employment in the NPS went from 2,207 to 7,341 between 1933 and 1940. In many parks, CCC people served as wildlife technicians, and there were many projects involving wildlife and habitat restoration. Between 1934 and 1941, CCC assistance included over two hundred work-years on wildlife development projects, including emergency feeding (Paige 1985). By 1936 there were twenty-three CCC wildlife technicians on the Wildlife Division staff. Some of these were headquartered in the parks, but most were placed in regional offices and given responsibility for the supervision of extensive field territories. During this period, Wildlife Division biologists reviewed all proposed management and development projects involving wildlife or its habitat and evaluated their impact on the environment (Smathers and Sumner 1975). Throughout the thirties park naturalists were also involved in scientific study, and they contributed to the knowledge of parks through observation, collections, and inventories of park resources, and on occasion through some basic research (Robbins et al. 1963).

The money and labor provided by the CCC greatly improved natural-resource management in the parks. By 1938 there was a wildlife ranger in each national park. Their primary duty was to keep the park superintendent and the Wildlife Division informed about wildlife conditions in that park. However, even with the energy and guile brought by Wright and others to the program, and the infusion of dollars and personnel from the CCC, many problems remained. NPS field managers, comfortable in tradition, were often reluctant to implement the recommendations made by the Wildlife Division, particularly with respect to the ecological role of fire and the management of native insects. Superintendents resented biologists telling them how to run their park.[7] That the Wildlife Division could veto CCC projects that adversely impacted the environment was a major source of controversy (Robbins et al. 1963). This factor reinforced the opinion of many administrators that biologists offered nothing positive and were a hindrance to large-scale plans for park development (Sumner 1967).

Changes in the Wildlife Division

The Wildlife Division was transferred to Washington, D.C., in 1935, allowing administrators to have more control over the program. Both Wright and Thompson moved to Washington, while Dixon remained in California as a field naturalist. Victor H. Cahalane, formerly a Wildlife Division biologist at Wind Cave, joined the Washington staff as did Adolph Murie and Lowell Sumner. In early 1936, George Wright was killed in an auto accident while touring Big Bend National Park. After his death, friction between biologists and administrators became even more pronounced. Cahalane became chief of the Wildlife Division, and Dixon returned as assistant chief. Cahalane continued to vigorously push the division's program, but he lacked Wright's personality and charm and had great difficulty in dealing with the agency bureaucracy. From that point on, the status of science in NPS slowly began to erode. The advent of World War II four years later cemented the demise of the program, eliminating any hope that science in NPS could continue to retain its high stature. It is interesting to speculate whether or not the era of enlightenment and progress in research in the NPS might have continued had Wright lived. It probably would not have. Power in the NPS as it had been and would continue to be lay with the superintendents and ranger corps. The NPS commitment to research and scientific management was not strong, and as the move to Washington indicated, there was an active movement to deemphasize the role of science. Indications are that the biological research program flourished as much because of the vast infusion of CCC dollars (e.g., by the end of the thirties some two-thirds of the NPS annual expenditures were being financed by CCC funds) as it did because of the talents of George Wright.

World War II eliminated funding for research, the military draft obviated the need for the CCC program, and many positions were lost. As a consequence of prewar mobilization and in accordance with a departmental reorganization initiated by President Roosevelt, the NPS Wildlife Division, now consisting only of Cahalane, Dixon, Sumner, and Murie, was transferred to the Bureau of Biological Survey (now the Fish and Wildlife Service) in December 1939, where it was called the Office of National Park Wildlife. The NPS Branch of Research and Education was dissolved. Although the positions and duty stations of the transferred employees remained the same, the individuals reported to the supervisors of the Biological Survey. This was a difficult situation, for they were now in an agency whose emphasis and funding came not from programs to protect animals but often to exterminate them. As a result there was little the few remaining NPS biologists could do about park wildlife problems. A decade that began with promise and great expectations for science in the parks ended in disappointment and frustration.

Other Changes in NPS Administration

The thirties was a dynamic time for growth in the Park Service and changes in administrative structure. In 1933 the monuments and national historic military parks (principally battlefields) under the jurisdiction of the Department of War were transferred to the NPS. This was a long-term goal of Albright, who was a history buff and who believed that the NPS had a responsibility to preserve significant aspects of the nation's history (Unrau and Williss 1983). In 1936, the Park, Parkway, and Recreational Areas Study Act was authorized by Congress. This made possible the addition of national parkways, national recreation areas, and national seashores to the national park system. In 1936, Lake Mead, the first recreation area, was established, and the following year Cape Hatteras, the first national seashore, was established. These new land-management categories brought new challenges to NPS resource management.

In 1933 Albright resigned as director and Arno Cammerer took over the leadership of the NPS. At the time of Albright's resignation, there were 137 units in the park system. Within the NPS, the flush of emergency conservation programs during the thirties brought about the establishment of regional offices in Richmond, Virginia; Omaha, Nebraska; Santa Fe, New Mexico; and San Francisco, California. Although regional boundaries have since changed, all but the Richmond office remain today. Regionalization of the agency was a concept that had been fought by the superintendents because it thwarted their direct access to the director, but they did concede and the change was put into place in 1937 (Henneberger 1965).

NOTES

1. The Seattle Mountaineers Club, in an attempt to show the fallacy of the proposals, offered its Puget Sound lawns and local golf courses for sheep if they were kept out of the park. This ploy was sufficient to stop this proposal. However, because even the White House grounds were opened to sheep grazing by President Wilson, the NPS faced a stiff battle in keeping the parks free of grazing by domestic sheep.

2. The success in solidifying the agency is even more remarkable in that the fledgling agency had to weather not only World War I but also the Roaring Twenties, a time when the emphasis was on private enterprise and development and which, in the words of Righter, required a "certain messianic zeal to be an ardent conservationist" (1982:43).

3. In light of the times, this should not be surprising. Land-grant universities were still young, and few had programs of study or research in the natural resources. Thus there was little expertise to build on. Adams, a professor of wildlife science and director of the Roosevelt Wild Life Experiment Station at Yellowstone, summarized the situation: "that wildlife is more or less an elusive subject for the public and the administrator to understand, and it cannot be understood merely by inspection—it must be known intimately, and therefore great damage can be done before it is realized" (1922: 143). To accomplish this he advocated a private endowment on the order of $1 million each for Yellowstone and Yosemite, the income of which would be devoted exclusively to research and education in those parks. His plea went unheeded.

4. The most prominent group was the Committee on Educational Problems in the National Parks, appointed in 1929 to examine the research and educational programs in parks. This was the first explicit NPS recognition that research should have a role in park management (Bryant and Atwood 1932).

5. Wright used funds from his inheritance to support the work.

6. Based on a recommendation by the ecologist Victor Shelford, Albright requested a plan to establish research reserves in specific parks (Shelford 1933). Subsequently, twenty-eight research reserves in ten national parks and monuments were designated between 1933 and 1940 (Kendeigh 1942). There

is no evidence, however, that any of these were ever formally used for that purpose.

7. At the time, most parks were independent of any central authority. Park superintendents were often influential figures and had considerable latitude in interpreting national policy in their own parks (Hydrick 1984). For example, in 1937 Yellowstone administrators again initiated control of coyotes to help park ungulates.

2

Science Program Administration in the Succeeding Decades

The advent of World War II had a drastic and immediate effect on the NPS science program. NPS funding, personnel, and park visitation were greatly reduced. Appropriations declined from $21 million in FY 1940 to $5 million in FY 1943. Visitation declined from 21 million in 1941 to 6 million in 1942. Between 1942 and 1943 the number of permanent, full-time NPS positions decreased from 4,510 to 1,974. NPS central offices were moved to Chicago in 1942 to make room for military functions in Washington and did not return until 1947. Newton B. Drury was appointed director in 1940. He was a staunch preservationist who helped the Park Service deflect most external wartime demands made on park resources. The NPS, for example, successfully challenged the attempt to harvest old-growth spruce from Olympic National Park for aircraft construction, the establishment of an artillery range along a trumpeter swan flyway in Idaho, and the proposed use of important bighorn sheep habitat in Joshua Tree as a bombing range. The Park Service also resisted demands to open parks up to additional grazing or to the use of game for food.

In retrospect, despite the neglect of parks, or maybe because of it, most park natural resources were not adversely affected during the war years, even though most resource-management problems were ignored. Knowledge about park resources, however, increased little because research was discouraged to conserve personnel and funds (Smathers and Sumner 1975). Scientific publications decreased dramatically from the levels of the thirties. The monitoring programs established by the Wildlife Division in the thirties were terminated. Plot locations and data were discarded, eliminating any possibility that the programs could be revived in the future.

One of the most serious and lasting consequences of the war was the influence it had on the structure of the science program. The program failed to recover from the personnel and funding cuts suffered. In 1947 the Office of National Park Wildlife in the Fish and Wildlife Service was abolished, and the eight scientists, (six biologists, a geologist, and a volcanologist), were moved back to NPS (Robbins et al. 1963). Rather than recreate a wildlife or science division, these scientists were placed under the direction of the Division of Interpretation and assigned relatively trivial activities, such as producing periodic reports on wildlife conditions in the parks (see, e.g., NPS 1947, 1948, 1949, and 1950). These reports contained often spurious wildlife population estimates in the parks and discussed suspected problems such as deteriorating range conditions, the need for greater protection from poaching, and malnutrition in some species. They also itemized needs for additional programs and for personnel to help protect wildlife, gather information, and develop management and restoration plans.[1]

Resource-management problems were dealt with only when they became too large or too politically sensitive to be ignored. As a consequence, staff scientists were used solely as a troubleshooting force on brushfire problems. Similarly, Adolph Murie was sent to Lava Beds to investigate a meadow mouse outbreak—after local ranchers had begun to pressure the Park Service into a poison program; Coleman Newman was sent to Olympic to study elk—after a local sports group had made a public-relations problem for the Park Service over the question of elk management.[2] However, despite the war, new parks continued to be added to the system. Mammoth Cave was established in 1941 and Grand Teton was created in 1943.

The Mission 66 Program

The fifties were a vexing time for resource scientists in many agencies. Following the war, attention was turned to rehabilitating the physical infrastructure of the nation, which had badly deteriorated. Focus was given to building new homes for the parents of the baby boomers, to developing an interstate highway network, and to the manufacture of consumer goods, particularly automobiles. Environmental concerns were generally ignored, but the new freedom of mobility enjoyed by the American public after World War II brought about a tremendous growth in park visitation. Like most of the nation's infrastructure, park facilities were in no condition to handle this increase. Park roads, trails, campgrounds, and buildings had received little maintenance since the thirties and were in gross disrepair. In response, NPS director Wirth asked Congress in 1956 to fund a ten-year program designed to rehabilitate and expand facilities throughout the system to handle the increases in visitation. Called the Mission 66 Program for the date of its expected completion on the fiftieth anniversary of the Park Service, it was enthusiastically approved by the administration, and over the ensuing years had a significant impact on virtually every unit in the system. It resulted in the construction of almost 2,800 miles of new and reconstructed roads, 936 miles of new and reconstructed trails, 330 new parking areas, 575 new campgrounds, 742 new picnic areas, 114 visitor centers, and hundreds of employee residences (Wirth 1980). Today many of the facilities in parks are a direct result of this program.

NPS scientists had accepted the lack of support for science in the forties as a consequence of the war effort. Not so in the fifties, when they saw the agency spending millions of dollars on development and virtually none on research.[3] The cadre of Park Service scientists who had suffered through the forties in the hope that postwar conditions could be better were often bitter. The frustrations of dealing with these inequities eventually caused Chief Biologist Victor Cahalane, arguably one of the most productive biologists ever employed by the NPS, to resign in 1955. Gordon Fredine assumed his position.

The problems that the materialism of the American culture was causing in terms of ignoring environmental values, and park resources in particular, slowly gained national attention as the fifties wore on. Criticism over the neglect of park resources specifically was led by prominent academic scientists, such as Starker Leopold and Stanley Cain, and conservation groups, such as the Sierra Club. The first signal that NPS was beginning to listen to its critics and was starting to recognize the need for a better natural-science program occurred in 1958 when it established its first official research budget, $28,000 (later reduced to $26,880) (a figure ironically little different from that given to George Wright in 1932). In 1959 new resource technicians called "wildlife rangers" were hired to work in various parks. Their responsibility included animal reduction, reintroduction of extirpated species, censuses, appraisal of browse and forage conditions, protection of endangered species, and elimination of exotics (Olsen 1986). Both the research and resource-management functions were also reorganized at this time. The territorial domains of both branches were clearly identified; resource management was not to do research; the research section was not to do any management.[4]

The forties and early fifties proved to be one of the bleakest periods in the history of science in NPS. Essentially no new information was produced, and the most lasting legacy of this era was the creation of an attitude toward research that persisted for many years. Research was viewed as simply a tool to solve immediate management problems, and once a specific crisis was dealt with, interest in it soon waned and attention was turned to other concerns. Each resource problem was a distinct situation to be solved and disposed of. This approach to problem solving became the hallmark of science and resource management not only in national parks but in most resource-management agencies. The result was that resource "problems" were rarely anticipated, were commonly ignored until they reached crisis proportions, and were hardly ever viewed in an ecosystem context. The fifties did end with a ray of hope in terms of larger budgets and more personnel for the science program in the parks. These factors were, however, only cosmetic. There was still no commitment by the Park Service to manage the parks according to ecological principles.

Revival: The NPS Science Program in the Sixties and Seventies

A new spirit of optimism embraced the NPS science program as the sixties began. The new presidential administration appointed Stewart Udall, a noted conservationist, as secretary of the interior, and there were indications that environmental concerns would be given equal weight with other interests in the government. Thus, for the first time in over three decades, NPS scientists held out real hope biological research in the Park Service would gain the financial support it needed. This attitude was strengthened when Howard Stagner, the able administrator of the successful Mission 66 Program, was appointed chief of the Division of Interpretation and National History, which then included the natural scientists. He did not disappoint his colleagues. Using tactics proven to be successful in selling the Mission 66 Program, he immediately took up the fight to make scientific research a paramount concern of the Park Service. Accordingly, over the next few years Washington office biologists devoted their time to developing congressional budget presentations to justify and sell a biological program—ironically the same kind of program that had been officially approved and financed in the early thirties and then forgotten. These efforts finally paid off in 1964 when Congress budgeted $80,000 for

NPS research, a significant increase from the $29,000 annual appropriation of preceding years. Subsequent years saw more increases. Several new programs were initiated, including studies of threatened species and the feasibility of reintroducing extirpated species in various parks. The long-dormant NPS Fauna Series was revived with the publication of the *Bighorn of Death Valley* (Welles and Welles 1961).

A major reason for the resurrection of science in the sixties was the heightened sense of environmental awareness that emerged during the decade. There was a growing affinity for nature and opposition to the unwarranted exploitation of natural resources and the increases in air and water pollution. The first pictures of Earth from outer space, portraying the planet as a small green orb in a lifeless environment, exemplified the fragility of its biological systems and strengthened public environmental awareness (Lee 1972). Concern for the management and protection of federal lands was a minor part of the environmental movement that developed at this time (Shanks 1984). However, for the first time scientists began to recognize the value of national parks as biotic reserves preserving integral parts of the global ecosystem and for their role as genetic storehouses and natural laboratories (Simmons 1974). This recognition led in turn to renewed interest in the biological properties of parks and the role played by NPS scientists.

A new vitality emerged in the Washington science office as the skills of recently hired individuals were combined with the wisdom and understanding of some remaining veterans in the science program. In 1962, this staff undertook a thorough evaluation of the entire science program, paying special attention to the administrative inadequacies of the existing program and the deficiencies in the way research was conducted. Their report cogently described the changes necessary to enable NPS to meet the challenges of the future (Stagner 1962).

Since many of the contributors to the report had suffered through several decades of frustration, they, more than any outside group, had a clear understanding of the deficiencies in the program. The report categorized NPS research as piecemeal, designed only to solve immediate problems, and lacking in continuity, coordination, and depth. Past research lacked an ecological perspective. It was descriptive rather than analytical, identifying and cataloging problems and providing little insight on the ecological integrity of the parks.

The report urged the development of a program of scientific study because of the speed with which parks were becoming isolated islands bounded by intensively managed and manipulated lands. This appears to be the first time the fragmentation of parks in the natural landscape was recognized as a real threat. Finally, the report outlined a comprehensive long-term research plan for all units in the system, including funding and staffing needs for the first five-year period.

Stagner used this report to convince Secretary of the Interior Udall of the need to have an impartial review of the NPS research program conducted by a committee of outside scientists (Sumner 1968; Robert Linn, interview with author, Ft. Collins, Colo., July 16, 1986). Udall was sympathetic to the problems confronting NPS science programs,[5] and he quickly established two advisory committees in 1962. He requested that the National Academy of Science conduct a review of the entire NPS natural-science program. He also appointed the Special Advisory Board on Wildlife Management to review wildlife policies.[6]

National Academy of Sciences Research Council Report

The report produced by the National Academy of Science (NAS) was a blunt condemnation of the past and present NPS research program.[7] The authors concluded that "its status has been and is one of many reports, numerous recommendations, vacillations in policy and little action, [or] financial support" (1963:24) and that NPS research "lacked conformity, coordination, and depth. It has been marked by expediency rather than by long-term considerations. It has ... lacked direction, has been fragmented between divisions ... has been applied piecemeal and has suffered because of a failure to recognize the distinctions between research and administrative decision making, and has failed to insure the implementation of the results of research in operational management" (Robbins et al. 1963:31). The report emphasized the role that research should play in supporting resource-management planning, park planning, and development. It recommended that park scientists and research should be administered separately from park administration and operations.

Most of the twenty recommendations in the report dealt with the mechanics of how an NPS research program should be administratively structured,[8] although the report did make specific biological research suggestions for Everglades, Yellowstone, and Grand Teton parks. It also recommended that an inventory of all park resources be made and that specific attention be given to significant changes in land and resource use on areas adjacent to national parks.

The report did not fully endorse the idea that NPS scientists should conduct basic research in parks, but instead suggested only that park research be long-term and capable of detecting problems before they became critical. It did recommend that NPS research should be mission oriented and directed to work only on park problems. In this respect, the report differed significantly from the feelings of the Washington office scientists. They maintained that many of the problems facing parks at the time could have been anticipated and dealt with if the Park Service had previously maintained a good basic research program (Linn interview). NPS management appeared to be quite pleased with the NAS report (Wirth 1962) and accepted most of its recommendations even though most were not enacted.

The Special Advisory Board on Wildlife Management

The primary reason Udall established the Special Advisory Board (SAB) was the growing public criticism over the herd reductions of elk in Yellowstone and Rocky Mountain by NPS personnel.[9] The committee was asked to determine whether these actions were necessary, and if so, who should carry them out. This was the first time a group outside NPS had been requested to evaluate agency wildlife programs. The SAB far exceeded this narrow directive. Its report, typically referred to as the Leopold Report, turned out to be a comprehensive examination of park wildlife-management goals, and most important, what policies would best achieve those goals and what methods would most suitably implement those policies (Leopold et al. 1963). The report was the first cogent statement in thirty years of NPS resource management policy, or at least what that policy should be (see chapter 3).

The Leopold Report was stronger than the NAS report in its endorsement of applied research and in its rejection of basic research. This was in part a reflection of the strong management orientation of the group and a recognition of the fiscal realities of the times. Leopold was one of the strongest proponents of applied research. He was more familiar with NPS problems and realized more than the others that management-oriented research was often the only way to solve park problems. His later views reflected this: "The NPS research program is intended to be mission-oriented. It is not science for science's sake. If on the whole we are not producing knowledge that will lead to better park management, we had best reconsider our commitments. There is no clear line between mission-oriented research (intended for application) and purely theoretical research, but we should be leaning always toward the former, without, however reducing the dignity of our work to simple troubleshooting" (Leopold 1963:6).

Though the Wildlife Protection Branch developed its program around recommendations in the Leopold Report (Smathers and Sumner 1975), there are several indications that personnel of the primarily park-based branch interpreted the recommendations of the report far too narrowly or literally. They emphasized the "what," e.g., listing the fauna of parks, describing the natural history of an area, and identifying resources that had disappeared in historic time and determining what that date was. Actions included reintroduction of formerly extirpated species. They ignored the "why," e.g., understanding why the species had disappeared in the first place (Wauer and Supernaugh 1983). As a result, many attempted species reintroductions met with failure, and "successes, where they occurred, frequently required heroic efforts. Desert bighorn died of livestock-induced parainfections. Elk migrated out of the area and were subject to hunting, poaching, or traffic accidents. Some species were maintained only by supplemental watering or feeding programs" (Wauer and Supernaugh 1983:15).

Many of the recommendations called for in the reports proved to be difficult to carry out without additional staff and funding. Although there were some increases in the funding and staffing of wildlife-management programs, personnel and budget shortages often meant piecemeal implementation of the recommendations on a project-by-project basis, rather than an overall service-wide commitment to solve a given problem (Reid 1968).

Changes in the Administration of the NPS Science Program

Several changes in the administration of the science program did occur in the early sixties, reflecting various attempts to implement the commission recommendations. There was a concerted effort to build bridges between NPS and the scientific community. The Advisory Commission in Natural History Studies was established in 1964, made up of Starker Leopold, Stanley Cain, and Siguard Olsen, to help guide the science program. Unfortunately the committee met irregularly, in part because of the geographic separation of its members, and in retrospect had little impact. It was responsible for the 1964 hiring of George Sprugel as chief scientist of the Division of Natural Sciences, who had supervisory authority over all NPS scientists. Sprugel was a renowned scientist and the biological sciences director of the National Science Foundation, but had no NPS experience. He was immediately caught in a cross fire between the expectations of the secretary of the interior and the realities of the science program. For example, there were constant demands from the secretary's office asking "when are you going to implement the Leopold Report?" (Linn interview). Yet he realized that there was little chance of doing that without increased staff and funds. Sprugel, recognizing that the research program was not receiving the support he had been led to expect, resigned in 1966. He was replaced by Robert Linn.

During the late sixties a number of new resource-management and wildlife technician positions were created. Many positions were largely attributable to the addition of new parks to the system, a healthy national economy that supported new positions, and the requirement to manage the additional facilities created through the Mission 66 Program. A subtle influence was the simultaneous retirement of park rangers who had been hired during the late twenties and early thirties. Most of these individuals were trained by the original rangers, and thus had a strong sense of tradition of what they thought the Park Service should be. Unfortunately, this view was often narrow and often stymied the growth of science, resource management, and interpretation. The loss of these individuals opened up many new positions and opportunities for employees who were less tradition-bound, usually college graduates, and better schooled in ecological theory (Roger Contor, interview with author, Ellensburg, Wash., Apr. 17-18, 1986). Most of these replacements were considerably younger than their predecessors and brought with them vastly different viewpoints on the mission of the Park Service. Supplementing this new mixture of employees was the initiation of lateral transfers among the parks. In response to this growing science program, Linn convened a meeting in 1968 at Grand Canyon of all thirty-eight NPS research scientists and management biologists (nineteen employed as wildlife biologists). This was only the third such meeting in the history of the NPS and was the first opportunity many of the recently hired individuals had to meet each other.[10]

The growth of the science program, however, concerned many senior park and regional managers who retained a management philosophy that hearkened back to the early days of the Park Service. They still wanted complete control over all personnel working in their respective parks and over the activities these individuals were engaged in. A science program based in Washington made up of individuals who reported to a chief scientist was a threat to this management style (Smathers and Sumner 1975). Director Hartzog was sympathetic to these concerns, and in 1971 he fundamentally altered science-program administration by terminating the supervisory authority of the chief scientist over NPS scientists and placing them instead under the supervision of respective regional directors or the superintendents of the parks where they worked. Regional chief scientist positions who reported to the respective regional directors were established in the six existing regional offices.[11] The change was in direct opposition to the recommendations made by the National Academy of Sciences report eight years earlier.

Most scientists and resource-management personnel were shifted from the Washington office to the various regional offices to implement the plan. The administrative structure that the reorganization established had several important repercussions. It diffused the power that the science program had accumulated over the previous decade and diminished the ability of scientists to react in a unified manner to service-wide problems. By having scientists supervised directly by managers, it created a staff of "management scientists" who were required to work on those projects management considered to be important and not to work on those projects management did not want done or want to know anything about (Glenn Cole, telephone interview with author, Aug. 28, 1986). Some regional directors and superintendents, well aware of the importance of scientific research in parks, actively supported and even expanded research programs, others did the opposite. The end result was the creation of an autonomous and unequal science program among regions and parks. Some regions and parks continued to maintain an adequate program, but others did not. Contact between scientists in the field with Washington often became nonexistent. The breakdown in communication among NPS scientists was, more than any other factor, the real causality of regionalization. (William Robertson, interview with author, Everglades National Park, Oct. 16, 1986).

Equally as important, the Washington office lost its ability to provide oversight and guidance to a national science program. While the Washington office often pretended it had control over the scientific research in the NPS, it did not. Even in the allocation of research funds, priorities were usually set by the regions. As a consequence of its ineffectiveness, Washington science and resource management offices have undergone an almost constant series of reorganizations since 1971, all ostensibly done to improve communication with the field and to reassert its dominance. It has been only in recent years that the Washington office has assumed some dominance over the science program. However, it still must contend with the divergent priorities of the ten regional offices and larger parks.

Cooperative Park Studies Units

The only major change in the science program has been within some individual regions where some scientists have been removed from direct park supervision and placed at Cooperative Park Study Units (CPSU) at regional universities, where they generally report to a regional chief scientist. The practice of placing NPS research scientists at universities began fifty years ago when scientists in the Branch of Research and Education were stationed at the University of California at Berkeley between 1929 and 1933. The first formal NPS affiliation with academia started in 1952 when the Jackson Hole Research Station was established in conjunction with the University of Wyoming.

The contemporary establishment of CPSUs was in 1970 at the University of Washington. The concept recognized that the number of scientific personnel in the NPS is limited. CPSUs were a way to broaden the base for acquiring scientific information and to complement the existing network of park-based science (Agee, Field, and Starkey 1983; NPCA 1988). Scientists at CPSUs generally have more latitude in assisting in problem solving for a spectrum of parks, particularly smaller parks with no in-house scientific staff. A major benefit of the units is that a single scientist can bring to bear the talents of many scientists on a given problem. The unit scientist also has access to libraries, labs, computer facilities, and other support services of the university. Since their initial creation, the number of CPSUs has varied from ten to twenty.

NOTES

1. Because there was little opportunity for field research or reconnaissance, most biologists placed little faith in the accuracy of these yearly summaries. As a joke, one biologist listed a giraffe as present in one park, and it was dutifully added to the records (Richard Prasil, interview with author, Seattle, Wash., Nov. 5, 1986).

2. Even this assignment was opposed by the regional director because he wanted more stenographers, not more biologists (Sumner 1968).

3. Even scientific overview was treated lightly. The Mission 66 Programs, unlike the CCC projects, never received rigorous review by biologists. Thus, many developmental mistakes were made, such as placing campgrounds in important wildlife habitats.

4. With the limited biologically trained staff available to NPS, this subdivision made little sense to those working in the agency. As Lowell Sumner in-

dicated, "How the biologist in a park was supposed to divide himself and his daily activities into these separate compartments was the subject of much speculation at the time" (interview with author, Glenwood, N. Mex., May 9, 1987).

5. In an April 1962 letter to Dr. D. W. Bronk, President of the National Academy of Sciences, Udall used portions of Stagner's 1962 report to write, "During recent decades, . . . research undertaken by the Service has of necessity, consisted largely of projects stimulated by crises in park management, planning, protection, and interpretation. No coordinated or long range plan of investigations has been developed. As a result, the needs of some areas have been fairly adequately met; in others, the accomplishments bear a haphazard relationship to actual needs; while for the remainder, comprising far too many areas, little has been done."

6. Udall also commissioned a third study on the ecological health of parks by the Conservation Foundation. This report was not published until 1967 (see Darling and Eichhorn 1967). The report was broad in scope, containing few specifics. It primarily criticized the lack of biological input to NPS visitor-management and planning programs as contributing to the declining ecological quality of parks. It made few specific comments about wildlife management or policy in NPS and although widely read, had little impact on the way parks were managed.

7. William J. Robbins chaired the evaluation committee, and the final report, known as the National Academy of Science Report or Robbins' Report (Robbins et al. 1963), was submitted August 1, 1963.

8. Recommendations included the establishment of a permanent independent research unit to conduct and supervise all research in the parks. The research unit was to be directed by an assistant director for research reporting to the director and containing a chief scientist who would supervise all field research personnel. It recommended that at least 10% of the annual NPS budget be devoted to research.

9. Members of the Special Advisory Board included A. Starker Leopold, Assistant to the Chancellor, University of California, Berkeley; Ira N. Gabrielson, President of the Wildlife Management Institute and a former director of the U.S. Fish and Wildlife Service; Clarence Cottam, Director of the Welder Wildlife Foundation and a former assistant director of the U.S. Fish and Wildlife Service; Thomas L. Kimball, Executive Director of the National Wildlife Federation; and Stanley A. Cain, Professor, Department of Conservation, University of Michigan.

10. Previous meetings of the limited number of scientists had occurred in 1929 at Berkeley, California, and at Grand Canyon in 1940. A fourth meeting also occurred in 1970 at Grand Canyon. Subsequent national meetings took place in 1976, 1980, 1984, 1988, and 1990 that encompassed all research in parks and were replete with numerous oral presentations. Unfortunately, because of costs, not all NPS scientists were permitted to attend these latter four meetings, a fact that continues to contribute to a communication problem in the agency.

11. The first regional chief scientists were Nicholas Chura, Northeast Region; Gary Clemons, National Capital Parks; James Larson, Southeast Region; Neil J. Reid, Midwest Region; Garrett Smathers, Pacific Northwest Region; and Othello Wallis, Western Region.

3

The Evolution of
Resource-Management Policies

The 1916 act establishing the NPS provided the agency with the initial framework for a unified set of management policies that applied to all parks and monuments. The following management actions were authorized in the legislation:

1. Selling or disposing of timber required to control insect attacks, diseases, or to conserve natural or historic objects
2. The destruction of animals and plant life detrimental to the use of the areas
3. Cattle grazing in all areas except Yellowstone

Parks were to be managed with the objective of protecting the most important resources. This philosophy was a consequence of the fact that most of the early parks and monuments were established primarily to protect unique scenery, natural curiosities, or historic works. It was also because from the beginning most of the threats, such as poaching, market hunting, theft of resources, vandalism, and trespass grazing, were resource specific. The focus of management and protection in almost all cases was at the species, rather than the community or ecosystem, level. This was particularly true where animals were concerned. The "good" or beneficial species—generally the large or unique species, such as elk, were protected, and in the case of bison, partially domesticated. Popular sport fish, often non-native, were stocked. The "bad" species, such as predators, were killed. The focus of forest management was primarily on trees rather than forest communities. Trees were protected from fire, insects, and disease. Management of geological resources was also single-feature oriented, with protection from vandalism and theft receiving priority. Because of this approach, most of the management practices manipulated park ecosystems to achieve management objectives.

Manipulation versus Natural Processes

One of the most important management issues in the Park Service has always been the degree to which managers, in carrying out actions, should interfere with the natural functions of park ecosystems. The long-term trend of NPS management has been to progressively minimize management interference and to allow natural ecosystem processes to operate freely. However, this trend has not been smooth and has never been free of controversy (see Figure 3.1). Depending on the type of resource and the magnitude of the particular problem, there were often sharp transitions in the intensity of management. Economic and administrative constraints on the NPS program also played a major role in the funding provided for resource management at various times. This trend also represents a learning process. Knowledge of ecosystem functions have helped managers understand the implications of management policies and optimally will help them, in the future, avoid some of the mistakes of the past.

Criticism over intensive management of natural resources in parks

Figure 3.1. Trends in Management Interference with Natural Processes in Parks

arose as soon as the Park Service was established. Grinnell and Storer argued in a 1916 paper that human manipulation of park environments should be minimized and suggested that a park's greatest value was that it was an example of a natural ecosystem as it existed before the advent of whites. They felt parks should be left in a pristine condition whenever possible, visitor harassment of animal life minimized, alien species eliminated, and all animals, including predators, protected.

A 1921 resolution from the American Association for the Advancement of Science (AAAS) also argued for minimal management interference, suggesting that

> the maintenance of the national parks in an absolutely natural condition is of utmost importance for a reason as yet but little understood by the general public. . . . The national parks are rich fields for the natural sciences . . . because on them the native fauna and flora may be found more nearly undisturbed than anywhere else. Many interesting plants and animals will survive in the parks long after they have been exterminated over the rest of the country. [This] . . . opportunity will aid in the solution of difficult scientific problems. (AAAS 1922:63)

The AAAS was particularly concerned with the Park Service's lack of concern about the impact of non-native species. The AAAS criticized actions involving the release of game animals not native to the region and passed the following resolution:

> Whereas one of the primary duties of the NPS is to pass on to future generations for scientific study and education, natural areas on which the native flora and fauna may be found undisturbed by outside agencies; and Whereas the planting of non-native trees, shrubs or other plants, the stocking of waters with non-native fish, or the liberating of game animals not native to the region, impairs or destroys the natural conditions and native wilderness of parks; Be it Resolved, that the [AAAS] strongly opposes the introduction of non-native plants and animals into the national parks and all other unessential interference with natural conditions, and urges the National Park Service to prohibit all such introductions and interferences. (Moore 1925:353)

The Ecological Society of America passed a similar resolution in 1922.

Although the Park Service recognized the legitimacy of this recommendation, it did not have the resource-management personnel or expertise to correct the situation, and thus many introductions, purposeful or accidental, continued. Control of existing alien species was even less feasible. Except for limited controls of burros in Grand Canyon and feral pigs and goats in Hawaii Volcanoes (see chapter 6), it would be many years before any concerted action was taken against alien species in the parks.

The Policy of Predator Control

One of the most significant manipulations of park processes was the effort to control predators. A policy of predator removal began soon after Yellowstone was established. Early control actions of wolves, cougars, and other carnivores were sporadic, primarily for self-protection and protection of personal possessions and food supplies. Protection of ungulates, however, soon became the chief reason for predator control. After 1916, predator control in several western parks grew markedly, and the list of species classed as predators increased to include the lynx, bobcat, fox, mink, weasel, fisher, otter, and marten. All of these species were hunted for almost a decade, with the intensity of the campaigns largely determined by the individual park superintendents.

Changes in Park Service predator control policies evolved slowly and can be traced in the decisions made in the yearly superintendents' conferences in the twenties. Control programs were gradually terminated in some parks, and the definition of predatory animals was narrowed to include only wolves, coyotes, and cougars. Joseph Grinnell, Director of the University of California Museum of Vertebrate Zoology, was a strong advocate for predator protection in parks and waged a continuous campaign to end predator control (Cahalane 1939). He argued that predators played an important role in the balance of nature and that they should not be killed except where they were threatening the extinction of other animals.

Throughout the twenties the campaign to end predator control in parks gained momentum. The Park Service received numerous resolutions and letters from many national conservation and scientific organizations, such as the National Parks Association, the Boone and Crockett Club, the American Society of Mammalogists, and the New York Zoological Society, condemning its predator control programs. Park Service scientists such as William Rush also argued in favor of retaining predators in parks to help control ungulates (1929).

A concurrence with these views was expressed in a reply by Director Albright, stating, "predatory animals have a real place in nature, and all animal life should be kept inviolate within the parks" (1931:185).

The policies concerning predatory animals were similarly revised:

1. Predatory animals are . . . an integral part of national parks and no widespread campaigns of destruction are to be countenanced. The only control practiced is that of shooting coyotes or other predators when they are actually found making serious inroads upon herds of game or other animals needing special protection.
2. No permits for trapping within . . . a park are allowed.
3. Poison . . . is banned from national parks except where used . . . in warfare against rodents in settled portions of a park.

It is [our] duty . . . to maintain examples of the various interesting North American mammals under natural conditions for the pleasure and education of the visitors and for the purpose of scientific study. (Albright 1931:185–86).

All superintendents were notified soon after that this statement defined the official policy of the NPS (Cahalane 1939). It was the first indication that NPS managers were beginning to understand the value of natural ecosystem processes. The new policy, however, had little real impact, for it was adopted at a time when there were few, if any, major predators of consequence left in parks in the continental United States. Cynics could conclude that this was, in fact, the only reason the policy was changed. This policy also, as with all others, left the actual management decisions to the discretion of the park superintendent. As a result, change in the parks was slow. Coyote killing continued in Yellowstone until 1933. Policy was further defined by Wright, Dixon, and Thompson to state:

No native predator shall be destroyed on account of its normal utilization of any other park animal, excepting if that animal is in immediate danger of extinction, and then only if the predator is not itself a vanishing form. When control is necessary, it shall be accompanied by transplantation, or if necessary by killing offending individuals, and not by campaigns to eradicate the general population of a species. Species predatory on fish shall be allowed to continue in normal numbers and to share normally in the benefit of fish culture (1933:147).

Although this was acknowledged as official NPS policy (Cahalane 1939), even this statement did not put the issue to rest, since the problem surfaced again in 1946 with calls for the extermination of the wolf in Mt. McKinley. Today, all predators are completely protected in parks, and there are even attempts to reintroduce species, such as the wolf (see chapter 8). These views are part of a more enlightened attitude toward predators by both wildlife-management agencies and by the general public.

Policy Shifts as the Result of Wildlife Division Surveys

The next change in Park Service thinking came with the publication of Fauna 1 in 1933 (Wright, Dixon, and Thompson 1933).
Although this report specifically addressed wildlife-management policies, it went far beyond those in its concerns and recommendations.
The report concluded that the problems facing park wildlife could be
traced to three general sources: (1) adverse impacts prior to park establishment; (2) lack of habitats for all seasons; and (3) conflicts
between visitors or management and animals that resulted in displacement, injury, or death of animals. Within these general areas, the
survey identified sixteen major problems confronting park wildlife,
which are summarized in Exhibit 3.1. Soon after the report was published most of the recommendations were "officially" adopted as NPS
policy, however, many were never carried out and others were far too
advanced for management to accept.

Revolutionary in its day, Fauna 1 remains remarkably contemporary. In reading it, one soon recognizes that the problems confronting
park animals have not changed in almost sixty years. Unfortunately
long out of print, the book is largely unavailable and unknown to most
current biologists and administrators. Fauna 1 was the first document
that defined a clear rationale for managing wildlife in national parks.
It recognized the fallacy of single-species management. More important, it placed recommended actions in an ecosystem framework that
recognized the role that natural processes played in achieving management objectives.

Policy Changes as a Result of the Leopold Report

It would be almost thirty years before Park Service thinking about
natural processes and their role in ecosystems was again challenged.
The challenge came from the report of Secretary Udall's Special Advisory Board on Wildlife Management and at a time when intensive
management actions, particularly ungulate control, were at a peak
and were the subject of growing public criticism. The committee was
established in response to this criticism and the question the group
was asked to address was how far the NPS should go in utilizing the
tools of management to maintain wildlife populations (Wauer and Supernaugh 1983). The committee went far beyond this narrow mission,
essentially replacing the words *wildlife populations* in its mandate with
the words *natural systems*. In what has become the most widely quoted
passage of the report,[1] the authors concluded the primary goal of

Exhibit 3.1. Wildlife Recommendations Made in Fauna 1

---

1. Based on the availability of stock, their potential for survival, and political feasibility, reestablish, where possible, species extirpated from parks.
2. Institute special management needed for threatened species, including protection of young or artificial feeding at critical periods.
3. End current livestock grazing in parks and restore previously overgrazed habitat.
4. Control abnormally large populations of ungulate species and restore overbrowsed and grazed habitat.
5. Seek boundary changes or artificial controls to better manage animals separated from their winter range.
6. Cease killing predatory animals both within and near parks.
7. Control the encroachment of exotic species into parks.
8. Restrict all transplants in parks to species native to the area and avoid diluting the genetic stock of native species.
9. Solve the problems caused by the exposure of native species to diseases born by domestic or exotic animals.
10. Control animal damage to plants important to the scenery or landscaping around buildings or unique in their rarity.
11. Stop the control of animals that may deplete the fish populations of parks and strive to maintain at least some park drainages free of stocking by exotic fish species.
12. Improve the management of animals that are potentially injurious to life or property and educate visitors on the proper relationship with wild animals.
13. Improve the management and mitigation of impacts and disturbances caused by park developments.
14. Protect animal breeding grounds from visitor disturbances.
15. Avoid overgrazing associated with the pasturing of saddle horses.
16. Avoid unnatural displays of wildlife such as bear feeding shows.

Source: G. Wright, J. Dixon, and B. Thompson, *A Preliminary Survey of Faunal Relations in National Parks*, National Park Service Fauna Series, no. 1 (Washington, D.C.: GPO, 1933).

park management was that "biotic associations within each park be maintained, or where necessary recreated, as nearly as possible in the condition that prevailed when the area was first visited by white man. A national park should represent a vignette of primitive America" (Leopold et al. 1963:32).

The report recommended that NPS adopt a diversity of management procedures to preserve the enormous complexity of ecological communities represented in parks. The report concluded that successful management for habitat within national parks is dependent on maintaining the ecological processes producing the habitat. It concluded that because of internal changes in park systems as a consequence of fire suppression, predator reduction, alien species, and species extinction, some habitats had deteriorated or had been destroyed and species had been extirpated. It suggested that active management might be necessary to restore pristine conditions. The report advised that management of resources should be limited to native plants and animals, and artificial means of managing or displaying animals, such as keeping animals in fenced enclosures or feeding programs, should be minimized.

Although the Leopold Report also dealt extensively with methods to control animal populations,[2] its lasting legacy was the profound influence the report's ecological orientation had on NPS resource-management policy. The recommendations of the report were widely accepted. The report's influence can be attributed in part to the reputation of its chair and the wide distribution and publicity given the document. It was reprinted by several outdoor magazines, and many thousands of copies were distributed. The simultaneous study by the National Academy of Sciences never received the same recognition though its committee was equally well qualified and its findings were similar. Today, copies of the NAS report are scarce.

One reason the Leopold Report received wide acclaim was that it was a bold statement, just bold enough to make many people in and outside the agency very nervous. It was also ably expressed. Most such commissions usually fail because their members do not recognize the need to do more than simply state a conclusion—they must state it very well and convincingly to sell their goals. The Leopold Commission did that superbly (Schullery 1989a). The impact the Leopold Report had can be seen in the present-day references by environmental groups and NPS scientists who call for a "new Leopold Commission" to review NPS research and on the references to the National Parks and Conservation Association study on research in the parks (NPCA 1988) as the "new Leopold Report."

Putting Natural Processes to Work

The concept of using measured interference in ecosystems, with a reliance on natural processes and other ecological principles, was first tested on a large scale starting in 1967 in Yellowstone as an outgrowth of an NPS agreement to stop killing elk in the park. A long-term research program was designed to enable scientists to test and evaluate the impacts of curtailing a variety of management actions that had been in effect for years by allowing the resources to be subjected to the actions of natural processes. Major actions included closing park garbage dumps used by bears to force them to return to foraging on natural foods and to reduce bear-human conflicts (see chapter 7), the initiation of a natural fire program in place of total suppression, and the elimination of elk control.

All actions were controversial. However, in terms of lasting controversy, the effects of eliminating elk control in the park has probably been most important. In what rightfully could be called an experiment, Yellowstone scientists were interested in seeing whether, in the absence of control, elk numbers would continue to increase and for how long, and whether limitations on available winter forage, periodic severe winters, or other ecological processes, such as intraspecific competition, would eventually naturally limit elk numbers at some equilibrium level (Cole 1971).[3] The group reasoned that if this equilibrium were attained, zootic disclimaxes, some soil erosion, and site deterioration would be inevitable and that ranges in less-than-optimal range condition were therefore not necessarily an indication that the density of animals was excessive (Cole 1971, telephone interview with author, Aug. 28, 1986).

These views of ungulate use of the range were directly counter to traditional range-management theory, which held that habitat degradation was unnatural and was evidence that the rangelands were being used by an excessive density of stock. As a result, there was widespread disagreement both within and outside NPS over whether the research program and the respective management actions were appropriate. Even Robert Linn, the NPS chief scientist, disagreed with some of the park's ideas and was not convinced they would work (Robert Linn, interview with author, Ft. Collins, Colo., Aug. 16, 1986). Others were even more critical, maintaining that the ideas were simply a "white-wash" for a failed elk management policy (Beetle 1974). In subsequent criticism of the program, that the scientists were advocating the implementation of research hypotheses, not management policies, was lost sight of.

The dramatic and continued growth of the elk and bison herds, the movements and harvests of animals outside the park, the influence of the 1988 fires, and the effect that wolf reintroduction might have on the herds have all served to keep ungulate management at Yellowstone, and other parks with abundant ungulates, in the spotlight. The controversy has been heightened by publications alleging gross mismanagement of the natural resources at Yellowstone because of the park's policy of relying on natural processes (e.g., Chase 1986). Thus

far, despite the criticism, the NPS has stayed the course in its maintenance of a management policy that recognizes the importance of natural processes. There have been some retrenchments, such as a
curtailment of the natural fire policy following the unprecedented
1988 Yellowstone fires, however, as scientists gain greater understanding of the unique situation that produced these fires, the appropri-
ateness of NPS policy is being reaffirmed (Christensen et al. 1989a).

Current Administrative Policies

Current administrative policies for the NPS reflect the knowledge
learned at Yellowstone and other parks in working with and understanding natural processes, as well as the recommendations of past
advisory committees. They state in part:

> The primary objective . . . will be the protection of natural re-
> sources . . . with a concern for fundamental ecological processes. . . .
> Managers . . . will not attempt solely to preserve individual species (ex-
> cept threatened or endangered species) . . . rather they will . . . main-
> tain all the components and processes of naturally evolving park
> ecosystems.
>
> Interference with natural processes in park natural zones will be al-
> lowed only (1) when directed by the Congress, (2) in some emergencies
> when human life and property are at stake, or (3) to restore native ec-
> osystem functioning that has been disrupted by past or ongoing human
> activities. . . .
>
> Natural processes will be relied on to control populations of native
> species to the greatest extent possible. Unnatural concentrations of na-
> tive species caused by human activities may be controlled if the activities
> causing the concentrations cannot be controlled. Nonnative (exotic)
> species will not be allowed to displace native species if this displacement
> can be prevented by management. (NPS 1988:4:1–6).

How Far Can Natural-Processes Management Be Extended?

Current NPS policies are obviously quite vague in terms of telling
managers what to do in a given situation. In the absence of precedent
and guidance, managers often decide for themselves the appropriate
course of action. The result is that policy in the Park Service is often
generated from the bottom up, as problems dealt with in the field test
and even shape the mandate and principles of the agency (Schullery
1989). Today, as in the past, the question of how much reliance to
place on natural processes, particularly when managing sensitive park
resources where biological, ethical, economic, and even political considerations enter the picture, is not always clear. Schullery poses an

interesting situation: "The basin of Yellowstone Lake is tilting; in a few years the nesting islands of white pelicans may be submerged, drowning one of the great nesting sites in North America. Should we be hauling gravel out there, or celebrating the imponderable power of natural processes?" (1989:46).

Isle Royale poses a similar but real-life question. There, after a five-year decline, the wolf population has inexplicably sunk to a level where extinction is a real possibility. This decline has arisen from constant high mortality coupled with a steady drop in reproduction. The reasons for the decline are not clear; they may be natural, they may not be. The decline may be the result of a decrease in food supply, mortality from new diseases, or the loss of genetic variability (Peterson and Krumanaker 1989).

For the last thirty years, Isle Royale has maintained a strict hands-off style of managing wolves and moose on the island. This approach was fully compatible with the management policies of the NPS. In 1988 this approach was changed to allow capture and handling of animals to get blood samples and place radio collars on them. Preliminary results are indeterminate with respect to exposure to canine parvovirus. Genetic variability studies are now underway.

Faced with the possible extinction of the wolf, several management options are available. Depending on the "naturalness" of the decline and the dictates of the Endangered Species Act, some or all might be compatible with NPS policy. These options include inoculation for canine parvovirus, supplemental feeding, augmentation with additional breeding animals, and capture for captive breeding (Peterson and Krumanaker 1989). If wolves were to be extirpated, additional management options might include allowances for natural recolonization, introduction of new wolves to repopulate the island, and control of the moose population via artificial means.

The maintenance of wolves on Isle Royale exemplifies the difficulties managers face in situations where policy doesn't tell what to do and precedent is absent. What is happening on Isle Royale will probably happen in other areas sooner or later. While these circumstances do not diminish the value of attempting to allow natural processes to guide management of the parks, they do point out the degree to which flexibility in their interpretation is needed.

Natural Processes and Cultural-Resource Management

Parks and monuments set aside to preserve cultural resources, e.g., battlefields, historic sites, and historic structures, are typically managed with the aim of preserving the site as it appeared during the "historic period." This static management requires that natural processes that may induce change into the system be curtailed. Conflicts resulting from opposing philosophical concepts are increasingly common.

A current area of concern involves the dramatic growth of white-tailed deer populations in historic areas in the East and their impact on plant communities, many of which are maintained in a state that reflects the historic character of the site and are thus in a somewhat static growth form. NPS management policies state that "Animal populations . . . will be controlled in . . . cultural . . . zones when necessary to protect property or landscaped areas" (NPS 1988:4:6). Unfortunately, the actual landscape-management objectives for most cultural areas are often loosely defined, which makes a determination of habitat damage by deer or other species difficult. Lethal control of animals is also often impossible due to public pressure, and other methods of reducing the population are often unfeasible or too expensive. Thus, as discussed in detail in chapter 5, these sites often face a situation very similar to that confronting natural areas with abundant ungulate species.

The Evolution of the Policy Prohibiting Sport Hunting

A policy prohibiting sport hunting and trapping in national parks dates to the Lacey Act of 1894, which prohibited all hunting and killing of birds and animals in Yellowstone. This law superseded the 1872 Yellowstone Park Act, which had prohibited only the wanton destruction or capture of fish and game for profit. Prior to the legislation establishing the NPS in 1916, sport hunting in the other parks and monuments was usually based on the provisions of the Yellowstone Act, and thus restricted, though not technically prohibited.

The 1916 act was interpreted by the NPS to mean that hunting for sport was prohibited in national parks, however, because there were few parks and virtually unlimited sport hunting opportunities outside them, this interpretation was not questioned for several decades.[4] The only departure from this provision occurred with the authorization of Mt. McKinley National Park in February 1917. That legislation permitted mining on park lands and allowed prospectors and miners to hunt in the park to supplement their food supplies. This activity also made it very difficult to control poaching.

The first written policy statement regarding the prohibition of hunting in parks was in form of a letter from Secretary Lane to Stephen Mather in May 1918: "Mountain climbing, horseback riding, walking, motoring, swimming, boating, and fishing will ever be the favorite sports. Hunting will not be permitted in any national park" (Cameron 1922:15).

Pressures to Allow Sport Hunting in Parks

The policy of prohibiting sport hunting in national parks was first seriously contested in the forties as a consequence of the ungulate control programs begun in several Rocky Mountain parks. Advocate groups viewed sport hunting as an alternative to NPS control of these populations. The Western Association of State Game and Fish Commissioners adopted a resolution in 1944 calling for hunting in the parks under licenses issued by the states, a resolution rejected by Hillory Tolson, Acting NPS Director (Tolson 1944).

The pressures to open parks to sport hunting focused primarily on the big western parks, although all parks that had what were perceived to be excess animal populations were targeted. For example, Krefting suggested that public hunting on Isle Royale would be the quickest way of decreasing the moose population (1951). He suggested, however, that public criticism could be avoided if hunting were legalized only for the Native Americans of the nearby Grand Portage Reservation who once hunted on Isle Royale.

Interest in sport hunting in national parks accelerated with the passage of Public Law 81-878 in 1950, which permitted sport hunting in portions of Grand Teton National Park by licensed hunters deputized as rangers (see chapter 10). The provision that the hunters be deputized was apparently passed to circumvent the 1942 international treaty (Cole 1969). Murie (1951) was convinced that the Wyoming senators who wrote the bill (PL 81-878) did not mean to have it construed as a precedent for hunting in national parks, but as soon as it passed Congress, the Colorado Game Department expressed hope that it might also lead to the opening of Colorado parks for hunting. The state of Washington expressed similar feelings for Olympic National Park.

The sport-hunting controversy in the Rocky Mountain parks grew more heated in the late fifties and early sixties as a result of the large NPS elk reductions at Yellowstone and the obligation of many state game departments to assume financial responsibility for crop damages caused by park animals outside the parks. Proposed plans to expand the National Park System added to the controversy. There were indications that NPS would face a stiff challenge in Congress on any expansion of the system if the new areas were closed to sport hunting. There was a fear that NPS could end up with two wildlife policies, one applying to existing areas and another to proposed areas.

Opponents of park hunting argued that sanctioning this activity would also leave the parks vulnerable to mineral exploration, water development, logging, and other exploitative uses. Supporters of park hunting spurned this argument, pointing out that "carefully managed big game hunting, where needed as a control measure, could add materially to the recreational value of these superb areas . . . [and] . . . would come at a time when the majority of the recreational visitors had left these areas" (Skibby 1960:93).

The Western Association of State Game and Fish Commissioners was a strong advocate of hunting in parks and urged "carefully controlled public hunting in cooperation with the states involved as the most acceptable solution to such problems as too many elk, deer, antelope, moose, or bighorn on too-limited range" (Carhart 1961:37). As part of this campaign, the superintendent of Yellowstone was sued by local guides in 1961 as a result of the ongoing reduction program. The court dismissed the case, stating that the disposition of animals at Yellowstone should be determined by the NPS (Reich 1962).

In 1961, the Western Association of State Game and Fish Commissioners passed a resolution urging "the National Park Service to reexamine and reappraise its policy relating to the removal of surplus game populations and to give consideration to the values of utilizing carefully controlled public hunting . . . as the most acceptable solution to such problems" (1961:289).

The focus of the conflicts over hunting in parks shifted in the early sixties to Rocky Mountain National Park. The state of Colorado was angered by what it considered to be its subservient role in the controversial elk reduction programs at that park. The state was also faced with increasing numbers of elk damage claims from ranchers outside the park, which had to be paid from hunter-license fees. Hunters objected to the idea of paying damages for animals they were unable to harvest (Teague 1972). To solve this problem the state pressed for policy change to allow sport hunting inside the park (Harbour 1963).

NPS Director Wirth appeared to capitulate to such demands and shocked many conservationists and NPS personnel when he stated at a national wildlife meeting in 1961 that "in searching for a solution to the problem [of overuse by animals] it may prove necessary to seek the cooperation of responsible citizens in local areas to participate in herd reductions" (52). Wirth further pointed out that the program would be carried out "only in those portions of a park where in the judgment of the Secretary of the Interior such participation is practical, desirable, and may be carried out safely and effectively" (52). Wirth noted that under existing laws, the secretary of the interior was empowered to permit hunters in parks. Wirth's statements were immediately criticized and countered by articles from individuals within the agency (Cahalane 1961) and by conservation groups, such as the National Park Association (Kilgore 1962). Faced with this pressure, Wirth rescinded his statement, and the NPS released a statement in October 1961 supporting its long-standing policy that banned sport hunting in national parks and monuments.

This did little to quell the controversy. In September 1962, Colorado Game Department director Harry R. Woodward proposed a pilot elk hunt in Rocky Mountain National Park at the fifty-second annual meeting of the International Association of Game and Fish Commissioners. In October, the Colorado Game Department pursued the matter in a letter to the secretary of the interior, suggesting that an experimental hunt be held in Rocky Mountain in the fall of 1963 to serve as a basis for determining what could be expected from similar hunts in other national parks and monuments because previous hunts in Grand Teton National Park were not meaningful "pilot" hunts. Such hunts would broaden the recreational use of parks and monuments. The Colorado Game and Fish Department staff would assist in planning and executing the hunt, with the number of permits to be determined jointly by the Fish and Game Department and the NPS. If NPS was still concerned about "dangerous and unreliable" hunters in the park, then cadets from the U.S. Air Force Academy's Rod and Gun Club might be used since they were thoroughly trained in hunter safety and could hunt under strict military discipline (Musselman 1971).

The validity of these ideas was further supported by a Department of the Interior solicitor's opinion that concluded that NPS laws did not prohibit the secretary of the interior from using public hunting as a tool to reduce surplus numbers of animals in national parks (Henning 1965).

The controversy over hunting in the parks was also heightened by the introduction of Senate bill S 2545 in 1962, which would have required the secretary of the interior to consult at least once a year with the governor of each state containing an NPS area to determine whether big-game-animal reductions were necessary. The bill provided that if reductions were needed, the secretary could enter into an agreement authorizing the state to issue licenses to hunters to hunt in parks and remove their kill. Though pressures by conservation groups forced the defeat of this bill, these threats were a major factor behind Secretary Udall's appointment of the Special Wildlife Advisory Board on Wildlife Management in 1962. In a May 23, 1962, press announcement Udall stated, "Until now this Administration has not had the opportunity to conduct the kind of study which would lead to an objective determination of the issue of hunting in the National Park System, but definite plans have been made for the conduct of such an analysis by a panel of unbiased and thoroughly expert persons. . . . From that analysis we hope to reach a general conclusion on the issue of hunting which can be applied to the National Park System" (USDI 1962:1).

After thorough deliberation, the committee concluded that the national parks should not be open to public hunting. Regarding population control, the report of the committee stated: "Where . . . excess park ungulates must be removed by killing . . . it is [our] unanimous recommendation . . . that such shooting be conducted by competent personnel, under the sole jurisdiction of the National Park Service, and for the sole purpose of animal removal, not recreational hunting" (Leopold et al. 1963:39).

The publication of this report, which obviously disappointed advocates of park hunting, marked the end of much of the controversy, as did the termination of most park control programs. Public support was also slowly turning in favor of the parks, and in the end most state game authorities were left with no alternative but to recognize NPS responsibility for the conservation and management of the wildlife within the boundaries of the national parks and monuments (Evison 1964).[5]

One state that continued to litigate was New Mexico, which in 1969 took the Park Service to court for killing mule deer in Carlsbad Caverns without first getting a collecting permit from the state. The state submitted that it owned the wildlife and that the management, regulation, and killing of wildlife were thus its sole responsibility. The U.S. District Court for New Mexico upheld the state's argument, but, in rendering this decision, the court ignored the ownership issue and ruled only that NPS did not have the authority to kill state-owned animals.

The Park Service appealed this ruling by arguing that (1) for it to perform its management responsibilities, research must be performed—the killing was part of a research project; (2) that the state did not own wildlife within the park boundaries; and (3) that when federal and state interests collided in the performance of a federal activity, the state laws must yield. The Tenth Circuit Court of Appeals ruled in favor of NPS, finding that the secretary of the interior was responsible for the proper management of park wildlife populations, which included conducting research. The ownership question was ignored. The court concluded that in protecting the park it was immaterial whether the United States had exclusive jurisdiction over said lands.

A definitive ruling on the ownership of animals on federal lands came in 1972 as a result of a request by New Mexico to have the 1971 Wild Horses and Burros Act declared unconstitutional because it placed animals on public lands under the protection of the secretaries of interior and agriculture. In 1972 the Supreme Court upheld the constitutionality of the act and affirmed the power of Congress to manage wildlife on public lands (*Kleppe v. New Mexico* 1972). A more recent court decision also affirmed NPS authority over wildlife even in areas where the agency does not own all of the land within a defined boundary.[6]

There have been few major controversies concerning the subject of sport hunting in established parks in recent years. However, there are special-interest groups always ready to challenge existing policy, as in 1984 when the National Rifle Association (NRA) filed a suit against the Department of the Interior challenging NPS regulations against hunting and fishing. The NRA argued that since Congress had not specifically prohibited these activities in park legislation, they should be permitted. In 1986 the U.S. District Court ruled in favor of NPS.

The ability of the sport-hunting lobby to influence policies in existing parks has diminished in recent years. This is not surprising since surveys such as Shaw's in 1974 have repeatedly shown that a majority of people are opposed to killing animals in parks and since the proportion of people who sport hunt in the United States has progressively decreased over the last two decades. Therefore, today as in the past, national parks and related areas remain one of the few large categories of public land that are specifically closed to the sport harvest of all terrestrial vertebrates. Current management policy states, "Hunting and trapping wildlife will be allowing only in parks where such use is specifically authorized. In areas set aside with legal authorization for hunting, trapping, . . . or other harvest of native wildlife, the NPS will still seek to perpetuate native animal life and to protect the integrity of natural ecosystems" (NPS 1988:4:7). Sport hunting continues to influence efforts to create new parks. This was particularly true for the new Alaskan parks as well as parks in the continental

United States.[7] One recent "solution" has been the use of the "national preserve" land classification (see chapter 10).

The Policy for Subsistence Hunting in Parks

The first subsistence hunting in parks dates to the early days of Yellowstone. The major reason hunting was permitted there was the belief that this was the only way that visitors and concession operators could obtain sufficient food. Those days are obviously long gone, and until the new parks were created in Alaska, subsistence hunting in parks was prohibited. Subsistence hunting in general in Alaska has been a highly controversial topic mixed with racial overtones. It has been acerbated by the grants of large land areas to Native American groups as part of the Alaska National Interest Lands Conservation Act (ANILCA). Approximately 18 million hectares are now owned by the twelve native corporations established under ANILCA. Many non-native groups in the state have argued that with these extensive land holdings there is no reason for Native Americans to have preferential subsistence hunting rights in parks and on other public lands. There have even been unsuccessful attempts to repeal all subsistence rights.

The right to hunt for subsistence purposes in NPS areas was an integral part of ANILCA.[8] Although ANILCA has no racial bias, it seemed apparent during the legislative process that lawmakers saw subsistence as applying only to native Alaskans. The state of Alaska recognizes no racial distinctions relative to the rights of individuals to follow a subsistence lifestyle; thus, anyone living in a bush situation can claim the right to harvest animals for subsistence. ANILCA gave subsistence uses of fish and wildlife priority over other consumptive uses. Reasonable access to subsistence resources was assured, including the use of snowmobiles, powerboats, and other "traditional" means of transportation. The subsistence clause is a source of controversy, particularly in times of game scarcity. It is also complicated by the fact that in and around many of the new parks more people seem to be pursuing a subsistence lifestyle by choice rather than for economic reasons.

There appears to be little doubt that the subsistence provisions in ANILCA have the potential to pose great problems in the Alaska parks. Many individuals believe that the provisions of ANILCA are unworkable or will have to be repealed as the greed of a few destroy the rights for many. Others point out that there is no need to hunt in the Alaskan parks for meat since there are sufficient areas in the state to do this, including the national preserves that adjoin all the parks. To date there have not been significant problems with subsistence users. However, as their numbers invariably increase, conflicts with other park values are inevitable. To deal with this problem NPS needs to develop educational programs that will prepare the visitor for encounters with different user groups and will explain the present management policies. Such programs can offer visitors a glimpse of lifestyles with deep historical roots but that are now foreign to most people. If properly structured, the interaction among park staff, local people, and visitors can generate pride in a unique way of life, protect the ecosystems, and perpetuate cultural traditions (Wright 1984a).

Policies Concerning Native American Hunting Rights

Over the past decade there have been numerous challenges by various tribes in the continental United States seeking proprietary use of fish and wildlife resources on park lands. More recently these demands have been extended to some national parks based on historic treaty rights. In Olympic National Park in November 1983, two enrolled members of the Quinault tribe were charged with illegally killing several elk within the park (Holt 1986). The killings took place within traditional hunting grounds ceded by the Quinault tribe to the government in 1855. The defendants claimed that the charges should be dismissed because the treaty reserved their right to hunt in that portion of the park. In January 1984, in a surprise ruling, the chief district judge dismissed the charges against the tribal members.

The settlement resulted in a great deal of public concern that Native Americans could be allowed to hunt in a national park. As a result, less than a month later Washington member of Congress Swift introduced legislation to overturn the court decision and extinguish any existing Native American hunting rights remaining in the park. The government also quickly filed a motion for a rehearing of the decision. It argued that as Olympic National Park was established expressly to protect Roosevelt elk and since hunting would endanger Congress's purpose for the park, it was clear that hunting was incompatible with congressional intent for the area. In April the district court reconsidered its initial decision and issued an opinion supporting the government's position.

Holt pointed out that although several tribes asserted their belief that the court decision was wrong, they did not appeal (1986). It is not clear why they did not appeal, although "political pressure seems to be the only answer coupled with the belief that the time was not appropriate for Indian assertion of rights, especially in national parks" (253). Holt pointed out that determinable hunting rights are compensable property interests, thus, the 1938 legislation that established Olympic National Park and preserved treaty rights also preserved those hunting rights in the park. In addition, since hunting was not banned in the park by the 1938 legislation, it was thus not incompatible with the purposes of the park. At least until 1942, when Congress passed additional legislation, the Quinault tribe retained the right to hunt on ceded lands in the park. He concluded that the 1942 legislation destroyed the Quinault tribe rights on those lands, abrogating the treaty and entitling the Quinault tribe either to the right to continue to hunt or to compensation.

Policies Concerning Sport Hunting in Other NPS Areas

Sport hunting is specifically authorized by law in all national preserves and in forty-five recreation areas, seashores, and lakeshores administered by the NPS. Trapping is legally permitted in twenty of these areas. In fourteen of the remaining areas the authorizing legislation prohibits trapping; no mention is made of trapping in the other eleven areas. Prior to 1982, park managers in these eleven areas had customarily interpreted the authority for sport hunting to encompass trapping. In an effort to clarify this situation, NPS established a policy that permitted hunting and trapping only in areas where it was specifically authorized by federal law. This was done because the agency concluded that it did not have the administrative discretion to broadly interpret hunting to include trapping. Even though these areas were small and seldom used by trappers, there was strong opposition to this change from the National Trappers Association, the NRA, and from Assistant Secretary of the Interior Arnett. The secretary signed the rule in 1983 but it was not imposed until 1987.

In general, there appear to be few problems or conflicts with sport hunting policies in most national recreation areas and equivalent sites. In most areas state agency officials set seasons and bag limits and enforce hunting laws. NPS retains the right to close certain areas to hunting for visitor safety or to protect unique resources.

Policies Concerning Fishing in National Parks

Although sport fishing in parks is not an integral part of this book, it is worth commenting on the policies that have developed to manage sport fishing since they differ significantly from those of other resources. The policy permitting sport fishing in national parks dates from the time Yellowstone was established. Not only was sport fishing allowed, it was generally enhanced whenever possible. The first known stocking of trout in a park occurred in 1889 when acting Yellowstone superintendent Boutelle reported on the stocking of young trout as a supplement for fish infected with parasitic worms (Hampton 1971). In the California parks acting military superintendents also sought to replenish "barren" waters by stocking young trout. Working in concert with the state of California, some 55,000 trout were planted in steams of Yosemite and Sequoia in 1902. Subsequent years saw additional plantings (Hampton 1971). These numbers were small in comparison to what was occurring in Yellowstone and Glacier, where by 1920, 2 million trout and 1.5 million grayling fry were being planted in respective park waters (Cameron 1922). To assist in these efforts, federal and state fish hatcheries were constructed in Yellowstone, Glacier, and Rocky Mountain, and the tradition of maintaining or expanding park fishery resources became firmly entrenched. By 1940, some 22.3 million fish were being planted yearly in twenty different parks.

In 1936, the Park Service issued its first formal policy statement on fisheries. In reviewing the history of fisheries management in parks, the statement recognized that fisheries policies were at variance with those of other resources. It found that as a result of NPS activities, no less than twenty to thirty non-native species of fish had been permanently established in park waters. Some stocking had been done in virtually every park. The new policy called for the protection of all park waters that remained free of non-native species. The policy also favored the management of native species over non-natives in waters where the two coexisted. Finally, this policy restricted future stocking of fish in parks by states and other federal agencies without NPS approval and direction. By the early sixties the NPS initiated a new fisheries-management concept called "Fishing for Fun." This program focused on the recreational benefits of fishing, and the importance of the catch was diminished. Regulations were issued governing the use of artificial flies and lures, and fish were returned alive to the lakes and streams.

Today, many people recognize that fishing is on a shaky philosophical ground in national parks. Schullery has pointed out that there is "no reason except hoary tradition that we should be out there harassing some wildlife populations [in parks] just because they had the ill fortune to be hairless and lacking big brown eyes" (1989:45). For the present, fishing seems to be viewed as an acceptable compromise of the Park Service's underlying principles, and although more restrictive regulations are certain, it is unlikely that fishing will be banned in national parks in the near future.

NOTES

1. The Washington office science staff objected to what they considered to be the racially biased phrase *white man* in the statement, and they disputed the idea that an ecosystem could be frozen in time. NPS scientists unsuccessfully advocated the following replacement wording in the report: "be maintained, or where necessary recreated as nearly as possible in that ecological condition that would now prevail were it not for the impact of the activities of Post Columbian North American culture" (Robert Linn, letter to author, Sept. 21, 1988).

2. The report considered trapping and transplanting excess ungulates unfeasible because of the costs involved and because there was often no place to put the animals. It suggested that excess animals that migrated outside the parks could be controlled by sport hunting, even though this method might favor the survival of nonmigratory animals. It reaffirmed the role of predators and of the need to intensify their protection in parks. However, it considered that predators alone were incapable of controlling park ungulate populations.

3. The Yellowstone scientists had many years of cumulative experiences with ungulate management in several Rocky Mountain parks (see, e.g., Houston 1968; Cole 1969; Stevens 1970; Meagher 1971; and Martinka 1969b). The group included Glen Cole, Douglas Houston, Clifford Martinka, Mary Meagher, Don Despain, Dave Stevens, and Bill Barmore. Their ideas were further reinforced by conversations with visiting scientists, such as B. C. Fitzgerald and John Owens (Serengeti National Park), who had, based on observations in their own areas, reached similar conclusions (Glen Cole, telephone conversation with author, Aug. 28, 1986).

4. In 1942, Congress did amend the authorizing legislation for Olympic, Rainier, and Glacier to specifically prohibit sport hunting. Also in that year, the International Treaty for Nature Protection and Wildlife Protection in the Western Hemisphere was signed by the United States and seventeen other countries. These governments agreed to prohibit hunting, killing, or capturing of all the fauna in national parks except as directed by park authorities or for authorized scientific investigations (NPS 1947).

5. The findings of the committee should not have been unexpected. In terms of the five-member committee's feelings on sport hunting in parks, D. H. Henning ranked their opinions as follows: Leopold and Gabrielson, neutral; Cain and Cottam, against; Kimball, prohunting (1965).

6. In 1986 NPS sought a court injunction to prevent the West Virginia De-

partment of Natural Resources from spraying a pesticide inside the boundaries of New River Gorge National River to kill black flies without an NPS permit. The National River contains 24,800 hectares of which only 2,360 are federally owned. The state submitted that it owned the river bed and all the wild animals in it. The court granted the injunction, maintaining that the authority of the United States is not limited to the 2,360 hectares of which it has legal title, but that it also includes the 23,620 hectares designated as the national river. The court further found that the federal regulations that prohibit the destruction of wildlife in national parks pertain to black flies, concluding that black flies, although annoying to humans, are clearly wildlife and their destruction is therefore banned (*USA v. Arch A. Moore* 1986).

7. For example, efforts to create a national park in the Sawtooth Mountains of central Idaho in the seventies were thwarted because it would close a large area to sport hunting. Similarly, opposition for many years prevented the establishment of a national park encompassing the Wheeler Peak area in Nevada. The recent establishment of the Great Basin National Park in this area came only after the park size was reduced and limited to high elevation lands.

8. ANILCA defines subsistence uses to mean "the customary and traditional uses by rural Alaskan residents of wild renewable resources for . . . consumption as food . . . for fuel, shelter, clothing, tools, transportation; for the making and selling of handicraft articles . . . for barter" (sec. 803, p. 1. 96–487).

4

Animal Control in the National Parks

The complete protection that all native species of animals enjoy in national parks today is of relatively recent origin. In years past, incredible numbers and kinds of animals have been killed in national parks (see Table 4.1). Animals were historically killed for five major reasons: (1) because they killed other desirable or beneficial animals (predators); (2) because they were considered to be in excess of the capacity of the habitat to support them and thus it was feared they would starve if numbers were not reduced (ungulates); (3) to prevent them from harming park visitors or employees (grizzly and black bears); (4) because they were classified as alien to the native ecosystems they occupied and were implicated in the damage of indigenous ecosystems (feral pigs, goats, and burros); and (5) because they disturbed park habitats or may have carried disease (several small mammals).

The killing of any type of animal in parks has long been a controversial management action. Even attempts to eliminate predators in parks, which met with relatively little controversy in the twenties (and in some areas still does), was eventually stopped because of public criticism. The ungulate control programs have been by far the most enigmatic. Undertaken with altruism and the welfare of the populations at heart, these were truly programs designed to destroy single animals to save the species. While initially enjoying broad management support, the often ugly carnage associated with these programs stirred immense public outcry from two divergent groups, those who were totally opposed to the actions and those who thought they should do the killing. Most recent animal large-scale reductions have been aimed at eliminating or reducing certain alien species. Although these operations generally have had a sound management basis, even these have enjoyed only limited public support. The growth of the animal-rights movement has complicated these actions as well as all other types of animal control.

Programs to Eliminate Predators

The most intensive animal control actions in parks have been waged against predators. Yellowstone, as the first national park, was by default the first to kill predators. These programs started immediately after the park was established and continued throughout the period of military and early NPS management. Predators were first killed in Yellowstone ostensibly to protect the lives or personal posses-

Table 4.1 Recorded Estimates of the Species Killed or Removed from National Parks

Date	Number	Park	Reference
Bison			
1942-61	120	Colorado	NPS (1962)
1940-62	20	Platt	NPS (1962)
1939-76	900	Wind Cave	Powell (1977)
1901-68	4,092	Yellowstone	Meagher (1973)
Black Bear			
1964-73	13	Crater Lake	McCollum (1974)
1919-87	4	Denali	Dalle-Molle (pers. comm.)
1960-63	15	Glacier	NPS (1963)
1960-63	38	Grand Teton	NPS (1963)
1960-77	161	Great Smokies	Singer and Bratton (1977)
1960-63	8	Mt. Rainier	NPS (1963)
1970-86	16	North Cascades	Park Files
1960-63	7	Olympic	NPS (1963)
1890-1986	771	Sequoia	Park Files
1885-82	973	Yellowstone	Schullery (1986)
1960-80	875	Yosemite	Cella and Keay (1980)
Bobcat			
1906-31	554	Grand Canyon	Park Files
1920-24	40	Rocky Mountain	Park Files
Burro			
1946-87	463	Bandelier	Allen (pers. comm.)

Table 4.1 Recorded Estimates of the Species Killed or Removed from National Parks (continued)

Date	Number	Park	Reference
1920-68	6,640	Death Valley	Douglas (pers. comm.)
1924-80	3,677	Grand Canyon	Grand Canyon (1980)
		Cougar	
1950	2	Big Bend	NPS (1962)
1921-24	30	Glacier	Park Files
1906-31	781	Grand Canyon	Park Files
1924-30	2	Mesa Verde	Park Files
1909-14	6	Mt. Rainier	Park Files
1920-24	15	Rocky Mountain	Park Files
1920-39	17	Saguaro	NPS (1939)
1894-1935	32	Sequoia	Park Files
1872-1935	201	Yellowstone	Cahalane (1939)
1917	25	Yosemite	Park Files
1926	14	Zion	Park Files
		Coyote	
1929-34	7	Denali	Park Files
1921-24	33	Glacier	Park Files
1906-31	4,889	Grand Canyon	Park Files
1920-24	25	Rocky Mountain	Park Files
1872-1935	5,452	Yellowstone	Schullery (1986)
1961	38	Yosemite	Park Files
		Elk	
1954-63	228	Glacier	Wasem (pers. comm.)
1944-69	455	Rocky Mountain	Park Files
1937-41	36	Wind Cave	NPS (1962)
1892-1966	14,304	Yellowstone	Park Files
1928-79	16,419	Yellowstone	Houston (1982)
		Feral Goat	
1930-87	1,700	Haleakala	Ohasi and Stone (1987)
1927-82	85,075	Hawaii Volcanoes	Katahira and Stone (1982)
		Grizzly Bear	
1919-87	18	Denali	Dalle-Molle (pers. comm.)
1910-82	44	Glacier	Martinka (1982)
1962-86	11	Katmai	Katmai (1987)
1885-1985	343	Yellowstone	Park Files

Table 4.1 Recorded Estimates of the Species Killed or Removed from National Parks (continued)

Date	Number	Park	Reference
		Moose	
1934-37	71	Isle Royale	Krefting (1951)
		Mule Deer	
1975-76	118	Bandelier	Park Files
1947-62	103	Grand Canyon	NPS (1962)
1952-56	139	Mesa Verde	NPS (1962)
1944-45	129	Rocky Mountain	Park Files
1952-75	1,253	Sequoia	Sequoia (1987)
1965	908	Yosemite	Park Files
1938	117	Zion	Dixon and Sumner (1939)
		Pronghorn Antelope	
1947-51	1,015	Yellowstone	Park Files
		White-Tailed Deer	
1960-61	161	Acadia	NPS (1962)
1960-61	5	Colonial	NPS (1962)
1936	75	Glacier	Aiton (1938)
1980-81	77	Great Smokies	Park Files
1957-63	1,497	Mammoth Cave	NPS (1963)
		Wild Boar and Wild Pig	
1959-85	2,418	Great Smokies	Park Files
1916-86	>1,000	Haleakala	Stone (pers. comm.)
1916-86	>1,000	Hawaii Volcanoes	Stone (pers. comm.)
		Wolf	
1919-84	86	Denali	Singer (1986)
1906-31	30	Grand Canyon	Park Files
1872-1935	163	Yellowstone	Schullery (1986)
1915	2	Yosemite	Park Files

sions of the employees or visitors. Superintendent Norris reported that poisoned carcasses were put out to kill wolves and wolverines, and mountain lions were killed to prevent them from molesting the riding and pack stock (1881).

Protection of ungulate populations soon became the most important motive for predator control. Secretary of Interior Noble appointed a predator hunter for Yellowstone in 1891, and in 1895 Acting Military Superintendent Anderson instituted a systematic campaign to kill coyotes. The attitudes of park managers in Yellowstone and presumably other areas during the early years were summarized by Murie: "In examining the annual reports of the superintendents of Yellowstone it has been exceedingly interesting to observe the attitudes concerning predators which have been held in years past. Almost from the beginning, a feeling against predators has existed. Only occasionally is a voice raised in their defense and then it speaks apologetically and with deference" (1940:11).

After the Park Service was established, predators, particularly wolves, cougars, and coyotes, were excluded from the policies governing the protection of wildlife, and the new agency initiated a wholesale predator control program. Having virtually no internal scientific expertise on this matter, NPS actions were influenced strongly by prevailing public attitudes, which were strongly supportive of predator control. Many individuals were undoubtedly convinced by the literary style of popular wildlife writers such as Hornaday who strongly condemned the murderous acts of predators (1913). Park Service policy was also influenced by ranchers and settlers outside the parks who wanted to protect their livestock, by hunters who wanted to protect game, and by park superintendents who wanted to ensure large game herds to show the public (Cahalane 1948b).

Even some wildlife professionals who generally took a more balanced view of predation became emotional when the situation warranted. Heller, a game naturalist with the Roosevelt Wild Life Forest Experiment Station in Yellowstone, usually condemned the shooting of coyotes in Yellowstone, indicating that park officials did not understand the idea of a balance of nature. Yet he too felt that "any coyote caught killing fawns . . . should . . . be separated from his spirit at the point of a bullet as an undesirable citizen. [Only those] . . . normal mouse-hunting coyotes . . . should receive the protection and encouragement of everyone." He also did not blame park rangers who "love to have some live object on which to try their marksmanship and the coyote is their legitimate prey under the present rules" (1925:422). Leopold also said that while he was glad to see NPS predator control being reduced, he was "certain . . . that some control is necessary even in the Parks. . . . It would be indefensible . . . to let lions decimate an unproductive herd of rare animals such as the Yellowstone antelope or the Yellowstone sheep" (1927).

With these types of influences, it is therefore not surprising that support for predator control existed at the highest levels of the Park

Service, such as Director Mather's response to a plea to curtail coyote control in Yellowstone: "That brings in a great many problems. In Yellowstone if Mr. Albright didn't kill off his 200 to 300 coyotes a year, it might result in their being the developing group for coyotes and wolves spreading out over the country and cattle or sheep men getting much greater losses than they ordinarily would" (1928:3).

Predator control policies in other western parks generally followed the example set at Yellowstone. The extent of the control programs was generally at the discretion of the park superintendent, who was influenced by local conditions and attitudes. Predator control was discontinued at Mt. Rainier and Sequoia by 1918 because those managers no longer felt it was necessary. However, in most Rocky Mountain parks, administrators pressured by outside groups used every resource at their disposal to eliminate predators, principally wolves, coyotes, and cougars. These parks entered into a cooperative agreement with the Federal Biological Survey, permitting their personnel to work in the parks to control predators. This program was unfortunately very successful, and by 1924 the wolf was extinct in Yellowstone, Rocky Mountain, and Glacier National Parks, and cougars were nearly exterminated.

As major predators decreased in numbers, emphasis shifted to other species, and at one time the official NPS list of undesirable predators included lynx; bobcat; badger; mink; weasel; wolverine; fisher; marten; otter; and red, gray, and swift foxes, as well as hawks, owls, kingfishers, and pelicans (Cahalane 1939, 1947).[1]

The first recorded use of poison as a control was in 1898, when it was placed in elk carcasses in Yellowstone to kill coyotes. Poison was used in many parks by the early 1900s. A number of coyotes were poisoned in Yosemite in the winter of 1910–11. Strychnine was used periodically in Glacier from 1914 through the early thirties. Compound 1080 poison stations were used along the eastern and western boundaries of the park as recently as 1952 (Singer 1975). The last recorded use of poisons to control predators was in Rocky Mountain in 1922 (Cahalane 1939), and it was banned in parks in 1930.

Trapping was another widely practiced method of predator control, first used in 1904. Public sentiment turned against the use of the steel trap in the twenties, and in 1928 the superintendents' annual meeting adopted a resolution against its use. The resolution was put into effect in Grand Canyon in 1930, in Yellowstone in 1931, and in Yosemite in 1932. After trapping and other predator control programs were eliminated in the thirties, outside groups maintained a vigorous campaign to have coyote control reinstated. Prominent among these groups were the national and state associations of wool growers.[2] Shooting, however, was always the most widely used means of predator control, and after the use of traps was discontinued, it became the sole method of control in parks.

Park rangers were generally responsible for predator control activities. Special civilian hunters or personnel from the Biological Survey were called in only when a park felt additional control was necessary or to train park staff. In the early days, to make the control activities more attractive to rangers, there was an unwritten rule that they could keep some of the animal furs as special compensation. (It was believed that without this special reimbursement, the rangers would not pursue the control work with sufficient vigor.) In Rocky Mountain, for example, rangers were allowed to retain about 25% of the funds derived from the sale of pelts taken in the control programs. This was offered as compensation for expenses involved in obtaining poison, traps, and feed for horses and ammunition, all of which came out of the ranger's salary of about $900 per year (Musselman 1971). Later, the government sold the pelts at auction and the rangers were reimbursed only for expenses.

Predator control surfaced again in 1946 with calls for the extermination of the wolf in Mt. McKinley. The role of wolf predation on Dall sheep populations in that park had long been a subject of controversy and speculation. After the park was created, the cessation of market hunting combined with a series of mild winters caused the sheep population to expand greatly. In 1923, the Dall sheep population was estimated at 10,000 (Cahalane 1946). Within a period of five years, however, a series of harsh winters caused the population to drop drastically to a level estimated to be between 1,000 and 1,500.

Continuing uncertainty about the situation caused NPS to ask Adolph Murie to make a study of the relationships of wolves and Dall sheep in the park in 1939 (Murie 1944). He concluded that wolf and Dall sheep numbers in the park had been relatively stable over the preceding ten years and saw no need for predator control. He felt that continued monitoring of the Dall sheep population was desirable so that management could quickly take appropriate corrective measures if necessary.

Unfortunately, during the next five years the demands of World War II limited NPS ability to carry out monitoring activities. Murie was again detailed to the park briefly in the fall of 1945 to check on the situation. He then estimated the Dall sheep population at five hundred. He concluded "that the population had been drastically reduced" (1945:2). He could not ascertain any change in the wolf population nor did he find clear evidence that the wolves were responsible for this reduction. He did suggest that "as a precautionary measure it would be wise to control the [park] . . . wolves to assist the mountain sheep herd to recover to a more favorable status. For the present, . . . it would be wise to decrease the number of wolves. Even 10 or 15 wolves to begin with, taken from the heart of mountain sheep range, would supplement the 'outside control' by trappers along the park boundary. The amount of control in the future can be adjusted to the observed results" (3–4). The Park Service estimated that the recommended removals would constitute about 50% of the wolves that occupied the sheep range in the park (Drury 1946.)

A skilled local hunter was employed for this mission. Five wolves were killed that year. However, wolves were considered to be uncommon in the park, and NPS suspended the use of professional hunters in April 1946, leaving park personnel responsible for control. This method was considered inadequate by individuals who insisted that the park had to do more to protect the game animals. In a move reminiscent of the attitudes that prevailed in Yellowstone twenty-five years earlier, legislation was introduced in Congress (H.R. 5401) to amend the act establishing the park to include the following: "The Secretary of the Interior shall take such action as may be necessary, including the immediate reduction in the number of wolves, coyotes, and other predators in Mount McKinley National Park, to the end that the said refuge shall become and be maintained as a safe sanctuary for the Dall sheep, caribou, and other wildlife, except predators, native to the area" (Cahalane 1946:21).

Cahalane, then NPS chief biologist, lobbied hard against passage of the bill, pointing out the obvious fact that Mt. McKinley was the only national park where the wolf had not been exterminated and it deserved to remain in this condition (1946). The efforts of Cahalane and others succeeded and the bill failed to pass. Wolf control in the park, however, continued until 1952. Between 1946 and 1952 twenty-six wolves were killed in the park and at least twice that many had been killed outside the park (Singer 1986).

Today, all predators are completely protected in parks, and there are even attempts to reintroduce some species, such as the wolf, back into some parks (see chapter 8). This movement combined with a more enlightened attitude toward predators by both wildlife management agencies and by the general public tempts one to conclude that predator control in parks is a thing of the past. This may be wishful thinking. Although there have been no efforts to control predators in parks since 1952, requests for this action and minor instances of predator control in parks continue to arise. For example, in 1961 the Bureau of Sports Fisheries and Wildlife investigated complaints that local ranchers were losing animals to "wolves" near Pea Ridge National Military Park, Arkansas. The animals were actually coyotes. After obtaining NPS approval, an agreement with the Arkansas Fish and Game Commission allowed the state to trap coyotes within the park for one year, with a maximum quota of five coyotes. Trapping in 1962 was unsuccessful and only one coyote was trapped outside the park.

If predator control in parks again surfaces as a controversy, it will undoubtedly be in Alaska. A portend of the future was seen in the 1977 attempt by the state to initiate an aerial wolf hunt in the northwest in areas proposed for park protection under the Alaska Native Claims Settlement Act. This effort was thwarted because the Bureau of Land Management (the existing land management agency) was taken to court for failing to have filed an Environmental Impact Statement on the hunt. However, even though the areas are now national parks and preserves, requests for wolf control continue as more and more demands are placed on game resources by subsistence and sport hunters.

NOTES

1. The case of white pelicans on the Molly Islands in Yellowstone Lake is an interesting example of NPS attitudes of the time. The U.S. Commission of Fish and Fisheries had established a cutthroat egg collection station on the shore of Yellowstone Lake in 1901. Over the next twenty-two years 187 million trout eggs were taken from this station to transplant throughout the world. This impact on the local fisheries was combined with the harvest of trout for park hotels and camps—a practice that resulted in the taking of 7,500 pounds of trout in the summer of 1919 alone (Culler 1931).

By 1917, the park began to note a decline in the fish populations in the streams between Thumb and Lake Hotel. Despite the harvests described above, the white pelican colony on Molly Island in Yellowstone Lake, numbering approximately five hundred birds, was implicated as the causal agent. M. Culler summarized the rationale that was common at the time: "It is my opinion that the pelicans of Yellowstone Lake destroy four times as many fish than are caught. Before the tourist traffic became so great and before any commercial fishing was allowed . . . [this did not present a problem]. But now due to the greater number of tourists and the more intensive fishing it will be necessary to curb the predicious [sic] bird so that the toursits [sic] will continue to enjoy good fishing at all times" (1931).

Accordingly, a control program was implemented in 1926 when all eggs (about 200) were destroyed, and in 1927 and 1928 about 214 young were killed (Schaller 1964). Lick reported that in 1927 "a lot of the early hatch got away, but in 1928 we killed every young pelican on the island, that year nothing escaped" (1932). This action occurred though there was considerable evidence from the Bureau of Fisheries that the birds may have harvested only a few hundred trout a year.

In response to pressures from national conservation groups, this program was terminated in 1932, and the superintendent issued an order prohibiting all boats from even passing close to the Molly Islands during the nesting season.

2. An interesting rebuke to the wool growers is seen in the address of Joseph Dixon to the annual meeting of the California Wool Growers Association (Dixon 1935). Dixon commented specifically on reports that Yosemite was teeming with coyotes that were reported to spread out from the park and destroy nearby flocks of sheep and other livestock:

I challenge any wool grower to show me six coyote dens containing young in Yosemite National Park, 1,176 square miles, in any one season. Four days ago I interviewed the man . . . who was given as your authority for the statement, and he voluntarily said that although he had lived in the Yosemite region for many years he had never set foot inside of the park and had never actually seen a single coyote in Yosemite National Park. . . .

I want to direct your attention to one important fact which I fear that you do not appreciate, namely that Yosemite National Park is one of your best markets for sheep products. The purchasing agent of the Yosemite Park and Curry Co. informed me that in one year, October 1, 1934 to October 1, 1935, 22,840 pounds of whole lamb and 23,510 pounds of lamb cuts were consumed by visitors in Yosemite. In addition to this [NPS] used about 10,000 pounds of lamb and mutton making a grand total of 56,000 pounds of lamb consumed annually in Yosemite alone. Even the rangers wear sheep-lined coats in winter. . . .

Thus it will be readily seen that visitors to Yosemite consume annually many times the entire sheep population of Tuolumne County. Gentlemen, you are all wrong! It is not the coyotes that eat the lambs at Yosemite. It is the visitors to the park that eat them and they pay a handsome price for every pound of mutton that they eat there. Many of the visitors come from distant states and from foreign lands to see Yosemite. I trust that the California Wool Growers Association is far-sighted enough not to try to cut off its nose to spite its face. (1935:3–5)

5

The Management of Ungulate Species

Of all the animal species found in parks, the large grazing and browsing animals are closest to the hearts of Park Service resource managers and, as a result, have by far received the most attention. Referred to somewhat facetiously as the "heroic species" by NPS personnel, species like elk, mule deer, and bison have been a principle management concern since the early days at Yellowstone when they were threatened with slaughter by poachers and market hunters. Even after this threat was reduced, the wildlife-management priorities of parks remained focused on the protection and enhancement of these species. Managers were deeply convinced that all that was needed to assure their survival and growth was complete protection. No animal or situation better exemplifies this than the program developed to manage bison at Yellowstone.[1] Management therefore sought to reduce or eliminate all feasible sources of ungulate mortality. Deaths that were considered preventable were a source of great frustration for park managers. The programs to eliminate predators discussed in the last chapter were one outgrowth of the desire to increase species survival. Another source of mortality that concerned park managers was losses of animals during the winter. Managers tended to view these deaths almost anthropocentrically as a loss of life that could have been avoided if only more food or better cover were available to the animals. As a consequence, one of the first management actions in national parks was the initiation of supplemental winter feeding programs.

Supplemental Feeding Programs

Programs to provide supplemental winter feed were first started in

Yellowstone in 1904 when deer, bighorn sheep, and antelope were fed hay because forage on the winter range was perceived to be insufficient. Animals fed were those that congregated along a fence line near the north entrance of Yellowstone. This fence had been built in 1899 along the northern boundary at Gardiner to help keep out local livestock and to keep antelope in the park to protect them from waiting hunters. By 1903 the number of antelope wintering in this area was estimated at one thousand, and the acting superintendent advocated that a supplemental feeding program for antelope and bighorn sheep be started. The source of the feed was a 50-acre field in the park north of Gardiner that had been planted in the early 1900s with alfalfa to be stockpiled in the event of a hard winter. Over the next decade, because of better protection, exclusion of domestic livestock, and supplemental feeding, the numbers of bighorn sheep, antelope, and deer increased, and by 1916, these species were consuming 200 tons of hay each year, and by 1919 with elk also being fed, 350 tons were used (Haines 1977).

The feeding program for Yellowstone elk was initiated during the winter of 1919 after storms had driven elk to the low country where they were slaughtered by hunters. Director Mather acquired $8,000 from the Department of the Interior and supplemented it with his own money to purchase feed (Shankland 1970). This program continued until 1937. Feeding operations caused large concentrations of animals with resultant heavy use of vegetation on and adjacent to the feedgrounds.

By the twenties, feeding grounds existed in several western parks. Most programs involved the use of hay cut in or adjacent to the parks. In some parks this activity persisted for several years. Ungulates were fed during some winters in Yellowstone between 1904 and 1945. White-tailed deer were fed at the Polebridge and Logging Ranger Stations in Glacier between 1930 and 1936 because winter-range forage in this section was deemed inadequate as a result of heavy use by domestic stock from privately owned ranches inside the park (Aiton 1938). Bighorn sheep were fed at the Many Glacier Hotel in Glacier during the early thirties. This program was terminated when it was realized that some sheep coming down to the hotel were being killed by coyotes.

These are but a few brief examples of the many supplemental feeding programs that were initiated by the Park Service in its first three decades. Looking back at these attempts, we can see that they were generally misguided but sincere. They were, however, minor in extent when compared with those undertaken over the years by state game agencies or by the U.S. Fish and Wildlife Service at refuges such as the Jackson Hole Elk Refuge. In 1935, NPS decided to limit artificial feeding in all parks only to cases of extreme emergency, and in the late thirties most artificial feeding was stopped with the exception of the buffalo herd at Lamar in Yellowstone, which was fed until 1952.

Ungulate Population Increases

Park managers hoped that as a result of strict protection, ungulate populations would increase throughout the twenties in most western parks. Though periodic counts of the major ungulate species had been initiated in Yellowstone as early as 1916, population-estimation procedures were relatively primitive and laden with many biases. The records show that managers and census takers greatly underestimated the difficulties of counting mobile and elusive animals that occupied the diverse habitats in a park like Yellowstone. Houston's examination of the elk counts in Yellowstone concluded that

> a review of the procedures and computations used in these pioneer census attempts casts serious doubts upon their accuracy. . . . Counts required three weeks or more to complete, were conducted in April and May by one to three scouts during the spring migrations of elk . . . and, most interestingly, were made while traveling in the same direction as the migrating elk. Numbers reported were "rounded" to the nearest hundred or thousand and represented general estimates rather than actual enumerations. The recorded itinerary of the individuals shows frequent overlap of counting units and the computations used to derive totals are obscure. (1982:13)

Although there are few data available today concerning the actual size of the park populations of the key ungulate species in the twenties there seems to little doubt that by 1930 there were substantially more mule deer and elk in most western parks than there had been fifteen years earlier. The increase in numbers of formerly threatened ungulate species was immensely gratifying to park personnel. They took a personal pride in this achievement and relished the satisfaction that viewing these species brought to visitors.[2]

By the thirties, however, this satisfaction began to be tinged with some trepidation. It was then that a consensus began to emerge that some ungulate populations needed to be artificially regulated to compensate for insufficient native predation, to prevent progressive winter-range habitat degradation, and to maintain an equilibrium among the various species of large herbivores (Cole 1971). This realization was supported by studies indicating that the capacity of the habitat to support these species was decreasing. Managers were told that if the herds continued to grow, the animals would face the possibility of starvation. This situation was considered to be the result of the combination of increasing numbers of animals and diminishing areas of winter range outside parks like Yellowstone and Rocky Mountain. The winter range was decreasing because increased development and harassment on lands surrounding parks blocked migration routes and the use of traditional wintering areas. This was viewed as concentrating greater than "normal" numbers of animals on the limited winter range of parks.

The idea that species that had been loved and protected for decades could now end up starving on denuded ranges thereby bringing about great public outcry frightened many managers. Many were already familiar with two dramatic accounts of large-scale ungulate dieoffs that had occurred as a consequence of starvation on the winter range. The most famous was the massive die-off of mule deer on the Kaibab Plateau, Arizona, in 1925.[3] Much closer to home were the stories that emerged from the winter of 1919–20 in Yellowstone when the deaths of fourteen thousand elk were attributed to malnutrition (Albright 1920; Skinner 1928).[4]

Evidence of Habitat Degradation

As a consequence of these fears, the condition of the winter-range habitat in western parks became the dominant scientific concern of the Park Service in the thirties. This was, as far as can be documented, the first time NPS management called on scientists for help in dealing with a resource-management problem.[5] Scientists in the Wildlife Division responded to this request, and studies by the division were conducted in most western parks. Most of these studies concluded that the range conditions in the parks were seriously degraded. For example, in observations made on the northern range at Yellowstone, Wright and Thompson wrote, "The range was in deplorable condition when we first saw it, and its deterioration has been steadily progressing since then. It is noticeably worse now than it was in 1929. . . . All observers who have been studying this problem are agreed that the northern elk herd is hovering on the brink of disaster. The first hard winter will bring hideous starvation and wastage. The longer the hard winter is deferred, the greater will be the catastrophe"(1935:85). This report was accompanied by several photographs depicting overgrazing at Yellowstone, which they felt would "portray the precarious sta tus of the Yellowstone elk winter range far more adequately and briefly than would a written description of these conditions" (75). Wildlife Division scientists concluded that to assure long-term survival of the species and the habitat, elk populations numbers needed to be reduced by about three thousand each winter until the herd could be supported by the range (Wright and Thompson 1935).

A similar finding was reached in Rocky Mountain, where the superintendent concluded that a serious winter-range problem existed for mule deer and elk and that herd reduction might be necessary to prevent later catastrophe (Musselman 1971). Extensive barking of aspen was noted, and he felt it was unlikely that a natural balance between animal numbers and available winter range could be established without removing excess elk (Wright, Dixon, and Thompson 1933). As an interim measure, Dixon, among others, advocated increasing the park's winter range through the purchase of 4,500 acres of winter range east of the park then used by domestic livestock (1931). The grasses on this new winter range responded immediately to the removal of domestic livestock grazing but the condition of the browse changed little, a factor attributed to the large deer population (Stevens 1980). This acquisition provided only a temporary cure, and it was not long before the numbers of deer and elk again were judged to exceed the carrying capacity of the range. A series of investigators (Ratcliff 1941; Cahalane 1943; Gray 1943; Packard 1947) all reported deteriorating range conditions and recommended that the number of deer and elk be reduced to protect the range and preserve the integrity of the herds.

Surveys in Zion also indicated significant overbrowsing and intimated that deer had ceased to migrate, were remaining in the canyon yearlong, and were increasing in numbers (Dixon and Sumner 1939). Field investigations by Sumner in 1937 and 1938 showed overbrowsing to have increased and the carrying capacity to be exceeded by a factor of three. A control program was recommended.

The Isle Royale moose population was also seen as "another example where an animal population exceeded its food supply" (Aldous and Krefting 1946:296). These scientists used Murie's estimates (1934) of between one thousand and three thousand moose on the island in 1930 and their own estimate of a population of two hundred in 1935 as an indication that a drastic reduction had occurred with tremendous "moose wastage" and suggested that repetitions of this cycle were likely. They concurred with Murie that controls such as hunting, state-controlled kills, or predator introduction were needed to preserve an already overbrowsed range.

In Sequoia there were reports as early as 1916 concerning a deterioration of the mule deer range. A continual decline in available browse was reported throughout the twenties. In 1934, the park used CCC labor in a failed effort to plant browse species in an attempt to alleviate the problem. This was also the year that the first exclosure was built to document the impact of the deer on vegetation. The rapid proliferation of vegetation inside the exclosures compared to the denuded areas outside affirmed the park's opinion that deer were a significant influence on the park flora and needed to be controlled if some plant species were to survive (Sequoia 1987). Similar conditions were noted in Yosemite Valley, and range conditions were considered so badly altered by overuse from mule deer that the "once famous wild-flower show [is] a memory, and even the brush was threatened with destruction. Deer were so common and so goat-like—having no need to be alert, and hence losing their charming wild behavior—that their interest to the visitor was greatly lessened. Crippled and diseased individuals which do not last long under natural conditions dragged around and added to the ugliness of the picture" (Wright, Dixon, and Thompson 1933:131).

In general, like the census and winter-mortality estimates, it is difficult in retrospect to evaluate the accuracy of most of the observations of habitat degradation. We do know that opinions were almost always based on qualitative observations rather than quantitative measurements. In addition, comparative analyses with past records were not possible. For example, the photographs taken by the Wildlife Division technicians were in many cases the first systematic photographic inventory of park resources ever made. Investigators such as George Wright, Victor Cahalane, and Joseph Dixon, while excellent scientists, could only make short-term inspections in the various parks. They were undoubtedly not familiar with the previous uses of the land at some of the sites they visited, such as domestic livestock care and wildlife feeding grounds. Likewise, they probably underestimated the effects of years of fire suppression and the more recent effects of severe drought on the range conditions they observed. In any event, whether or not the claims of habitat damage on winter ranges were accurate, the fear of massive die-offs they induced in park managers was real.

Ungulate Control Actions in Specific Parks

Yellowstone

Yellowstone initiated a major program to reduce the numbers of elk in the early thirties. At the start, "surplus" animals were commonly sent to other parks or natural areas, zoos, or reservations. Specifically, Yellowstone elk were sent to Rocky Mountain, Mt. Rainier, Crater Lake, and Guadalupe Mountains National Parks. Through the years, over fourteen thousand elk were eventually transplanted from Yellowstone to restock or initiate new herds in forty states and three Canadian provinces. Opportunities to place transplants diminished, and it soon became apparent that killing "surplus" animals was the only reliable way to assure population reduction.

The programs to kill animals, however, posed significant legal problems. Legal statutes provided the Park Service with only limited authority to kill wildlife. In 1923 Congress had approved legislation authorizing the secretary of the interior to sell surplus Yellowstone bison and to give surplus elk, bear, beaver, and predators to zoos and other institutions (Stat. 42, 1214). Between 1935 and 1938, about five hundred elk were killed for use by various public agencies. Legal authority also existed for the removal of surplus bison and elk from Wind Cave National Park (52 Stat. 708). Other than these laws, interpretations of the legislation establishing NPS suggested that the Park Service had the legal authority to control only those animals that posed a human health and safety problem (Cahalane 1941).

Some parks attempted to solve their animal control problems and avoid legal hassles by seeking an increase in the sport harvest of animals outside the park. These efforts met with varying success, but rarely solved the problem. Others developed informal, quasi-legal arrangements with other agencies. For example, surplus mule deer in Zion were transferred by arrangement with the state and Forest Service to the nearby Powell National Forest. The highly decentralized NPS decision-making process allowed superintendents to carry out their individual programs without much scrutiny.

Consensus on a program to reduce Yellowstone elk was finally reached in 1934 when a consortium of agencies organized under the Emergency Conservation Commission agreed that the northern herd should be "kept within the carrying capacity of the winter range; increase of this range through purchase should be continued; feeding of hay should be discontinued; and an annual reduction of 3,000 elk should be made by legal hunting, live shipments, and slaughter for Indians" (1933:2).

In the winter of 1934–35, the NPS, Forest Service, and Montana Game Commission started a cooperative reduction program to accomplish these objectives. Harvests outside the park were of course dependent on the highly variable numbers of elk that moved out of the park. For example, consecutive censuses identified only 67 elk north of the park in 1961 and 3,147 in 1962. Similarly only 43 were found north of the park in 1977 but 3,034 were identified in 1978 (Erickson 1981). Between 1935 and 1950 an average of 1,807 elk per year were removed from the northern herd by sport hunting, varying from 6,530 in 1943 to only 40 in 1950. During five of these years a small number of elk were also killed in the park.

The average low removal rate by hunters and the continued growth of the herd convinced managers to substantially increase removals in the park. By this time, the legality of killing large numbers of animals in the park was not questioned, although there was still no clear legal basis for the actions. The killing of animals in the park did pose serious ethical problems for many rangers forced to carry out the action. Although most rangers were philosophically convinced that in the long run reducing the numbers of elk would benefit the species, the actual killing was generally considered extremely unpleasant. Admittedly there were some rangers who enjoyed it and used control programs as an excuse to hunt in parks, but these individuals were in the minority (Roger Contor, interview with author, Ellensburg, Wash., Apr. 17–18, 1986).

Removals of elk from the park were intensified between 1956 and 1962 when a yearly average of 1,774 elk were killed (91% of them killed in the park). During this time the park probably killed a number of animals similar to that which would have been killed by sport hunters had the animals moved out of the park. Thus, this program created an uproar in neighboring communities that were dependent in part on the business generated by sport hunting (Haines 1977). Park removals continued at a high level between 1963 and 1968, averaging 1,649 each year, of which 71% were in the park. In 1963 a cooperative agreement was worked out between the NPS, Montana, Wyoming, and the U.S. Forest Service to develop a long-range management plan for the northern Yellowstone range and its wildlife (Howe 1963). This plan called for the removal of sufficient elk to maintain the level of the herd at 5,000. It also advocated removing up to 45 bison and about 200 antelope from the northern range to prevent range overuse.

Yosemite also sought to reduce mule deer numbers in the early sixties. At first the park requested a special hunt adjacent to the park in the fall of 1965 and hoped for a reduction of 1,400 deer. The state, however, refused to go along with that magnitude. The park undertook its own program, killing a total of 842 deer in the fall of 1965. Most of the carcasses were shipped to a California prison for inmate consumption (Yosemite 1965; Metherell 1966). Control programs ceased after 1965.

Rocky Mountain

Reductions in Rocky Mountain did not start until a decade after Yellowstone. The first management plan for reducing deer and elk populations at Rocky Mountain was written in 1943, and the first reductions took place in 1944, when 311 elk and 129 mule deer were removed (Condon 1944). Subsequent analysis of winter-range carrying capacity concluded that mule deer were no longer a problem, as their populations were declining, and that only elk needed to be controlled to prevent future problems (Grater 1945).

Because of its accessibility and proximity to urban areas, control programs in Rocky Mountain were, from the start, far more visible than those in most other parks. This visibility frightened some NPS officials. In 1946, the director's office cautioned park officials against a regular reduction program, urging that deer and elk not be reduced except for good cause (Musselman 1971). As a result, park management attempted to move the harvest out of the park, recommending, for example, the initiation of salt chains to induce more elk and deer to move out of the park and the establishment of a controlled, late-winter, either-sex hunt east of the park.

Further periodic reductions took place over the next ten years until in 1955 regional biologist Jim Cole considered the range in good enough condition to discontinue the control program. However, for political reasons he recommended continuation of the control program (Stevens 1980). Buttery's studies of range conditions on the east side of the park using exclosures built in the midthirties also indicated that range condition was improving, but he too felt that elk control should be continued (1955).

In 1962, the state of Colorado officially terminated all assistance by its personnel in the park's reduction program. There were several reasons for this action, not the least of which was that the state resented having to haul and dress the carcasses while the park did the shooting (Henning 1965).[6] The primary reason for this action, however, was because the state was also involved in an effort to introduce sport hunting in the park. The failure of state efforts to introduce sport hunting and the need to reach some accommodation with the park on elk control eventually resulted in an agreement between the park; the Colorado Department of Game, Fish, and Parks; and the Roosevelt National Forest to set up the Rocky Mountain Cooperative Elk Studies Research Program. An important goal of this study was to gain information on the seasonal movements and distribution of elk in and around the park and thereby see if it was possible to remove surplus elk through public harvests outside the park (Teague 1972; Guse 1966).

The first stage of the program was a sport-hunting season held early in 1963 along the east boundary of the park. This successful hunt killed 415 elk, 57% of which were adult females. Park biologist Guse estimated this kill would hold the elk in check for at least three years. By 1967 enough data had been gathered from the elk movement studies to recommend a series of early- and late-season hunts outside the park. The park decided that with some additional reductions, subsequent sport hunts could hold the herd in check. The last direct reductions thus took place in 1968, when a total of 175 elk were trapped and given to the state for transplanting (Teague 1972; Stevens 1980).

The Sierra Nevada Parks

Mule deer were the focus of control activities in both Sequoia and Yosemite National Parks. During the early forties some attempts were made to relocate deer to less-used portions of Sequoia. These efforts, never intensive, also met with little success. The first control took place in 1952, when fifty-two deer were killed. Special sport hunts were also initiated in the Mineral King area, which was then outside the park. A park-wide control program was initiated in 1955 and continued until 1971, with over one thousand deer killed.

The End of Control Activities

Criticism of Park Service management activities at Yellowstone began to grow in the late fifties and early sixties as more and more elk were killed. Opposition came both from humane organizations and sporting groups. Sporting publications and area newspapers, feeling that the reductions could best be handled through sport hunting, considered reduction programs a euphemism for "wholesale slaughter" (Hall 1970). Initially, NPS reacted defensively to attacks on its policies and ignored them (NPS 1962). Criticism of the program, however, reached national proportions in 1967 when a March 7 NBC-TV news program highlighted the elk control program in Yellowstone and critical articles appeared in *National Geographic* and other magazines (Allard 1967).

Concern over the reduction programs in the parks was the impetus for the establishment of the Special Advisory Board on Wildlife Management in the National Parks in 1962. Although the report of this committee advocated continued control of "excess" animals in the parks through shooting by park personnel, the pendulum was slowly swinging the other way. Public pressure for a cessation of wildlife control programs was increasing. The culmination of this pressure came with the Senate field hearings on the control of the elk in Yellowstone in March 1967. Faced with intense political pressure, NPS agreed at that meeting to immediately stop the direct killing of elk in the park (U.S. Senate 1967). This decision was soon applied to other parks, and there has essentially been no ungulate control in the parks since then.[7]

Contemporary Events

Artificial controls on the growth of ungulate populations in most parks have been absent for over twenty years. To date, except for Yellowstone, there has not been the dramatic increases in ungulate populations that were postulated by the proponents of the controls. As a result, except for Yellowstone, controversies over habitat conditions have largely disappeared.[8]

The Yellowstone Elk Population

Following termination of controls, an experimental management program for both elk and bison was established. As described in chapter 3, the program was based on the premise that over a period of years native ungulate populations would regulate their own birth and death rates in relation to available winter food and population size. The outcome of that experiment is still in doubt. The growth in the elk herd over the twenty-year period has been dramatic. In 1988, 22,500 elk from four herds were estimated on the northern winter range of the park. Elk from five other herds migrate into the park each summer, increasing the population to about 31,000 (Singer et al. 1989). Many observers have attributed the growth of the elk population in the last two decades to the milder-than-normal climate that has been the norm over this time period. While this cannot be documented, there seems to be little doubt that an extremely harsh series of winters will kill a large number of elk.[9]

These large numbers of elk have a dramatic effect on the habitat of the northern range, and habitat degradation remains a contentious issue. A cursory examination of the range with its extensive trailing, obvious browse lines, and large areas of sparse ground cover can easily cause one to conclude that elk are having an adverse impact on the range. This conclusion, however, is contradicted by the studies of Gruell (1973) and Houston (1982), which comparatively analyzed historic and contemporary photos of representative park landscapes. These pictures showed that despite large variations in the numbers of ungulates in Yellowstone over the years, little habitat change had occurred. Sites that were considered to be overgrazed in the 1930s and 1940s actually looked the same way in the 1870s and 1880s, presumably before Europeans had any effect on the system. Changes that did occur in some areas were explained by recent warmer and drier climatic conditions, fire suppression, or abnormal uses of the area, such as for feeding grounds.

Other long-term studies on the northern-range grasslands have supported the contention that precipitation patterns influence grasslands more than elk grazing. From 1958 to 1981, total plant cover more than doubled on grazed and ungrazed study sites apparently due to a pattern of wetter-than-normal summers, though elk numbers quadrupled during this time (Singer 1989). Conclusions about the effects of elk grazing on the summer range are less certain. One study has suggested that the summer-range grassland standing crop, as determined from LANDSAT imagery, is significantly correlated to the depth of winter snowpack and not to elk numbers (Singer 1989).

The first significant decline in elk numbers in recent years occurred in the winter of 1988–89 following the summer fires of 1988. The fires themselves appeared to cause relatively little mortality of large mammals. A total of 261 large mammals were found dead in the areas of four of the fires in the park—246 elk, 2 moose, 4 mule deer, and 9 bison (Singer et al. 1989). None of the 68 radio-collared park elk died in the fires (David Vales, interview with author, Moscow, Id., Apr. 14, 1989). The die-off occurred the following winter as a result of lack of forage and hunter harvest of elk that moved outside the park. The drought reduced forage production on the summer range 60% to 80% and winter-range production about 22%. Fire burned 34% of the range and about 9% of the dry grasslands (Singer and Schullery 1989). The northern herd declined between 38% and 43% (about 6,000 elk) during the winter of 1988–89, of which 14% to 16% were harvested by humans and 24% to 27% died in the park. For comparison, during the mild winters from 1986 to 1988, elk mortality was less than 5% (Singer et al. 1989).

The fires present a unique opportunity to document how the ungulate populations will recover from the winterkill and to study the response of the animals to large-scale burns. At the present, it appears that elk are responding quite favorably to the improved habitat (e.g., greater forage production, more nutritious forage, and enhanced plant diversity). Aided by the relatively mild 1989–90 winter, elk numbers have increased significantly and are probably now at their prefire levels (Francis Singer, interview with author, Yellowstone National Park, Apr. 5, 1990). Whether this increase will continue will depend on the severity of winter conditions and on the ability of the herd to naturally regulate its population.

In the end, the fires represent only one of a series of natural processes that have always influenced elk numbers in Yellowstone. The fires and their subsequent effects on wildlife populations tested Park Service resolve to stand by its policy of allowing natural processes to function unhindered. For example, the park was confronted with demands to provide supplemental feed for the elk during the winter after the fire and to keep animals in the park to avoid their harvest outside. In adhering to its policies and rejecting the above demands, the Park Service position has been strengthened. The NPS position was also supported by the conclusions of the panel of ecologists commissioned to evaluate the ecological impacts of the 1988 fires. The panel stated that "dynamic processes take avenues which may seem cruel and wasteful by some standards, but not from the standards of stewardship of natural ecosystems. The tendency to interfere is an understandable altruistic human response. However, in the case of our national parks . . . this interference does not serve a useful purpose in the long-term scheme within which wildlife populations are being allowed to exist" (Christensen et al. 1989b:58).

Bison Populations in Yellowstone

There are three more or less discrete bison populations in Yellowstone. The Pelican and Mary Mountain–Firehole herds appear to be contained in the park. The Lamar herd on the northern range moves in large numbers across the park boundary. The Lamar bison herd is expanding, and its movements, possibly enhanced by additional road plowing in the winter, may be an effort to recolonize former historic range (Mary Meagher, interview with author, Yellowstone National park, Apr. 5, 1990). Because of their physical size and the brucellosis they carry, bison are not compatible as are other ungulates with the ranching communities surrounding the park (both Montana and Wyoming are classified as brucellosis-free states).

Following the cessation of population controls, the park proposed a boundary-control program in 1968. This program relied on shooting bison that approached specified boundary areas. Under this program, three animals were shot in 1974 and two in 1978. At the time, there seemed little likelihood of large-scale bison movements to the boundary areas. The situation changed during the severe winter of 1974–75 when about eighty bison moved to the northern boundary. Similar movements continued in subsequent years, and since 1984 increased numbers of bison have attempted to cross the western and northern boundaries. The park tested numerous fencing and hazing techniques, including noise, rubber shot, and baiting to alter the movements, all with no avail (Meagher 1989). Approval to shoot bison was rescinded in 1978 by the Department of the Interior.

In 1985, in an attempt to control animals outside the park, the Montana state legislature established a permit-based state bison hunt. Despite attempts by animal-rights groups to stop it, the hunt took place in 1985, with about fifty animals being killed. Between 1986 and 1988 an additional thirty-eight animals were shot. This action, however, failed to curtail subsequent movements, which reached a climax during the winter of 1988–89 when most bison from the northern herd left the park. During that year's public hunt 268 bulls, 224 cows, and 53 calves were killed out of a population of about 700 (Meagher 1989). Whether this kill will reduce movements in subsequent years remains to be seen, since only limited movements and a limited harvest were reported during the winter of 1989–90.

What is clear is that NPS management options are limited. Bison repopulation of the lands north of the park is not politically feasible. Keeping bison within the park appears equally impossible. Fencing the park's northern boundary could have serious effects on elk, pronghorn, and mule deer. Hazing and herd activities have only demonstrated that "bison can be moved only where they want to go" (Meagher interview). The current public hunt outside the park remains one of the few viable alternatives to lessen local conflicts, but it too remains controversial and probably will not cause bison to change their movements (Meagher 1989). The bison hunt has been very popular with hunters, but has outraged animal-rights groups. The bison is a powerful and emotional symbol, and the public does not take kindly to television news footage of hunters crippling cow bison only 30 meters away.

White-tailed Deer Management Problems
in the Eastern Parks

In the past decade, the National Park Service has gained an increased awareness of white-tailed deer populations and their influence on the resources of parks in the eastern United States. This new enlightenment emanates from a growing concern among resource managers that as deer populations increase dramatically in parks, they have potentially irreversible impacts on park resources. In the East, this concern has focused in particular on sites preserved to commemorate historic events, such as Civil and Revolutionary War battlefields, or in historic settings in natural areas, such as Cades Cove in Great Smoky Mountains National Park. Deer densities in Gettysburg, Saratoga, and Morristown have been estimated at 44, 41, and 52 deer per square kilometer (Storm et al. 1989; Cypher, Yahner, and Cypher 1985; Underwood et al. 1989).

The majority of these sites are small, often less than 1,970 hectares. In addition, they are often set in a complex landscape surrounded by residential areas, highways, and small farms. The surrounding landscapes are typically becoming more and more fragmented by urban development. Most of these parks are too small to maintain naturally regulated populations, and their high boundary to area ratios (parks like Shenandoah and Blue Ridge Parkway are long and narrow) make them susceptible to external influences.

The NPS faces a quandary in its management of historic areas. It needs to strike a balance between the protection of deer and the preservation of the site. It must determine if deer are having an adverse impact on the resources and if so, how serious it is. Deer may cause damage to native plant communities; damage to historic plant communities and agricultural crops; damage to unique, rare, or endangered plants; accidents with vehicles; accidents with pedestrians; and disease (Wright 1990). Some of these impacts are easy to document, some are not, and the existence of others is questionable. It is the lack of consensus on the validity or seriousness of some of the impacts that has complicated deer management in parks, particularly in situations where management programs may recommend a reduction of deer.

Until recently, the Park Service has not been philosophically or operationally equipped to deal with this kind problem in these parks. As we have seen, wildlife management was an issue primarily in the large western parks. Concepts such as a reliance on natural processes to govern animal populations have not been applied to most eastern parks. In part this is because they were not needed, and in part because parks lacked natural-resource personnel. Natural-resource management was usually only undertaken as a collateral duty along with many other activities.

Another complicating factor is that the management emphasis of historic sites is different from that for natural areas. Historic sites are managed primarily for their cultural resources rather than for their natural resources. Vegetation is typically managed to either maintain static conditions, i.e., those existing at the time period a site commemorates, or if those conditions have changed, to restore that condition through habitat manipulation. Maintaining the "historic scene" is important. Visitors can better understand the events that took place on a site when they can see the area as it actually existed during the period. For example, on battlefields, the vegetation mosaic during the time of the battle often played a pivotal role in the outcome. Deer (and other animals) are generally not managed as a component of the ecosystem at historic sites but as an adjunct to it. When the actions of native animals interfere with the preservation of these cultural resources the actions of the animals must be altered or eliminated.

In recent years, eastern historic areas have transcended their role as monuments to a historic event and have become important as regional recreation areas and open spaces and, in some cases, as wildlife sanctuaries. This in turn attracts visitors who come primarily to view wildlife. This new role tends to broaden the actual, if not the legislated, mission of the park and further complicates management objectives.

Deer-Vehicle Collisions

In Pennsylvania, reported deer deaths on highways are over thirty thousand per year, and actual deaths may be much higher. Parks bisected or bordered by major travel routes often have deer-vehicle collisions disproportionately higher than those in surrounding areas. For example, 108 deer were killed on roads in Gettysburg in 1987 (Storm et al. 1989), and 88 were killed during a two-year period at Valley Forge (Cypher, Yahner, and Cypher 1985). This mortality has been shown to be a major factor regulating populations in these areas. At Gettysburg and Valley Forge most collisions do not involve park visitors.

Disease

Reports of human Lyme disease infections have increased dramatically in the eighties, and as a result public concern about the relationship between deer and the spread of the disease has risen. The apparent overlap in the distribution of the deer tick and white-tailed deer in the northeast has implicated deer as a critical link in the maintenance and spread of Lyme disease. As deer populations and human disease cases have both been increasing the association between deer and the deer tick, at least to the general public, has become stronger. Though deer tick densities have been correlated with the presence of deer in several areas, the presence of deer ticks appears to be independent of deer densities (Cypher and Cypher 1988).

Initially, researchers recommended removal of deer to reduce deer tick populations in certain areas. Evidence now suggests that this may be futile because immature stages of the deer tick are found on a variety of hosts, most commonly the white-footed mouse, a species that appears to be an important reservoir for the causative agent of the disease, *Borrelia burgdorferi*. There are indications that visitors to parks with high deer densities may be concerned about health hazards. If concern over Lyme disease increases, pressures for deer reduction might increase and visitation to some areas might decrease.

Impact on Agricultural Plant Communities

Several parks retain some lands planted in agricultural crops or pasture grasses to maintain the character of the land as it was during the historic period. Gettysburg has the largest of these programs, maintaining 1,870 acres in corn, wheat, milo, and pasture grasses. There is little doubt that when unprotected by fences or other devices, these crops can be devastated by high densities of deer.

The damage to corn in the southern portion of Gettysburg and on the adjoining farms of the Eisenhower National Historic Site has been so great that farmers can no longer successfully grow it. Wheat crops have also been severely damaged. Switching to alternative crops, such as milo, has been attempted, but these too are being eaten (Wright 1990). Though damage to crops can be rectified by next year's planting, there is more at stake than cosmetic concerns. Most historic croplands are leased to local farmers who need to harvest a crop to subsist, partly because most park budgets do not permit the maintenance of agricultural fields on a permanent basis without such arrangements.

Deer protected in parks can also forage on private farm lands adjacent to parks. There they affect the ability of those farmers to make a living. The long-term impact of the loss of farming opportunities on lands adjacent to a park like Gettysburg could mean changes in the adjoining landscape, e.g., housing developments, that would be detrimental to the historic scene and may raise demands for additional land acquisition.

Impact on Native Plant Communities

It is in the analysis of the impacts on native plant communities that real difficulties arise. Most historic parks don't have a clear idea of what vegetal conditions they want to manage for. Part of the management objectives for Gettysburg are to preserve and "restore the general landscape to its appearance as it was seen through the eyes of visitors in the last decade of the 19th century" (NPS 1989:31). Obviously such a statement is open to many interpretations, ranging from maintaining an exact replica of the structure and composition of the original plant communities to maintaining a landscape mosaic similar to that which existed in the past. In actual practice, most parks strive for some compromise.

Whatever the ultimate management goal, there are problems in achieving it. Parks often have poor detailed knowledge of the plant communities that historically occupied the site. They also often have no records of the changes that might have occurred in these communities in intervening years. Finally, management sometimes fails to recognize that it cannot compensate for externally influenced changes to those communities, for example, the loss of a dominant species like the American chestnut. Though Gettysburg probably has a better understanding of the land uses and plant communities at the time of the 1863 battle than any other area since the army mapped the area in 1868, this effort was biased toward the agricultural lands. We know what crops were planted and where, but we can only make educated guesses about the composition and age structure of the historic woodlots (Wright 1990).

The impacts of deer browsing on woody vegetation can be viewed at two levels. One is the influence deer have on the regeneration of dominant species. There is solid evidence that deer, even at moderately low densities, can have a profound influence on the regeneration of many woody species (Marquis and Brenneman 1981; Tilghman 1989). However, most of the numerous studies documenting this condition have been undertaken out of primary concern for healthy populations of deer or commercial timber species. Research has shown that the regeneration of dominant woody species in eastern parks is being curtailed by deer (Marquis 1981, 1983). Subtle long-term shifts in species composition and even the loss of key species are possible results that would adversely impact historical interpretation and the natural ecosystem. On the other hand, if one seeks to manage for only a general historic landscape, this shift in composition may not be a problem.

The historic woodlots at Gettysburg now have a relatively sparse understory. These historic woodlots were probably not in pristine condition 125 years ago, but were instead an integral part of the farmsteads that occupied the battlefield. They provided heating and cooking fuel as well as building lumber. They were also used periodically for grazing domestic stock. In the years before federal protection, evidence suggests that some of them were burned and clear-cut. Old photographs reveal that the visual mosaic has changed very little. If anything, understory growth is more sparse in the original photos than at present. Some original photos show a distinct browse line that is lacking today. Other photos indicate of areas of deforestation. In viewing old and contemporary photos, one can conceivably draw the opinion that perhaps deer at the present time are serving the same function as cattle and woodlot management did in the historic period. High deer numbers may in fact be a positive element in the maintenance of a historic scene. In essence, an examination of comparative photos makes it hard to draw the conclusion that deer are having an impact on forest cover (Wright 1990).

A second concern is for the influence of deer on the density of minor components of the plant community, particularly unique or rare species. Studies in the Sunken Forest at Fire Island, Cades Cove (Bratton 1980), and elsewhere have documented dramatic declines in the cover and frequency of species unique to these areas. Most of the plants are herbaceous species that may flower and die quickly and therefore may not play a role in the historic interpretation but may be significant to the biological diversity of the area.

Conclusion

To support a deer management program that may include controversial actions such as herd reduction, the impacts that deer are causing in parks need to be well documented. To date, they have not been. Much of the white-tailed deer research conducted in the eastern parks seems to have been designed primarily to support a preconceived idea that deer were in fact a problem in the area studied. Emphasis has been placed on deer biology and not on habitat-related parameters. As a result, although the studies provide important information to park management, they fail to help define a rationale for management.

Management objectives for defining desired biological conditions therefore remain ambiguous. Clear statements of these objectives are the necessary first step in developing a deer management program. They need to be based on historic landscape studies and take into account the ecological effects of past human use and disturbance. The environmental conditions that result from deer use in many historic parks may or may not be acceptable to managers, however, these conditions cannot be rectified until there is a clear understanding of what the management goals are.

NOTES

1. There was more concern for bison in the early years of Yellowstone than for any other animal species. The mountain or wood bison native to the park were nearly exterminated at the turn of the century as a result of sport, market, and table hunting. In 1902 only forty to fifty bison survived in the park out of a historic population estimated to be about one thousand (Meagher 1973).

In an attempt to bolster this herd and save the bison from extinction, plains bison purchased from privately owned herds were brought into the park in 1902. The introduced animals were held in a fenced pasture at Mammoth until 1907 when they were moved to a corral in the Lamar Valley, whose facilities became known as the Buffalo Ranch (Cahalane 1944). From 1907 until at least 1915, these animals were closely day-herded and put in a fenced pasture at night. Since the objective was to maximize the production of buffalo, they were essentially managed as domestic animals and were for all intents isolated from the wild population. Calves were removed from mothers at an early age to guard against injury, and some were even bottle-fed. Surplus bull calves were castrated, and the animals were fed hay throughout the winter months. In the intervening time, the wild herd persisted and gradually increased as a consequence of protection from poaching (Meagher 1973).

By 1915 the ranch herd was too big to keep the animals fenced during the summer months, so they were allowed to roam, where they intermingled and probably interbred with the wild animals. They were periodically returned to the vicinity of the ranch. As the managed herd increased in size, more emphasis was placed on returning them to a natural state (Cahalane 1944) and the intensive management measures were gradually phased out. However, throughout the thirties and forties the main management concern was to ensure that there were sufficient bison numbers in the park to guarantee perpetuation. Through 1938, horseback riders drove as many bison as possible into the corrals in the fall for feeding and selective reductions. Disabled, aged, and brucellosis-infected animals, or those otherwise considered undesirable, were removed to improve the herd. All vestiges of artificial management except herd reductions were eliminated by 1952. Herd reductions continued at irregular intervals through 1968.

2. These achievements were even more noteworthy in view of the declines in game species that had occurred during the same time period on other public and private lands in the country.

3. The Kaibab Plateau situation was used as the classic example of what happens to a mule deer herd when predators are removed. The population was variously estimated to have increased from four thousand in 1906 to one hundred thousand in 1924. Thereupon with food resources theoretically depleted and the animals weak, over the next two subsequent harsh winters 60% of the herd was assumed to have died (Russo 1964).

4. Both Caughley (1970) and Houston (1982) have cast considerable doubt on the accuracy and interpretations of both events. Caughley stresses that inconsistencies in the original population estimates make it difficult to place much confidence in any interpretation of what happened on the Kaibab. He concluded that "little can be gleaned from the original records beyond the suggestion that the population began a decline sometime in the period 1924–1930, and that this decline was probably preceded by a period of increase" (1970:56). Houston suggested that there was no conclusive evidence that the Yellowstone decline ever occurred.

5. The question, of course, that immediately arises is whether this interest in science was because of a real concern for the resources or because managers were looking for a way to protect their own backsides.

6. Teague, a state employee, wrote that "we were referred to as the 'gutting crew' by the imported 'expert park ranger shooters' from Yellowstone" (1972:55). He had intense memories of the unpleasantness of dressing and loading elk in freezing winter weather.

7. In 1981, seventy-seven white-tailed deer were killed in the Cades Cove area of Great Smoky Mountains National Park to reduce the population. Concern about an overpopulation of deer was first voiced in 1969 when severe browse lines were noted in adjacent woodlands. A loss of most of the deer in 1971 due to hemorrhagic disease contributed to suspicions that the herd was too large (Fox and Pelton 1973). Subsequent investigators (e.g., Burst and Pelton 1973; Kiningham 1980; Bratton 1980) all concluded that because of a lack of natural controls, shooting was the only viable option to control further habitat degradation.

Implants of a synthetic progestin hormone to block contraception was tested at Mammoth Cave National Park in 1974 (Matscheke 1980). The implants worked effectively for two breeding seasons, but the high costs of capture and treatment and the short lifespan of the implants made the technique unfeasible for large-scale application.

8. There has been a small but persistent controversy over the effect of high densities of elk in winter-range aspen stands in Rocky Mountain (Olmsted 1979; Stevens 1980). There is no doubt that elk heavily browse the aspen stands, but whether this is natural or not is hard to determine. It is equally clear that elk densities would not be altered if all of the aspen were to disappear.

9. Up to 60% of the northern herd was reportedly killed during the severe winter of 1919–20 that followed the drought of 1919. Houston (1982) ques-

tioned the accuracy of these estimates, but Singer and others (1989) believed that a large winterkill did occur. During the relatively cold winter of 1974–75, two thousand elk were alleged to have died (about 10% of the northern herd), and weakened animals were visible along the park boundary. State game managers used this situation to criticize the park's policy, asking rhetorically, "are we as managers really 'managers' or just observers? Can we afford to allow a food resource as massive as this to periodically winter kill, sometimes in large numbers, just to preserve a place where man can view natural regulation?" (Erickson 1981:96). Schullery has pointed that that an interesting thing about this supposed die-off was that few people were aware of it. He asked regularly at campfire programs for several weeks if people had heard about it and received only one positive response (Paul Schullery, letter to author, Nov. 28, 1989).

6

The Management of Alien Animals

The terms *alien, exotic,* and *non-native* are commonly used to describe plant and animal species that inhabit areas in which they did not evolve or spread to naturally.[1] Typically, alien species are introduced by direct human introduction, either purposeful or accidental, or by human-induced changes in the environment that facilitated the establishment and survival of the species.[2]

There are four general categories of alien animal species. First are those animals that upon introduction to a new environment find it inhospitable and soon disappear or barely continue to exist without continued reintroductions. Second, there are alien species that do establish viable populations in the new area but do not play a major role in the ecological community. They have a negligible impact on the native species, and the net effect of their introduction is a slight increase in the complexity of the community.

A third category of alien species consists of those that find their new environment much less limiting to their spread or growth than their original habitat. Such species, generally because of a freedom from factors that controlled their numbers in their native habitat, may rapidly expand and proliferate to the point that they threaten the existence of some native plants and animals. When the damage to "valuable" native species becomes severe enough, alien species often become the target of long-term, expensive, and sometimes controversial control or eradication programs.

A fourth category contains those species that are capable of hybridizing with native stock. These species are potentially the most troublesome of all because their impact is more difficult to detect, and losses of pure native genotypes are permanent. Examples include the hybrids resulting from the introduction of Rocky Mountain elk into

Roosevelt elk ranges, of plains buffalo into mountain buffalo ranges, and hatchery-reared trout into streams and lakes.

Whenever alien species cause economic disruption or threaten human health, natural resources, or valuable native species, there is generally widespread support for programs to control or eliminate them. Conversely, when such species are viewed as beneficial because of their aesthetic, economic, or recreational values their propagation is supported. In many states, alien species are stocked or transplanted by state game agencies and form an important part of the sport hunter's bag.

The problems caused by alien species in parks has long been recognized, and alien animal control programs in parks date back to the twenties. However, these were often sporadic, frequently inadequate, and not necessarily supported by national policy. Throughout his career, Victor Cahalane, an NPS chief scientist, was troubled by the problems that alien animals caused in the parks and the inability of NPS to solve them. He was particularly frustrated when state game departments released alien birds and mammals in parks solely to "meet the demands of an ever-increasing army of hunters" (Cahalane 1948a). He felt the mountain goat would soon become established in Yellowstone and Rocky Mountain as a result of adjacent stocking by the states and lamented that "little or nothing can be done to guard against these threatened invasions or to eject exotics which are already established" (Cahalane 1948a:648).

Current NPS management policies seek to keep parks free of artificial influences, thus, alien species have no place in parks.[3] However, park officials also realize that the elimination or even control of highly mobile, ubiquitous species, such as the European starling and Norway rat, is impossible. Thus, in actual practice, the control of alien species, both plant and animal, is generally limited to only the most troublesome species.

Almost all parks have problems with some alien animal species, and the list of parks with significant populations of problem alien species is long (see Table 6.1). One survey showed that over three hundred NPS areas were threatened by some type of alien species (NPS 1980). These problems primarily involved habitat damage, such as trampling, overbrowsing, erosion, and threats to significant or rare plant species. Elaborate and expensive programs have or are being carried out in some parks to deal with the impact of specific alien species. It is difficult to estimate the money spent on alien species control programs because in most parks these programs involve a variety of park divisions including research, resource management, and maintenance. Such programs include the use of park rangers or deputized personnel to kill problem species, efforts to live-capture and transplant alien animals to areas outside the parks, projects to construct boundary or unit fences to keep alien species out, and live-capture and adoption programs used for animals that can be domesticated. Many of these programs have been quite successful, but others have been extremely difficult to carry out and represent little more than holding actions, effectively eliminating the current year's production while maintaining the overall population at a relatively constant level.

Public support for alien control programs in parks varies considerably depending on the species. Many problem species are the result of purposeful unsanctioned introductions by local hunters seeking to use the park as a reservoir of breeding stock. Attempts to eliminate these animals from the park thus engenders considerable local hostility. Killing animals that the general public views as cute or otherwise values can also generate a great public outcry and adverse publicity, particularly among animal-rights and humane groups. Their opposition to lethal controls was one of the principle reasons NPS adopted an expensive live-trapping and adoption program to remove unwanted burros.

Sensitivity to such protests has often limited the ability of the NPS to control alien species except by expensive methods, such as live-capture and removal. While these programs have spared NPS public wrath they have engendered professional criticism. Allen and others

Table 6.1 Alien Species in National Parks

Park	Years Present	Approximate Population	Management Measures	Reference
Burros				
Bandelier	>120	5–10	A	Allen (pers. comm.)
Big Bend	>50	unknown	—	Park Files
Carlsbad Caverns	>50	unknown	—	Park Files
Death Valley	>100	>25	A	Park Files
Grand Canyon	>150	<25	A	Park Files
Lake Mead	>100	>25	A	Park Files
Organ Pipe	>100	unknown	—	Park Files
Feral Horses				
Assategue Is.	>350	180	M	Park Files

Table 6.1 Alien Species in National Parks (continued)

Park	Years Present	Approximate Population	Management Measures	Reference
Cape Hatteras	>150	30	M	Bratton (1986)
Cape Lookout	>350	<50	M	Bratton (1986)
Cumberland Is.	<100	180	M, A	Finley (1985)
Mesa Verde	>50	6–14		Mierau and Schmidt (1981)
Theodore R.	40	40	M	Park Files
Gemsboks				
White Sands	15	57		Reid and Patrick (1983)
Goats				
Haleakala	200	<1,000	A	Stone (pers. comm.)
Hawaii Volcanoes	200	200	A	Hawaii Volcanoes (1986)
Mountain Goats				
Grand Teton	<10	~5		Wood (pers. comm.)
Olympic	60	1,175±170	R, T	Houston, Moorhead, and Olsen (1986)
Wild Boars and Pigs				
Big Cypress	>200	300–500	H	Duever et al. (1979)
Big Thicket	>100	unknown		Singer (1981)
Blue-Ridge	~40	unknown		Singer (1981)
Cape Canaveral	>100	>7/km^2		Singer (1981)
Congaree Swamp	—	unknown		Singer (1981)
Cumberland Is.	>300	>250		Singer (1981)
Great Smokies	~40	>2000	A, R	Walthen (pers. comm.)
Gulf Is.	130	<60		Baron (1979)
Haleakala	1,200	dense		Singer (1981)
Hawaii Volcanoes	3,000	dense	A	Hawaii Vol. (1986)
Pinnacles	—	unknown		Singer (1981)
Sequoia	<10	unknown	A	Sequoia (1987)

Table 6.1 Alien Species in National Parks (continued)

Park	Years Present	Approximate Population	Management Measures	Reference
Shasta-Trinity	20	common		Singer (1981)
Virgin Is.	—	<100		Singer (1981)

A = active control program including killing and transplants out of park.
H = hunted for sport.
M = managed or maintained as part of the historic scene.
R = research on control in progress.
T = some individuals have been transplanted from the park.

pointed out that "the much publicized catching and live removal of animals . . . is conditioning the public to believe that these expensive methods are the proper way to control nuisance animals. The National Park Service will never have money to handle most jobs in that manner. We wonder also about the priorities of a society in which contributions can be raised to rescue feral domestic burros at $1000 each while nearly all the wild horses of the Earth . . . are declining to extinction" (1981:20).

Burros

One of the most recognized problem alien species in national parks is the burro, which presently inhabits seven national parks. Although introduced to the North American continent as early as the 1600s by Spanish explorers, it was not until the latter part of the nineteenth century that large numbers of feral asses, or wild burros, began to occupy many areas in the southwestern United States (McKnight 1958). The feralization process was caused in some cases by escape or deliberate release, sometimes to serve as breeding stock to provide pack animals for prospectors (Bennett el al. 1980). Because many of the animals generally retreated to the rougher, drier, and more remote areas to escape the pressures of civilization, they often came to inhabit areas that were to be included in national parks. The protection provided by these areas, combined with the burro's relatively high rate of reproduction, allowed rapid population increases in many areas. For example, Margart and Ohmart estimated the burro population at Bandelier increased at a rate of 29% a year (1976).

The voracious and indiscriminate appetite of burros has been the biggest problem and has caused significant and relatively rapid habitat destruction in many parks. Where the burro's habitat overlaps those of mule deer, pronghorn antelope, or bighorn sheep, adverse competition with these native species often occurs. There has been particular concern over competition with bighorn sheep, in part due to the tendency of burros to degrade the habitat around water holes and foul the water. Wauer and Dennis (1980) also concluded that native bird populations at Bandelier were reduced because of burro-caused changes in vegetation structure. They also felt that burros damaged the archaeological sites that are the monument's chief resource.

In summarizing studies on burro-bighorn interactions at Death Valley that had been underway since 1935, Sumner stated that the picture was clear: "Where burros have increased markedly, the big-horn have dwindled or disappeared. On the other hand, places where bighorn still come to drink and in considerable numbers, seem to have one thing in common: they are not visited by wild burros" (1959:5).

Because such findings were often based on casual observations and were difficult to quantify, a research project was begun in 1973 to study the severity and potential consequences of burro-bighorn inter-actions in Death Valley. Gennett concluded that "the potential for for-age competition exists and that due to their more highly opportunistic patterns of feeding, burros should be expected to out compete desert bighorn sheep if a competitive situation were to exist" (1982:24). Dunn (1984) felt that the presence of burros at certain springs during summer might limit use of these springs and surrounding habitat by bighorn ewe groups, and concluded that there was no evidence that feral burros had any positive effects on native bighorn sheep. Laycock wrote that "the destruction of vegetation [by burros] may cut sharply into rodent populations, reducing food for birds of prey, while habitat for such small birds as quail vanishes" (1974:117). The results of these and other studies (Carothers, Stitt, and Johnson 1976; Blong and Pollard 1968) have left little doubt that competition between desert big-horn sheep and burros does exist and that it has been detrimental to the bighorn.[4] However, researchers have often reached differing con-clusions regarding the extent of direct competition between the two for food, water, shade, and space. Results of the research studies vary depending upon the area investigated, the number of burros present, available water, and type of vegetation (Grand Canyon 1980).

The solution to the burro problem in parks has been complicated by the sharply conflicting opinions held by the public about the value of burros. Burros are often depicted as cute, docile, harmless little creatures similar to those portrayed in *Brighty of the Grand Canyon*

(Henry 1963). The control has been further complicated by the passage of two pieces of federal legislation. The first was the Hunting Wild Horses and Burros on Public Lands Act of 1959 (Public Law 86-234), which prohibited the use of aircraft or motor vehicles to capture or kill any wild unbranded horse, mare, colt, or burro running at large on any public lands. The second act, the Wild, Free-Roaming Horse and Burro Act of 1971 (Public Law 92-195), was far more comprehensive and mandated the protection, management, and control of wild and free-roaming horses and burros on public lands. It was passed after an overwhelming public outcry protesting the capture and killing of wild horses for pet food and other commercial purposes. Testimony preceding the passage of the act dealt only with the treatment and management of wild horses. There was no concern evidenced for burros, and it is not clear why they were even included in the act (Pitt 1985). Lands managed by NPS were specifically exempted from this law, thus the Park Service retained the right to kill burros. However, letter-writing campaigns, injunctions, and court suits were brought against NPS by citizen groups whenever burro control programs were planned. This tactic worked, and because of a fear of adverse publicity, all lethal burro control activities were stopped in the early seventies.

Burro Control at Grand Canyon

As early as the twenties, rangers in Grand Canyon observed significant habitat destruction caused by a rapidly expanding burro population. They felt that drastic control measures were needed to restrict the population to preserve the range and save native wildlife. The Director's Annual Report for 1920 indicated that "these animals living down in the canyon have increased to such an extent that they form a veritable pest, denuding the plateaus of grass and other forage so that native wild game such as antelope has been forced out; it is even necessary for working and exploring parties to pack feed for their working animals. Furthermore they destroy the trails. The time is not far distant when radical steps will have to be taken to eliminate the burro evil" (NPS 1920:27). A burro control program was begun in 1924, and over the next forty-five years 2,860 animals were removed from the park (Ruffner, Phillips, and Goldberg 1977) The program was hampered throughout its existence by lack of financial aid and personnel as well as misunderstandings regarding the necessity of the program itself (Bendt 1957).

In hindsight, the control program probably did little more than remove some of the annual increase, so burro populations continued to grow. In response, the NPS issued a burro management plan and environmental assessment for Grand Canyon in 1976 (Carothers, Stitt, and Johnson 1976). The plan alleged that burros were significantly altering the native vegetation in the lower reaches of Grand Canyon and advocated that they be eliminated from the park by shooting. However, as a result of criticism of the plan because it advocated lethal control and because data on burro impacts were considered to be inadequate, the secretary of the interior suspended the plan and directed NPS to do a full Environmental Impact Statement (EIS) on the action.

The subsequent EIS and management plan (Grand Canyon 1980) also proposed to remove all burros from the park, primarily by live-removal. Qualified persons were to be invited into the park to capture and remove burros for their personal use and at their own expense. This program would be allowed to continue as long as it was effective. Burro-preservation groups and humane organizations were urged to cooperate and work actively in the program. The program also involved some fencing to prevent ingress of burros from adjacent Lake Mead. A shooting program was to be implemented only after the removal program was no longer effective.

In 1980 there were an estimated 350 burros in the park. During 1981, the Fund for Animals was successful in removing and putting up for "adoption" 565 burros. The operation involved a roundup, roping, and the use of a sling-equipped helicopter. Removal costs were placed at more than $1,000 per animal (Allen et al. 1981). The program was highly successful, and in July 1981 it was estimated that only a dozen burros remained in the park.

European Wild Boars

The success enjoyed by parks in controlling burros has in general not been achieved with the other major problem alien species—the wild pig, which inhabits at least thirteen NPS areas. Pigs related to the true domestic stock occur in ten areas; the European wild boar (a different subspecies) occurs only in the Great Smoky Mountains National Park; crosses between the two types are found in two parks. There are few data available on the numbers of wild pigs in most parks. In most areas, pig populations appear to be relatively stable except for the Great Smoky Mountains, where the wild boar population has been expanding for many years (Singer 1981). There is also a potential threat to Texas and California parks from wild pig increases in those states, and for the wild boar, which can withstand more extreme climatic conditions, to expand north into other Appalachian Mountain parks.

The ecological effects of wild pig populations vary greatly from area to area, depending on the density of pigs and the relative sensitivity of the ecosystems. Impacts have only been recently studied, and then in only a few areas. Baker (1979) and Bratton (1974, 1975) concluded that impacts were more severe in sensitive plant communities and where pig densities were high.

Populations of wild pigs have proven difficult to reduce or eliminate in the national parks. Only the smallest and most accessible areas have reported any success in reducing populations. Four of the areas that have wild pig populations are recreation areas where sport hunting is allowed. In these areas all but Congaree Swamp reported sizable harvests that were considered useful in reducing the populations.

Wild Boar Management in the Great Smoky Mountains

There is more known about the history and ecological impacts of wild boar in the Great Smoky Mountains than in any other area. The first wild boars in the region were brought from Europe to a private game reserve in North Carolina by a group of English hunters in 1912. For several years the wild boars were kept undisturbed in a large enclosure. In 1920, during an attempt to hunt them in the enclosure, the animals became excited and about one hundred escaped (Stegeman 1938). Over time, they mixed to a minor degree with feral domestic swine during their expansion outside the park (Rary et al. 1969). It is arguable whether the progeny of these animals formed the basis of the present park population. Singer and Coleman (1980) attributed the boars in the park to other releases, suggesting that all of the animals released in 1920 were dead by 1940 of a hog cholera epidemic (Stegeman 1938).

Whatever the source, wild boars were first observed in the southwest corner of the park in the late forties. From there they spread rapidly and are now found in all but the extreme eastern section of the park. The first control efforts began in 1959 in response to observations of extensive rooting damage on some of the famous mountaintop grasslands, or balds (Fox 1972). The park then entered into a cooperative agreement with the Tennessee Fish and Game Commission to capture boars and transplant them to state game-management areas. In 1962 a similar agreement was reached with North Carolina. These agreements acknowledged both the park's need to eliminate or reduce wild boars and the desire by the respective states to use wild boars whenever possible as hunting stock. Between 1960 and 1977, an average of sixty-two wild boars a year were removed by trapping or shooting. These efforts had a negligible effect on the eastward expansion of the wild boars in the park.

Bratton (1974) estimated that a yearly removal of 25% of the wild boar population would be needed to stabilize the population, and harvests of 50% would be needed to cause a population decline. With estimates of over 1,500 wild boars in the park, this level of control was clearly not being achieved, and populations continued to increase. Wild boars have been so successful in the Great Smoky Mountains mostly because of their omnivorous food habits that enable them to take advantage of the great diversity of foods in the park. Other factors include their high reproductive potential, great mobility, lack of natural predators, and nocturnal habits that shield them from humans (Duncan 1974).

By the midseventies the park recognized that the wild boars were causing extensive damage to important wildflower areas, reducing individual plant populations, damaging tree roots and seedlings, destroying portions of some of the balds, and preying heavily on unique invertebrates and small rodents (Bratton 1974). There was even an indication that feral pigs were preying on white-tailed deer fawns (Pavlov 1981). In 1976, the park initiated a broad-based research program on wild boars to determine their seasonal movements, home range, daily movements, activity patterns, and daily and seasonal habitat preferences in an effort to increase the effectiveness of the control programs.

Much has been learned about the ecology of the wild boar since then, and in recent years control efforts have improved dramatically (over one thousand captured in 1985). However, over the last decade the control program has remained embroiled in politics. Unlike those who were against burro control, boar control programs have been adamantly opposed by local residents who regard the wild boar as a game animal. As a result, the State of North Carolina Wildlife Resources Commission has long been opposed to the killing of boars in the North Carolina section of the park by park personnel. Although they have no legal standing in the matter, this opposition along with a "constant barrage of charges hurled at hog management through the media and of other acts (sometimes taking the form of vandalism)" have caused the park to terminate direct reduction activities on the North Carolina side of the park (Coleman 1984:16). Direct reduction does continue on the Tennessee side of the park.

As a trade-off to this action, a recent agreement with hunters from North Carolina allows interested private citizens under the supervision of park personnel and North Carolina officials to trap and remove as many wild boars as possible to acceptable release sites in North Carolina, where they may be harvested during the regular season. Though the volunteer program has successfully diffused much of the hostility toward the park, it has had several drawbacks. It has more than quadrupled the work force devoted to this issue. Volunteers only work when they can, leaving periods of no trapping effort. There are difficulties with the capture and release of nontarget species, such as native small mammals. Finally, the baiting techniques and trapping success are less effective per unit effort than when done by government personnel, partly because trapping has been restricted to areas of easy access, such as close proximity to roads and lakeshores. Remote areas receive little control (Coleman 1984; Goigel and Bratton 1983).

Most individuals have concluded that the elimination of the wild boar from the Great Smoky Mountains is highly unlikely because of the biological potential of the species and the relative inaccessibility of large portions of the park. In addition, boundary areas continually replenish the population, which is supplemented by illegal restocking efforts by local hunters (Bill Cook, interview with author, Great Smoky Mountains National Park, Oct. 14, 1986). Management will therefore concentrate efforts on specific portions of the park. The emphasis will be to increase the effectiveness of traditional techniques of trapping and shooting, to investigate alternative baits to enhance trapping success; to provide greater accessibility to remote areas, to investigate the use of well-trained dog packs; to rescind the moratorium on shooting in the North Carolina section of the park, to fence key areas of the park, and to explore the possibility of fencing large sections of the park boundary to prevent further immigration.

Mountain Goats in Olympic National Park

For years the NPS has struggled to develop a workable plan to eliminate the mountain goat from Olympic National Park. This effort epitomizes all of the problems that alien species can cause in parks and the difficulties the Park Service has in explaining and carrying out its policies.

Mountain goats are native to many of the mountainous areas of northwestern North America, but because of the isolation of the Olympic Mountains from the Canadian Rockies and the Cascade

Range, mountain goats never colonized the area. Surveys of the region in 1897 and 1899 by eminent biologists found no evidence that mountain goats existed in the Olympics. In 1909 the mountainous area of the Olympic Peninsula was designated as Mt. Olympus National Monument under U.S. Forest Service management. According to local sources, a group of local hunters was responsible for bringing the mountain goat to the Olympic area. They considered the mountains suitable for establishing a herd of mountain goats for hunting purposes, and in 1925, four adult mountain goats from the Selkirk Mountains in British Columbia were released in the northern foothills of the Olympic Mountains near Lake Crescent. Additional releases in 1927 and around 1929 brought the total number of transplanted individuals to about twelve.

In 1933, jurisdiction of the national monument was transferred to NPS. In 1938, Olympic National Park was established, and the mountain goat was protected from sport hunting. The mountain goats had few checks on their population. The great majority of goats resided in the park rather than on the more marginal habitat found on Forest Service lands surrounding it, which were open to sport hunting. The wolf had already been extirpated from the peninsula by this time. Other predators had been controlled by local game agents so their numbers were probably small. By the sixties a thriving mountain goat population existed over much of the northern and eastern parts of the park.

Concern that the goats were damaging subalpine vegetation caused NPS to initiate studies of the mountain goats in the seventies. Research throughout the seventies and eighties examined the impact of the mountain goat on plant communities and soils. Erosion from wallowing was documented, and plant communities near those wallows were shown to have been changed considerably. Mountain goat grazing reduced the dominance of several species in the climax subalpine plant communities. There was also concern that some species of unique endemic plants would eventually be eliminated. The first large-scale aerial census of mountain goats, conducted in 1983, estimated the population at between 1,000 and 1,350 (Houston, Moorhead, and Olsen 1986).

The park undertook its first control actions in 1980 when seventeen goats were removed. In 1981, the park began a three-year experimental management program to test the available options to control goat numbers. To date more than three hundred goats have been live-captured and removed from the park. Most of these goats have been given to the game departments of surrounding states for restocking ranges.[5] Another three hundred animals have been captured, marked, and released in the park as part of the ongoing research. A variety of capture techniques have been tested, including drop nets, drive nets, net guns, snares, and tranquilizer darts from the ground and from helicopters.

Several factors have combined to make control of the mountain goats in Olympic an extremely sensitive issue. First, mountain goats are a very popular animal and the most photographed one in the park. They are easily seen by backpackers (sometimes to the point of being an annoyance) and by motorists from the Klahhane Ridge overlook. Mountain goats are also a particularly attractive animal, and mountain goat kids are adorable. Second, the ecological damage the goats are causing is not readily apparent to the casual observer. Changes in plant dominance and species composition are factors plant ecologists deal with; they are not things that generally alarm the average visitor. This point is particularly vexing to those who view NPS policy on alien species control as inconsistent. They ask why some parks can have English sparrows or ring-necked pheasant but Olympic cannot have mountain goats. The fact that mountain goats are native in similar terrain in areas as close as 40 kilometers from the park also causes consternation. Finally, the state of Washington, which administers sport hunting of goats on lands surrounding the park, feels that a control program in the park will ultimately eliminate the sport harvest outside the park.

NPS also faces several complications in any program it might undertake. The Olympic Mountains are largely roadless, incredibly rugged, and often have long periods of harsh weather. All of the control options tested would require the use of helicopters in most areas of the park. On an operational basis, they would be prohibitively expensive. Costs for helicopter removal have averaged approximately $500 per animal and will increase as the easier-to-remove animals are eliminated. Shooting goats from the air would be by far the most cost-effective and expedient method of reducing or eliminating the population, but would probably be the most politically unpalatable solution.

The unacceptability of traditional population-control techniques has led to a search for other control methods, including sterilization (Hoffman and Wright 1990). Two fertility-control techniques have been tested on free-ranging mountain goats in the park. Females have been treated with silastic implants of melengestrol acetate—a synthetic hormone that inhibits estrous. This treatment is estimated to be effective for three to four years. Males were chemically vasectomized using a sclerosing agent (lactic acid) injected into the epididymus. This treatment renders the male permanently sterile, apparently without changing courtship and reproductive behavior. Beginning in 1982, twelve females were captured and sterilized. Subsequent monitoring of these females over four years of the study has indicated that only three kids were produced (see Table 6.2). This was a significantly lower reproduction rate than that observed in nontreated females.

Five males were captured and sterilized in 1985. An attempt was made to choose the largest males in the given area to ensure social and reproductive dominance. Unfortunately these males dispersed more widely than anticipated, making it difficult to measure their influence on the reproductive success of female goats in the area, though it was apparently not lowered. It appears from these findings that too few males were sterilized to have an effect on reproduction, particularly if the males disperse throughout a wide area. Given the uncertainties in male dispersal and reproductive behavior, the number of males that would need to be sterilized to lower the reproduction rate is not now known.

Table 6.2 The Reproductive Performances of Female Mountain Goats Sterilized with MGA Implants in Olympic National Park

| | | Year | | | |
1982	1983	1984	1985	1986	Years Effective
T[a]	0	0	0	0	4[c]
T	0	0	0	0	4[c]
	T[a]	0	0	0	3
	T	0	1	0	1
	T[a]	0	0	0	3[c]
	T	0	0	0	3[c]
	T[a]	0	0	0	3[c]
		T[a]	0	0	2[c]
		T[a]	0	1	1
		T	1	0	0
		T	0	0[b]	1[c]
Reproductive Success		0/2	0/7	2/11	1/10

T = The year of treatment of an individual goat.
[a]Female known to have bred successfully prior to treatment. (Reproductive history of the other females was unknown.)
[b]Female known dead.
[c]Minimum duration of effectiveness.
Source: R. Hoffman and R. G. Wright, "Fertility Control in a Non-native Population of Mountain Goats," *Northwest Science* 64(1990):4.

Since it involves the live-capture of mountain goats, sterilization, while possibly effective and a politically feasible method to manage the Olympic population, is presently an expensive option. New techniques presently in development and testing may someday eliminate the need for capturing an animal to be treated, thus removing the most expensive and difficult step in sterilizing wild animals. Should this occur, it would provide the NPS with a humane and politically viable control option to deal with what has thus far been an extremely difficult problem to solve. Currently NPS is relying on a live-capture and removal program to reduce the mountain goats in selected areas of the park. During 1988 and 1989, over ninety goats were removed and given to the state of Washington for transplant elsewhere.

Alien Animals in Hawaii Volcanoes National Park

Few areas of the world have had as much trouble with alien species as have the islands of Hawaii. Most isolated island ecosystems are fragile because their fauna and flora are developed from a few colonizers and often evolve into many small populations vulnerable to disturbance. The Hawaiian Islands are among the most isolated island groups in the world and have been extremely vulnerable to outside influences (Ames and Stone 1985). Prior to the arrival of humans, the only land mammal on the islands was the Hawaiian bat. Since then animals such as goats, cattle, domestic pigs, mongooses, and rats have become abundant and have caused immense damage to the island's natural ecosystems. Two of the state's national parks, Hawaii Volcanoes and Haleakala, have been especially susceptible to this damage. Principal concern is over the impact of two species, feral pigs and goats.

Feral Pigs

Feral pigs are probably the most important vertebrate modifiers of native Hawaiian ecosystems (Stone and Keith 1987). They were originally introduced to the Hawaiian islands by Polynesian peoples hundreds of years ago. Pigs were the most important sacred and secular animal in Hawaiian culture. They were the primary sacrificial animal, prominent indicators of wealth and status, and an important food source. Starting from the time the Europeans first discovered the islands in the late 1700s, European domestic pigs were also released on the islands. The result is that today there are feral pig populations in most habitats and on most islands in Hawaii. An estimated eighty thousand animals are present statewide, and ten thousand pigs per year are harvested by hunters (Stone 1985).

Feral pigs inhabit a wide variety of ecosystems, and their impact on native flora and fauna has been severe. The pigs select certain native species of plants, such as tree ferns, and have destroyed rare lobelioids, mints, lilies, orchids, and other taxa. They enhance alien plant spread through their digging and rooting activities and by carrying seeds in their feces. In suitable rainforest habitat, pig densities can reach 40 per square kilometer. At such densities, up to half of the forest floor can be rooted every six months. Pigs knock down and hollow out tree fern stumps by eating the starchy interior. This allows the stumps to collect water, permitting mosquitoes that may carry avian diseases to breed (Stone 1985; Stone and Taylor 1984). (Standing water is otherwise extremely rare in Hawaii due to the porous nature of the rocks and soils.) Pigs also affect endangered birds, such as the po'ouli, by altering the invertebrate fauna of the forest floor (Scott, Kepler, and Sincock 1985).

The damage caused by pigs in Hawaii Volcanoes was recognized soon after the park was created, and a limited, if sporadic, control program (mainly shooting by rangers) was initiated in the thirties (Lamb 1938). While this program removed over eleven thousand pigs between 1930 and 1970, it did little to reduce the pig population. In 1972 a citizens' hunter program, which allowed selected sport hunters deputized as park rangers to hunt in designated pig management units in Hawaii Volcanoes, was initiated. However, since most hunters stayed close to roads or trails, and because hunter success was related to pig density, this program was never successful in reducing pig populations. Only one pig management unit (around park headquarters) was successfully cleared (Barrett and Stone 1983). In 1980 an accelerated program involving several control methods was begun in Hawaii Volcanoes. Studies were initiated on the effect of trapping, snaring, and hunting by expert teams with trained dogs. Researchers often accompanied the hunters, detailed records were kept of effort expended, and data were obtained from the animals killed.

Well-constructed woven-wire fencing, although expensive ($9,000 to $16,000 per kilometer) has proven capable of excluding pigs and appears to be the best method to exclude pigs from adjacent lands and to subdivide the park into manageable sections. Between 1983 and 1985 the park constructed 50 kilometers of pig-proof fences that enclosed nine control units comprising 7,550 hectares. Pigs have been eliminated from eight units (7,156 hectares) and reduced to remnant levels in another other unit (394 hectares). At present, there are 77 kilometers of pig-proof fences in the park, and annual costs for pig fence inspection and maintenance are about $25,000 (Chuck Stone, interview with author, Hawaii Volcanoes National Park, June 10, 1989).

Once an area is fenced, pig control within the units has been most effectively accomplished through systematic hunting by NPS personnel using dogs (Stone and Keith 1987; Barrett and Stone 1983). The cost of removal in such a program (primarily hunters' salaries) was estimated at $95 per pig in 1986 (Hone and Stone 1989). Once the pig numbers in fenced units have been reduced to very low numbers hunting is no longer efficient or cost-effective. There is some evidence that pig populations reduced to a low density (less than 1 per square kilometer) may have difficulty surviving. Remnant animals in Hawaii Volcanoes do not seem to repopulate an area as rapidly as breeding potential would allow (Stone interview; Kituta and Stone 1986).

Feral pigs continue to occupy about 22,000 hectares of the park (28%) in the rain forest, mesic forest, seasonal montane forest, shrubland, and open grasslands. Populations are most dense in the rainforests, where they are believed to be 128 to 200 pigs per square kilometer (Hawaii Volcanoes 1986).

Feral Goats

The areas occupied by the national parks in Hawaii had been subjected to grazing by domestic stock with increasingly evident impacts for more than a century before the parks were established (Lamb 1938). Most of the grazing and damage was by goats that were probably introduced to the island of Hawaii in 1778 (Katahira and Stone 1982). Control efforts in Hawaii Volcanoes began in the twenties. Over seventy thousand goats were eliminated in the park from 1927 to 1970 by drives conducted by foresters and rangers, contracts to private companies, CCC personnel, and deputized hunts. Large numbers of personnel were devoted to this effort, and most rangers thought they were accomplishing a real reduction in goat numbers (Stan Schelgel, interview with author, Mt. Rainier National Park, Jan. 13, 1988). It was not until a 1970 aerial census showed that there were about fifteen thousand goats in the park (just as many animals as when control efforts began), that the ineffectiveness of the existing control program became evident (Katahira and Stone 1982).

As a result, many doubted that goat numbers in the park could ever be reduced. However, by late 1970, park researchers and management had developed a long-term systematic plan for goat reduction. The major steps in this plan consisted of the construction and maintenance of goat-proof boundary and internal drift fences followed by frequent organized goat drives and hunts, in part using a citizen hunter program. In all, about 100 kilometers of fences were constructed over a period of ten years at a cost of about $960,000.

Between 1971 and 1975, 12,976 goats were eliminated, and in June 1975 the last goat drive was conducted. As goats became difficult to locate, interest by the public in the citizen hunter program diminished. From 1976 to 1979, 1,596 goats were eliminated, largely by NPS shooters using helicopters. By 1980, 90% of the goat range in the park had been fenced, and the population estimate within was about 200 goats (Hawaii Volcanoes 1986). With so few goats remaining, these became so wary and elusive that helicopter searches became prohibitively expensive and impractical.[6] Radio transmitters were attached to captured goats, which were then released to the wild in areas where remnant bands of goats were suspected. If subsequent tracking revealed that a transmittered goat joined a wild band, the wild goats were shot and the transmittered goat was left to join other bands. This method has since succeeded in reducing goat numbers to near zero in all fenced areas (Taylor and Katahira 1988).

The program at Hawaii Volcanoes is unfortunately never ending. Since the reproductive capacity of the remaining goats is undoubtedly at maximum, even a few goats, if left within the fenced areas, could render all past efforts futile within a few years. Secondly, maintenance of the fencing remains a constant problem. Rapid deterioration occurs from sulfur fumes, salt spray, and high humidity. Fences are also destroyed by vandals, earthquakes, and rock and tree falls. Thus, constant inspection and reconstruction is necessary. It is estimated that within the next three to fifteen years, replacement of 64 kilometers of goat-proof boundary fences will be needed.

At present, goats in the Mauna Loa area above 2,200 meters elevation are not contained by fences. The estimated twenty-five to fifty animals in this area roam freely in the park subalpine zone, and are causing damage to the vegetation. The remoteness, rugged terrain, and frequently inclement weather in this area make it expensive to fence. Part of the area was fenced in 1989, and goats will be removed as soon as possible after additional fences are completed (Stone interview).

Conclusions

Although alien species control in parks can be a difficult biological problem, the main constraints on parks are financial and political. Political problems result in part from ambiguities in NPS policy toward alien species. Present policy is only a general guide and can have a range of interpretations. Clearly many alien species present in parks are tolerated or ignored. In addition, some species are questionably classified as alien, thus adding to the confusion.[7] Thus, NPS needs to make more careful evaluations before deciding on the status of given species, and such determinations need to include both temporal and spatial considerations. This process could eliminate many of the problems NPS has encountered with the public and interest groups over control programs.

It also seems clear that many of the problems are self-imposed. Park managers often refrain from imposing policies in the face of opposition from special-interest groups. Even though clear evidence of biological damage exists, managers are sometimes reluctant to take action. Lessons of the past also indicate that most control programs, lethal or not, are going to be expensive and long-term. Only in the Hawaiian parks has NPS faced up to this situation and spent the money necessary.

Political problems also exist because NPS has done a relatively poor job in educating the public on the damage alien species cause to natural ecosystems and why control programs are necessary. The public often does not understand why parks are managed as they are. The situation in the Hawaiian parks, where control programs are now tolerated by most people, understood by a few, and disliked by some, is common. As with the Great Smoky Mountains, the recreational pig hunters are the most hostile to the park's management plans (Brower 1985). One may never convince this group, but great opportunities exist for eliciting the support of the majority of park visitors for effective alien species control.

NOTES

1. I have chosen to use the term *alien* to designate such species. This decision is based on the opinions of several biologists (Smith 1985; Stone interview) who feel that the other terms do not convey to the public the dangers posed by such species. They feel, for example, that the word *exotic* is not appropriate because it often connotes species that are intriguing or unusual but not necessarily destructive to native ecosystems.

2. Technically, species are classified as aliens only when their existence in an area can be traced to some human influence. This definition can create ambiguities because it separates species that may, for example, inhabit remote islands as a result of natural wind-born introduction from those carried to the same island directly by humans or by human-introduced plants or animals.

3. In some parks, alien species are managed as an essential part of the area's historic scene. This is the case with the ponies on Assateague Island National Seashore (Keiper, Moss, and Zervanos 1980). Feral ponies have lived on Assateague Island since the mid-1600s. Their population presently numbers about 180, including 60 on the northern (Maryland) portion of the island in the National Seashore and about 120 on the southern (Virginia) end in the Chincoteague Wildlife Refuge.

Feral horses are also treated as part of the historic landscape at Cumberland Island National Seashore. This is in spite of research by Turner (1986) that has shown the horses have a major impact, reducing vegetation up to 98% of that in ungrazed areas. Her analyses suggested that the population of 180 horses is more than three times a realistic carrying capacity for horses on the island.

4. Only rarely have any researchers disagreed with these findings. Moehlman, for example, stated that "the burros I observed did not strip the land, foul waterholes or endanger other animals. . . . I do not deny that bighorn sheep might be affected by burro overpopulation, but to condemn the burro is to simplify a complex question, one that involves such things as climatic cycles and human population pressures" (1972:517).

5. An ironic twist to this story is that some of the mountain goats given to the state of Idaho and stocked in the southeastern portion of the state have apparently been seen in Grand Teton National Park, an area that was also never occupied by mountain goats.

6. Cost per goat taken increased from $1 to $5 in 1970 to $100 to $300 in 1982 (Katahira and Stone 1982).

7. The bison in Wrangell St. Elias National Park and Preserve are a species of such questionable status. This species went extinct within the park less than five hundred years ago. It was introduced into the area now administered as a preserve in 1950, and has been hunted as a game animal since. The park considers it an alien species, although Peek and others (1987) have concluded that the actual status of the bison is debatable.

The photogenic character of young mountain goats makes it easy to see why they are a favorite of visitors, which complicates control programs. (National Park Service photo by Roger Hoffman)

Mountain goat male in a wallow at Olympic National Park. Wallows such as these have caused widespread damage to fragile subalpine plant communities in Olympic. (National Park Service photo by Roger Hoffman)

Dall sheep in Wrangell St. Elias National Park. Balancing their habitats was one of the biggest issues facing planners working on the Alaska lands settlement. (National Park Service photo by Robert Belous)

Mature bison bull near Mary Bay, Yellowstone Lake. (National Park Service photo by Mary Meagher)

Early spring concentration of bison near the Lamar River in Yellowstone. (National Park Service photo by Mary Meagher)

Bighorn sheep at Yellowstone. They have posed difficult management problems because of their susceptibility to disease and disturbance by visitors. Sightings of these sheep are rare in many parks. (National Park Service photo by Douglas Houston)

Elk at Grand Teton National Park. (National Park Service photo by R. Gerald Wright)

Cougar in Glacier National Park. Rarely seen and more rarely photographed, cougars and other predators are more common in many large parks than is generally realized. (Glacier National Park Museum)

Park personnel feeding bears at Yosemite National Park in 1943. Such actions were common before the 1970s and made enforcement of feeding regulations much more difficult. (National Park Service photo by Joseph Dixon)

Black bear cubs at a concession stand in Glacier National Park. Their comic antics and human traits are major reasons for their popularity among visitors. (Glacier National Park Museum)

Visitor feeding a black bear in Glacier National Park. Visitors feeding bears from cars or at picnic areas was a common sight before the 1970s. (Glacier National Park Museum)

Monarchs of the parks, grizzly bears are a lasting symbol of the loss of wildness and wilderness in the United States and an attribute national parks seek to preserve. (Glacier National Park Museum)

Isle Royale wolf waiting for the immobilizing drug to wear off following placement of radio collar. Because of a dramatic decline in wolves on the island, a research program involving handling and placing radio collars to track movements was initiated in 1988. (National Park Service photo by Robert J. Krumenaker)

Fitting a radio collar to an Isle Royale wolf in the spring of 1988. (National Park Service photo by Robert J. Krumenaker)

7

Bear Management

More than any other animal, bears are inexorably linked to national parks. Public interest in and affection for bears was a major factor in saving them from the controls imposed on other predators in many parks (Johnson 1973). Public affection for bears first became prevalent during the Teddy Roosevelt era, and the unique relationship between visitors and bears in parks continues today. In many parks bears, more than natural features and scenery, are the principal item of interest to visitors. During the times when black bears frequented the roadsides of parks like Yellowstone and Great Smoky Mountains, "bear jams" were formed as visitors stopped to watch or feed bears. Parks now attempt to disperse bears from roads and campgrounds to minimize the problem of bears becoming accustomed to handouts from visitors. The policy, while good for the bears, has decreased the opportunity to see bears and has disappointed many visitors. This policy reflects the great difficulties encountered in trying to manage both people and bears in the same area. In doing this, the Park Service has spent more money on research and management actions for bears than for any other group of animals.[1]

Black and grizzly bears are quite different in their behavior and habits and, thus, pose distinctly different management problems. Black bears more easily become habituated to human activity, and therefore have historically been more visible along the roads and developed areas in parks. As a result, they are among the most adored and sought after of park animals, though their potential danger is generally poorly understood or ignored. Significant numbers of black bears are found in thirty parks and monuments. Grizzly bears are a more intractable species and more dangerous to park visitors, but are rarely seen. They are classified as a threatened species in the forty-eight contiguous states where they reside in only two national

'lacier and Yellowstone (though there are occasional transients
...i Grand Teton and North Cascades). They are also found in most
parks in Alaska.

Grizzly Bear Management in Yellowstone

The status of the grizzly bear population in the early years of Yellowstone is not known. Early explorers frequently used the term *bear* when referring to either blacks or grizzlies, thus making it difficult to determine the relative abundance of either species from historic records. Craighead and Craighead (1967) concluded that the grizzly was common in Yellowstone prior to 1900, whereas the black bear was apparently scarce. Most observers have concluded that grizzly bear numbers in the park were relatively stable between 1900 and 1960, although estimates were generally crude. Open-pit garbage dumps were established in the 1880s, soon after the first hotels were built. The growth in visitation over the years resulted in increased quantities in garbage, which provided an additional source of food for bears and probably enhanced population growth.

For many years bears caused few problems, so there was a limited bear management program. Accurate records of personal injuries and of bears killed were not kept until 1930. In those days, visitor injuries or problems with bears were usually considered to be the visitor's fault, resulting from foolish actions in which the visitor should have known better. Prior to the forties, it was relatively uncommon for problem bears to be killed; they were usually shipped to zoos. However, as the zoos became full, more and more problem bears were killed. Throughout the forties and fifties the number of bears killed yearly fluctuated widely, apparently reflecting management sensitivity to visitor complaints of injury or property damage.

There was no information on grizzly bear ecology or habitat use in the park. Olaus Murie's research in 1944 on grizzly bear habitat use was a first, and it was short-lived. A growing concern over the lack of knowledge about bears and the implications this had for the long-term survival of the species became the catalyst for the first long-term research study on the grizzly bears of Yellowstone carried out between 1959 and 1967 under the direction of John and Frank Craighead.

The Craighead Study

The Craighead study focused on the most visible grizzly bears—those using the park dumps. From them the scientists sought to develop an understanding of grizzly bear population biology throughout the park. Study goals were to

1. examine population characteristics, such as density, sex and age composition, mortality, and reproduction
2. determine distribution and movement and
3. determine carrying capacity and habitat requirements.

The study encompassed a time when there were dramatic changes in grizzly bear management in the park. Some of these changes were necessitated by the tremendous increases in visitation, particularly in the backcountry, that occurred in the early sixties. Others were the result of a controversial decision by the park to close the remaining park garbage dumps.[2]

The Craigheads and the Park Service disagreed on the importance and impact of closing the dumps.[3] The Craigheads concluded that most park grizzly bears fed at the dumps, that the dumps were an important source of nutrition for them, and that the dumps were important in concentrating bears safely inside the park and at places isolated from visitors (Craighead and Craighead 1971). They felt that any closures of the dumps should be gradual to permit bears to readjust to natural foods and to the loss of supplemental food.

The NPS position came from a gradual recognition that operating open dumps was wrong. The management program of the park was designed to restore a "natural population" of bears as compared to a population that was artificially fed or artificially maintained at a higher than normal density (Schullery 1986). The park felt that each year the dumps remained open another generation of cubs would be conditioned to depend on them. The Park Service took the position that an abrupt closure of the dumps was the best course of action. The time frame of dump closure thus became the crux of the argument. The Craigheads concluded that a rapid closure of the dumps would result in "increased grizzly incidents in campgrounds, accelerated dispersal of bears to areas outside the Park, and greater concentrations of grizzlies at the public dumps in Gardiner and West Yellowstone. . . . The net result could be tragic personal injury, costly damages, and a drastic reduction in the number of grizzlies" (1967:96). Cole, on the other hand, maintained that abrupt closures of the dumps actually decreased the long-term probability of human injury because habitual campground-feeding grizzly bears would be killed and young bears would have less opportunity to learn this behavior (1972). Thus, it was debatable which alternative—phasing out the dumps or closing them immediately—would result in the least impact to bears.

The Craigheads further felt that the hands-off management goal of NPS, while laudable, was not realistic, and that an active management program was needed to sustain a healthy population of grizzly bears. They suggested that "any purposeful management of wildlife populations or their habitats can be considered 'unnatural'. . . . Natural population regulating processes have been so altered since the establishment of the park that these are not now effective. Since there is no possibility of these being wholly restored, and since management must do the job, artificiality becomes inevitable. Maintenance or reestablishment of the natural situation, . . . [has] limitations that must be recognized" (1967:98–99).

NPS Management Activities after 1969

The Rabbit Creek dump was closed in October 1969, and the dump at Trout Creek was closed the following year. All garbage cans were bear-proofed. The park began an intensive public-education campaign describing the dangers of feeding bears and increased enforcement of bear feeding regulations. During the period immediately preceding and following the closing of the dumps, the number of grizzly bears killed in the park was three times the average of the preceding nine years. This fact combined with increased depredations in park campgrounds and in the communities around the park led many to conclude that the Craigheads' predictions were coming true. The Craigheads and their supporters frequently disputed NPS policy in the local newspapers and in a variety of magazines, (e.g., Craighead 1973), a tactic that angered NPS personnel, who were more limited in their ability to argue their viewpoint. A particularly sensitive point was accusations that NPS was secretly killing more grizzly bears than was officially recorded (see Chase 1983). This was a vexing situation because it was a difficult charge to prove or deny. Most of the accusers were anonymous, whereas the Park Service was in a highly visible position and was constantly placed on the defensive.

The Bear Management Controversy in the Seventies

As the number of grizzly bears killed in the park increased in the early seventies, concern over long-term survival of the grizzly bear in Yellowstone also grew, and this too became a point of contention. The Craigheads maintained that most park grizzly bears (75% or more) visited the dumps, and thus considered that their observations provided an accurate census of grizzly bears in the park. They estimated that about 230 grizzly bears occupied the park prior to the closing of the dumps (Craighead and Craighead 1971; Craighead, Varney, and Craighead 1974). On the other hand, NPS maintained that between 50 to 100 grizzlies stayed in the remote areas of the park, never visited the dumps, and were thus never counted by the Craighead team; this made the total population closer to 335 (Cole 1973).[4]

In response to the growing controversy, in 1973 the secretary of the interior requested that the National Academy of Science (NAS) establish the Committee on Yellowstone Grizzlies to evaluate population data. Their initial findings essentially supported both viewpoints. The committee concluded that some Yellowstone grizzlies used the dumps infrequently and thus were probably not observed or marked. They estimate that a minimum of 32% (approximately 57 bears) were in this category. However, they also concluded that the total grizzly bear population in the Yellowstone ecosystem had averaged 234 per year between 1959 and 1970, a figure concurring with the estimate of Craighead, Varney, and Craighead (1974).[5]

Another point of contention was over differing predictions for future trends in the population. The Craighead estimates came from a computer model of grizzly bear population dynamics, which predicted a decline from a peak of 245 in 1967 to 136 animals in 1974 (Craighead, Varney, and Craighead 1974). Further declines beyond this point were projected, along with more trouble in developed areas if park management policy was not changed. NPS disputed this model, suggesting that the population would increase because closing the dumps eliminated the high cub mortality (some estimates put it as high as 27%) that occurred as a result of cubs being killed by dominant males at the dumps or from ingesting toxic or other lethal items, such as broken glass, metal, or plastic.[6] Second, the Park Service maintained that females would begin to breed at a younger age due to the removal of stress caused by the high concentrations of grizzlies at the dumps (Stokes 1970).

The NAS report rejected the Craighead computer model and NPS suggestions, concluding that the "data are not at hand to make accurate predictions about population responses to various levels of adult mortality" (NAS 1974:35).[7] The committee did, however, feel that the high levels of bear removals between 1968 and 1973 made it "most probable that the grizzly population was reduced substantially during this period" (NAS 1974:37).

Although on the surface the NAS conclusions appeared to have settled little, after the publication of the committee's report, the controversy began to cool. One reason for this was that the number of bears killed and transplanted in the park declined dramatically after 1971, supporting NPS contentions that the new policies were working and that a truly wild population of bears was being established.

Formation of the Interagency Grizzly Bear Study Team

The controversy was also defused by the creation in 1973 of the Interagency Grizzly Bear Study Team (IGBST), made up of biologists from NPS, Forest Service, Fish and Wildlife Service, and the states of Montana, Wyoming, and Idaho under the direction of Richard Knight. The study team had two main objectives, to study the status and trend of the bear populations and to study the use of habitats by bears and the relationship of land management to the welfare of the bear populations.

The IGBST has since been involved in numerous studies in the Yellowstone ecosystem. Knight and Eberhardt (1984, 1985) summarized much of this work, and found that between 1974 and 1982, the average litter size for grizzly bears had been 1.9, and about 60% of the females produced first litters by age six. This compared with an average litter size of 2.2 and an age of first fecundity of five years from 1959 to 1970. They suggested that the earlier maturation between 1950 and 1970 was associated with more rapid growth rates probably made possible by the food available at the garbage dumps. Another contributing factor might have been a drying trend in the climate of Yellowstone in the seventies that resulted in smaller litter sizes and a general decrease in carrying capacity (Picton 1978; Picton et al. 1986).

Knight and Eberhardt used a population model to conclude that a population decline of between 1.7% and 1.8% a year had occurred between 1974 and 1982. An interesting facet of this model was that population changes were very sensitive to change in the number of adult females. They found that lowering the mortality of adult females by even one animal per year was roughly equivalent to shifting the litter size from the present value to that prevailing when the dumps were open. Knight and Eberhardt did not speculate as to what extent the declines in population size were due to dump closures and to what extent they were due to other factors, such as changing climate or habitat conditions.

Under the authority of the Endangered Species Act, grizzly bears were listed as a threatened species by the U.S. Fish and Wildlife Service in 1975.[8] In 1979 the preparation of a grizzly bear recovery plan was begun that would provide recommendations and actions necessary for the maintenance, enhancement, and recovery of this species in the contiguous forty-eight states. The plan, completed in 1982 (Fish and Wildlife Service 1982), spelled out for the first time specific actions needed to protect and enhance grizzly populations:

1. Identify grizzly bear population levels that signify measurable species recovery in regions determined to have suitable habitat for bears
2. Identify limiting factors in the population and habitat that have caused the population decline
3. Identify specific management measures that will remove the limiting factors and permit populations to increase
4. Establish recovery of at least three populations in three distinct areas to delist the species

As expected, the plan met with considerable controversy. One of the most adamant opponents was the National Wool Growers Association, which argued that the plan gave "far too much emphasis . . . to the welfare of the grizzly bear over the impacts of human and livestock welfare. The loss of one human life is not worth the entire grizzly population" (U.S. Fish and Wildlife Service 1982:185).

The three areas selected to receive priority funding for recovery were the Yellowstone ecosystem, which includes the park and surrounding lands; the Northern Continental Divide region, which includes Glacier National Park and surrounding lands; and the Cabinet Mountains–Yaak River Drainage in western Montana. Another area to be looked at if funding becomes available includes North Cascades National Park. Since the approval of the recovery plan, research on grizzly bear biology and habitat needs have expanded in the Rocky Mountains. The direction of grizzly bear research has shifted from site-specific, general biology studies to topical studies focusing on the effects of certain human activities upon the behavior and habitat use of grizzly bears. These studies are designed to supply information on how grizzly bears relate to specific activities so they can be more effectively managed (Servheen 1986).

Recent Trends

Recent evidence suggests that things are going well for the grizzly bear in Yellowstone. In 1988, a special task force headed by Richard Knight of the IGBST calculated that the minimum total population of grizzly bears in the region was about 170 to 180, a figure very close to the Craigheads' 1967 estimate. There is, however, much less talk today about bear numbers and more concern about reproductive rates and the quality of the habitat available to bears. Based on these conditions, the grizzly in Yellowstone is doing better than it has in many years (Schullery 1989b). Distribution of sows with young throughout the greater Yellowstone ecosystem is considered good. Between 1986 and 1988, known mortality averaged six bears a year, with an average of less than two adult females per year. Bears also appear to be using natural food sources quite well. At the same time that the garbage dumps were closed, elk and bison controls were terminated. It is now clear that grizzly bears are using those expanding food resources to a great extent. Recent IGBST reports have also documented a shift in denning sites to areas near known spring concentrations of ungulate carcasses (Mattson, Blanchard, and Knight 1986). Trout populations in the park, growing because of increased protection, are also being exploited, and bears are still exploring and discovering spawning streams they weren't fishing a few years ago (Schullery 1989b).

Grizzly bears are an incredibly valuable part of the Yellowstone ecosystem. Their ultimate survival will depend on how we adjust to their needs and our willingness to sacrifice some of our own wants. As Paul Schullery has said, "The jury is still out on whether or not we, as a people and as a government, are willing to make that sacrifice. In the last few years we've proven we *can* do it, but proving we *will* is something we must do again every year, forever" (1989b:29).

Black Bear Management in Great Smoky Mountains National Park

When Great Smoky Mountains National Park was created, black bears were scarce due to exclusive logging, unrestricted hunting, and the gradual loss of the American chestnut—an important food item. They began to recover quickly in the midthirties under the protection afforded by the park. Willis King, a park naturalist, wrote in 1935, "Ten years ago, before protection was given the animal life of the park area, bears were . . . rarely seen. [Recently] they have reproduced to the extent of becoming fairly common. They inhabit the high mountains and ridges and the more inaccessible stretches. . . . I believe bears are approaching the numbers which they normally should have" (2).

In 1940, Arthur Stupka estimated the population at about three hundred bears (1950). Such estimates are extremely suspect, since they are based almost entirely on chance observations along trails, roads, and in campgrounds. The number of bears observed in such instances was primarily related to food availability rather than density (Marcum 1974). During the late forties the first depredations began to occur and the first bear-visitor conflicts were reported. Since then, the number of black bears in the park has fluctuated according to mast scarcity or abundance. Years of major mast failures, such as from 1949 to 1958 and in 1968, 1972, and 1978, caused many bears to leave the park, after which they were often killed.

The population apparently stabilized at the present level (five to six hundred) in the seventies (Greg Walthen, interview with author, Great Smoky Mountains National Park, Oct. 14, 1986). Bear habitat in the park is good, and the population appears to be at carrying capacity. The park now has the largest protected population of black bears in the southeast. Beemen (1975) observed that reproductive rates were low, that only 17% of the females had cubs, and that there was substantial cub mortality in the first five to nine months of age.

There have been conflicts between black bears and visitors in the park virtually since its establishment in 1934. Over the years, these problems have become more numerous as the black bear population and visitation has increased. In recent years, Great Smoky Mountains has averaged 8 million visitors a year, one of the highest in the nation. During the first four decades of the park, bear management largely consisted of capturing, relocating, and occasionally killing problem bears. Visitor management included attempts at education and enforcement of laws preventing feeding. As in other parks, the seventies saw a tremendous increase in backcountry use, which caused a shift from primarily front-country to backcountry bear incidents. As a result, significant revisions in black bear management were made beginning in 1976. This coincided with a major research effort on bears that was conducted through the University of Tennessee.

As a result of this work, Great Smoky Mountains probably has the most thoroughly studied black bear population in the nation, and probably no animal species in any park has been the subject of so many individual research efforts. At least twenty-one graduate theses have been conducted over the past fifteen years. While some of these projects have emphasized basic ecological data, others have been invaluable in helping the park formulate management programs.

All bears in the park appear to rely to a degree on some human foods. Most of these foods appear to come directly from raiding garbage cans or visitor handouts. Unlike Yosemite, Sequoia, Glacier, and Yellowstone, Great Smoky Mountains has no formal overnight accommodations in the park that generate large quantities of refuse.[9] Beeman (1971) found at least some garbage in virtually all bear scat analyzed. He concluded that a truly wild group of black bears did not exist in the park. He subsequently found that there were two distinct cohorts of bears in the park—one in the backcountry that had a high proportion of adult bears and a nearly balanced sex ratio and a second, or panhandler, group conditioned to human activities and human foods (about 5% of the population), which had a lower proportion of adults and a high proportion of males (1975). Panhandler bears have long been a problem in Great Smoky Mountains (Eagar and Pelton 1979). Their significance far outweighs their small numbers, as they have been responsible for a majority of the aggressive encounters and equipment damage in the park.

To counteract the problem of panhandler bears today, the park maintains an active education and enforcement program designed to prohibit feeding bears. Garbage is picked up daily and hauled to areas far from the park. Problem bears removed from the park have in recent years been placed in isolated areas of Tennessee in a joint program with state management biologists. This program includes careful assessment of the transplant site to assure the survival and well-being of the animal. Released bears are tagged and monitored to assess their habituation to the new area. Thus far, survival of bears has been excellent and return rates low. To further reduce problems, many of the overnight shelters on the park's extensive trail system are surrounded by high fencing to keep bears out (a zoo in reverse). All cooking and sleeping is done within these shelters.

Conflicts between Bears and Visitors

Prior to the sixties, conflicts between bears and visitors were not considered to be a serious management problem in most parks. However, the dramatic increase in the use of park backcountry areas in the sixties and seventies greatly increased the opportunity for conflicts between bears and humans. Martinka (1982), for example, found a direct relationship between the total number of visitors to Glacier and the number of confrontations with grizzly bears. Incidents of property damage, injuries, and bears obtaining human foods increased from less than 2 per year prior to 1972 to 36 per year by 1982 in Denali (Dalle-Molle and Van Horn 1987).

Jope has pointed out that grizzly bear incidents with visitors fall into two distinct categories. One type of incident is food-related and most often involves campers, and its likelihood of occurrence may be enhanced by the bears' lack of fear of people. The other type is the surprise encounter that most often involves hikers and others moving through bear habitat (Kathy Jope, letter to author, Apr. 17, 1987). Most management has addressed the food-related incidents perhaps because they tend to involve the same bear repeatedly in incidents of escalating severity and because they result in the most severe injuries and in fatalities. Surprise encounters rarely result in severe injury, and this type of incident is unlikely to involve the same bear repeatedly since bears seem to avoid recurrence by leaving the area.

Park management programs designed to reduce food related-incidents have typically emphasized (1) public information programs on safe camping practices; (2) removal of artificial food sources; (3) enforcement of regulations regarding proper food storage and feeding of wild animals; (4) control of problem bears; and (5) continued research and monitoring of the effects of the above actions. Management actions to reduce the likelihood of surprise encounters have included public information programs on safe hiking practices, e.g., making noise in a dense area or carrying a bell, and closing specific areas to visitor use that are known to contain high densities of bears.

Aside from humans, bears are the most dangerous mammals in the parks. Injuries and deaths attributable to bears pale in significance when compared to other sources of fatalities in parks, such as drownings, falls, and auto accidents. However, human nature being what it is, people view incidents with bears much differently, and such encounters often receive widespread and sensationalized media coverage. Visitor injuries attributable to grizzly and black bears in major North American national parks were compiled by Herrero in 1970. Almost all of the serious injuries and deaths are attributable to grizzly bears. He found the death rate from grizzly bear attacks in such areas was 1 per 30 million visitors, and the injury rate was 1 per 2 million visitors. In parks, 11 people have been killed by grizzly bears (see Table 7.1).

Black bears have also been known to kill people (Beeman 1975), and there is one reported death in a U.S. park (Rocky Mountain) (Roger Contor, interview with author, Ellensburg, Wash., Apr. 17–18, 1986). Black bears cause far more injuries than grizzly bears. These injuries are, however, typically not severe because black bears are generally not as aggressive. Herrero's data in parks show that most injuries caused by black bears were minor—requiring less than twenty-four hours of hospitalization. Hastings, Gilbert, and Turner (1981) and Hastings (1982) found that among 5,784 reactions of bears to

Table 7.1 Visitor Injuries and Deaths by Bears

Park	Injuries	Deaths	Dates	Reference
		Black Bear		
Crater Lake	8		1960–73	McCollum (1974)
Glacier	14		1960–61	Park Files
Grand Teton	8		1959–82	Grand Teton (1986)
Great Smokies	164		1960–85	Park Files
Mt. Rainier	2		1961	Park Files
Rocky Mountain	—	1	1921	Contor (pers. comm.)
Sequoia	23		1959–86	Sequoia (1987)
Yellowstone	1,883		1931–84	Schullery (1986)
Yosemite	231	—	1960–86	Keay and Webb (1989)
Total	2,309	1		
		Grizzly Bear		
Denali	16		1917–86	Dalle-Molle and Van Horn (1987)
Glacier	28	7	1910–86	Martinka (pers. comm.)
Glacier Bay		1	1960–86	Park Files
Katmai	1		1966–86	Katmai (1987)
Yellowstone	84	3	1930–85	Schullery (1986)
Total	129	11		

visitors, only 1.2% could be categorized as aggressive. Bears responded to humans largely by walking away, watching, traveling around, walking toward, and running away from people. They found that the level of aggression was not correlated with age, size, or sex of the bear. Eagar and Pelton (1979) found that the most common factor precipitating an aggressive action in black bears in Great Smoky Mountains was crowding by visitors (see Table 7.2). However, of 624 acts of aggression, only 37 (5.9%) resulted in contact with, but not necessarily injury to, visitors. In contrast, 50% of the grizzly bear injuries that Herrero identified could be classed as major—requiring hospitalization for more than twenty-four hours or resulting in death. Incidents involving grizzlies conditioned to human food are typically serious or fatal. On the other hand, injuries by grizzlies involved in surprise encounters are typically less serious, usually requiring less than twenty-four hours of hospitalization.

Some park visitors when hearing about bear-inflicted injuries often express outrage at the failure of the parks to protect them. However,

Table 7.2 Activities Resulting in Physical Contact with Black Bears

Activity	Total frequency	Contact frequency	Percentage resulting in contact	Percentage of all contacts (n = 36)
Crowding	244	10	4	27
Petting	27	10	47	27
Petting—crowding	19	9	47	24
Harassing—crowding	30	2	7	5
Photographing	6	1	17	3
Handfeeding	11	1	9	3
Photographing—crowding	67	1	2	3
Handfeeding—crowding	13	1	8	3
Tossfeeding—crowding	2	1	50	3

Source: Adapted from J. T. Eager and M. R. Pelton, "Panhandler Bears in the Great Smoky Mountains National Park," Unpublished report, Great Smoky Mountains National Park, 1979.

Herrero (1974) found that even among individuals actually injured by bears, the majority of opinions favored the bear. In a survey of people injured by black bears in Great Smoky Mountains, Pelton (1976) found that 42% readily admitted they were entirely at fault in the incident. About 31% of this sample did feel that bears posed a serious problem for park visitors, although fewer than 1% felt that bears should be eliminated from the park. Part of this reasoning may be because violations of NPS regulations were a major contributing factor to personal injuries in the park between 1964 and 1976 (Singer and Bratton 1977).

Despite these findings, any bear injury and mortality generally receives sensational media coverage, and sometimes results in demands for the elimination of the offending animal or even the species. Moment (1970) has spoken for those who feel that grizzly bears should be removed from national parks because they conflict with human uses. Moment has maintained he is not "anti-bear," but only that his position on grizzly bears is similar to that for alligators: "I would advocate the preservation of the . . . species, but not in the same ponds where people are encouraged to swim" (1970:1019). Such views appear to represent a small minority. Demands for elimination of bears from parks are uncommon. It seems to be becoming generally acknowledged that people who use national parks and other public lands should be expected to assume some risk if sufficient warnings and precautions are given.

Conflicts with Grizzly Bears

It has been postulated that habituation of grizzlies to human presence in parks may be an important factor influencing confrontations or injuries. Habituation is defined as a decline in an animals' response following repeated exposure to an inconsequential stimulus (Jope 1985). Shifts in grizzly bear behavior in parks related to changes in the distribution of visitors have been documented in a number of studies. Jope (1979, 1982) described how bears lost their fear of visitors in heavy-visitor-use areas of Glacier. She felt that such habituation reduced the number of charges made by bears during surprise encounters with humans, thereby decreasing the injury rate to hikers. McCullough (1982), however, pointed out that because close encounters were more frequent with habituated bears, the probability of injury increased.

In an analysis of visitor–grizzly bear encounters between 1968 and 1982 at Glacier, Kendall (1986) found support for both viewpoints. She found that habituation did decrease the probability of human injury during an encounter and, thus, the risk was lower in high-visitor-use zones. Habituation, however, also increased the rate of encounters and thus there was a higher number of incidents and changes in high-use zones.

Conflicts with Black Bears

Black bears are a problem because they tend to damage equipment in their search for food. Such depredations in the backcountry appear to be much more common than realized by park managers. Hastings, Gilbert, and Turner (1981) found that for some backcountry areas in Yosemite, only 1.3% of the estimated damages were reported, while 2.8% of the financial loss was reported. Visitors appeared to be reluctant to report bear damage unless it was easy to do so. This unwillingness may have been accompanied by a fear of receiving a citation for improper food storage. For example, Cella and Keay (1980) found that 92% of the backcountry users stated that they stored their food properly while only about 3% actually did. Hastings, Gilbert, and Turner (1981), however, found that visitors who had suffered large dollar losses in equipment appeared to be more angry and more willing to risk a citation in the hopes of being reimbursed for their damages.

To reduce conflicts, Yosemite has had an intensive black bear management program in effect since 1975. The program has been notably successful in reducing black bear problems and injuries in the front country of the park. However, property damage in the backcountry has not been reduced. Like many parks, Yosemite offers limited opportunities for controlling bears in the backcountry because of the high costs, lack of alternative release sites for problem bears, reduced staffing, and limited visitor contacts to convey education and enforcement information (Keay and Webb 1989).

Management Techniques Designed to Minimize Bear-Visitor Conflicts

The continued increases in bear incidents in the national parks and the awareness that better management is necessary has led to the investigation of a number of methods designed to better inform visitors of potential bear problems, to safer storage of food in backcountry camps, to spatial separation of bears and visitors, and to conditioning to avoid humans (Jeff Keay, interview with author, Yosemite National Park, Mar. 2, 1987).

Visitor Information

All parks with bears now provide some literature on how to recreate in bear country to avoid problems. Pamphlets include information on how to properly store food, what actions to take if confronted by a bear, and other often very specific information.[10] Yosemite has an elaborate public information and education program that combines printed brochures with permanent warning signs at park entrances, discussions of how to avoid bear problems in the park newspaper, messages in park interpretive programs, and a taped radio message broadcast along all roads entering Yosemite Valley. The proper ways to store food in the backcountry are displayed at wilderness permit stations. Finally, a movie entitled *Forever Wild*, which graphically portrays improper visitor behavior that ultimately resulted in a bear's death, is shown weekly.

Unfortunately, there is little information on how effective park information programs are. Sundstrom (1984) found that the information campaign in Denali significantly increased the knowledge of what precautions to take for 74% of visitors. However, he found that many visitors did not apply that knowledge, and concluded that major efforts were needed to impress on visitors the critical need to use what they learned. Ironically, he also found that park and concession employees had lower understanding of what precautions to take than did visitors, pointing out the need for stronger attention to these users. Similarly, Keay and Webb (1989) concluded that although 90% of backcountry users who encountered bear problems had received information on avoiding bear problems, this information was not effective in instructing or motivating visitors to follow proper procedures when camping. They concluded that public information messages must be strongly worded to be effective.

Katmai has one of the most extensive visitor-information programs on bears. The park uses its interpretative program to manage visitor behavior in an attempt to contribute to desirable bear behavior and to prevent all conflicts between bears and visitors. The premise is that the development of conflicts indicates that park management has failed to meet its objectives. The unique geographic situation at Katmai, in which there are no roads to the area and most visitors arrive by float plane, allows a very personal interpretation program. Each plane is met by a ranger who welcomes the visitors and spends five to ten minutes discussing bear behavior, how a person should act in bear habitat, fishing regulations, and other important information (Katmai 1987). Since intense human activity commonly occurs along the Brooks River, a bear can have access to the river only if it can tolerate the presence of people or learns how to successfully avoid them. Thus, the concentration of visitors selects bears that can tolerate people. There is no intent by management to instill a fear of people in the bears of Brooks River since this would work against the environment the park has attempted to create for its bears. The objective of management is to avoid creating a situation in which only the boldest, most aggressive bears are able to successfully use the river. Visitors are thus requested to maintain a distance of at least 50 meters from any bear, to move out of a bear's way, and not to force the bear to move out of their way. The unique situation at Brooks River means that considerable staff time is invested in monitoring the situation and working with visitors. During July, one seasonal ranger position is diverted to patrolling the Brooks River area, ensuring proper handling of fish and proper behavior toward bears.

Safe Methods of Food Storage

Considerable study has recently gone into finding ways to safely carry and store food in backcountry areas inhabited by bears. Graber (1986) outlined five ways to protect food from bears that are being tested in California and Alaska parks (see Exhibit 7.1). At designated

Exhibit 7.1 Bear-Proof Food Protectors Being Evaluated in the Sierra Nevada Parks

1. Counterbalance: Two stuff sacks or a sack and a weight are balanced over a small limb at least 3 meters from the trunk, with the sacks at least 6 meters above the ground. This technique requires a proper kind of tree and is usually restricted to lower elevation camps.
2. Bear-proof cable: Aircraft cable is suspended between two trees, creating an artificial limb from which sacks can be counterbalanced. Cables installed in several Sierra Nevada parks have been proven to be successful and popular with users.
3. Bear-proof pole: This device looks like a tall metal hat rack with hooks at the top and is anchored in rock or concrete. A second free pole is used to hoist food sacks to the hooks. The device cannot be bent or climbed by bears, and the food is too high for bears to reach.
4. Food locker: These are heavy steel boxes that cannot be opened by bears. Installation for such lockers in eleven Yosemite campsites were accompanied by a 61% drop in incidents between 1979 and 1980. Such lockers are expensive and must be transported by helicopter to backcountry sites.
5. Portable food canister: Those tested in the Sierra Parks and in Denali are relatively light cylindrical or rectangular containers made of plastic, e.g. PVC, and have a latch that requires a tool to open. Dimensions are such that a black bear cannot open it with its teeth. The canister can be carried inside or strapped on a backpack.

Source: Adapted from D. M. Graber, "Backpackers, Backcountry Bears: The Sierra Nevada Experience" *Park Science* 7, no. 1 (1986).

front and backcountry camps, permanent food storage lockers are one of the most effective, if expensive, means to separate bears and human food. Since bears are opportunistic, the intent of food storage containers is to make it more difficult for bears to get people's food than to get their natural food. A second objective is to devise a storage method that people can use easily, since ease of use is correlated with the rate of use. Steel storage lockers have been installed in all but three front-country campgrounds in Yosemite from 1977 to 1988, where their use is mandatory. They are proving to be very successful in curbing bear depredations.[11] Such fixed-site containers have the drawback of leading to excessive trampling at the site, which is why some parks have focused on developing portable containers.

In wilderness areas of Yosemite, food suspension cables were installed in heavily used areas during the seventies. Food storage lockers were installed in one wilderness campground in 1979, and food storage poles were installed in selected sites in the mideighties (Keay 1990). Because of their low cost and flexibility, portable food canisters have shown promise. In 1982, Denali began conducting a program to test portable plastic food containers for backpackers to develop a model resistant to bears. In that park, because of the lack of trees for hanging food, hikers cache food on the ground where bears can easily find it. Bears also damage packs and tents while searching for food. Containers have been handed out to backpackers going into areas with the most problems. Thus far, the containers have proven to be very effective in reducing problems and visitor acceptance has been very high (Dalle-Molle, Coffey, and Werner 1986). Similar results have been achieved in an experimental program at Yosemite (Keay interview).

Spatially Separating Visitors and Bears

Controlling the distribution of backcountry visitors has proven to be a relatively effective way of curtailing conflicts with bears. This technique has long been used at Glacier, where selective areas of the park are closed for certain time periods, others are opened only when grizzlies are least likely to be present, and in other cases trails are re-routed and campgrounds relocated from critical habitat (Riggs and Armour 1981). Unfortunately, information on how and when to do this is often lacking. In a theoretical study, Stuart (1978) looked at backcountry travel patterns and trail and habitat characteristics in Glacier to develop models to demonstrate how various management options could reduce the rate of contact between grizzlies and visitors. Another study in Glacier, which mapped both grizzly habitat and backcountry use in the Two Medicine drainage of the park, has direct field application and shows promise in evaluating potential areas of conflict and developing ways of mitigating them. Integration of the two components revealed that at present a high number of hikers were concentrated in the best-quality habitat. Potential conflicts were minimized because most human use occurred during times of low bear use (Baldwin et al. 1985).

Aversive Conditioning

Several parks have tested various methods to condition bears to avoid humans and their food. Some parks have tried to deter bears from developed areas by making noise, such as using cracker shells or by hitting bears with rubber shot or with soft plastic slugs fired from a 12-gauge shotgun. These slugs cause discomfort to the bear but bounce off with only minor localized tissue damage. Dalle-Molle and Van Horn (1987) have reported that the use of this tool is a viable management technique, but it does not always work, and they have no evidence that such aversive conditioning will last without occasional reinforcement. Graber (1986) has suggested that while such techniques might work in a single campground with a few bears, they could not be applied over vast wilderness areas. However, an interesting experiment has been underway in Denali to do just that.[12]

In general, to be most effective, aversive-conditioning techniques need to address the specific undesirable behavior. For example, using methods that teach bears to fear people will have little effect on bears' propensity to see campsites as a source of food. Unless the food is made unavailable, adversely conditioning bears to fear people will only teach them to be sneaky.

A Synthesis of Bear Management Activities

More than any other land-management agency, the management of bears has been a legacy of the NPS, and the agency probably has the most experience in bear management. For many years this management could best be described as following seat-of-the-pants techniques. There was little research to guide management decisions and minimal coordination among parks. It was recognized early that feeding bears did cause problems. In 1902 Yellowstone enacted a policy prohibiting the feeding of bears at dumps, but enforcement of this regulation was generally lax. In 1938 a parkwide regulation forbidding the feeding of bears by visitors was instituted along with a program to install bear-proof garbage containers in parks. Again enforcement varied widely, but as there were few problems, this was not a concern.

The dramatic increases in visitation and backcountry use in the sixties and seventies changed the situation substantially. Visitor injury rates attributable to bears increased by a factor of four. In response, NPS established a national bear management program in 1960, which sought, by means of more efficient garbage removal, visitor information, removal of problem bears, and stricter enforcement of the feeding regulations, to reduce the number of personal injuries and the amount of property damage caused by bears. In recognizing that concentrations of bears along roads, in dumps, and developed areas were a problem, this program echoed acting NPS director Tolson's (1933) statement thirty years earlier: "We are now confronted with the problem of reestablishing a wholly wild population. . . . While visitors are entitled to see park wildlife in its natural habitat . . . unnatural bear populations concentrated along park roads and in campgrounds are not a proper display of wild animals for the visitor" (1933:57).

The recognition that parks had a bear management problem provided the impetus for a bear research program that has been remarkable in its scope. Today, there has been more research done on bears and on bear-visitor interactions than on any other set of species in the parks. This program has greatly increased our knowledge of bear biology. Recent studies have helped to develop a variety of ways to safeguard food storage and sanitize campgrounds, thereby enhancing the safety of visitors. Better and safer immobilizing drugs and methods of handling problem bears have also been developed, Communication among bear researchers has improved immensely as a result of meetings and international conferences on bear research and management. Some parks have also developed sophisticated computer data bases containing information on bear sightings, confrontations, control actions, etc., enabling them to track individual bears and to identify areas of potential conflict.

Despite the great volume of research in the parks, bear management appears to have changed very little over the years. Management continues to minimize bear-human conflict by removing garbage and other unnatural foods that might attract bears, by maintaining facilities that limit bear access to food and garbage, and by closing certain portions of parks to human use. However, in the end, the standard treatment for problem bears is to transplant them to remote locations either in or out of the park or kill them if they persist in causing damage or represent a risk to visitor safety. Likewise, despite the emphasis bears have received, data on bear populations, incidents and visitor injuries are nonexistent in many parks. Agency inertia and reluctance to change traditional techniques has worked against the adoption of meaningful management programs. For example, parks still spend more time on garbage handling than on all other categories of bear management activities combined (see Table 7.3).

Research findings on the effectiveness of different bear management techniques often does not filter down to those individuals in the field who are responsible for carrying out management actions (Jope letter). For example, transplanting problem bears away from a given area is expensive and time consuming, and it is only a stopgap activity that does not address the situation that actually caused the problem behavior (Jope 1981). Achieving a successful transplant, i.e., one

Table 7.3 Estimated Time Expended on Bear Management Activities

Task	Percentage of time spent
Communications with visitors	14
Garbage handling	72
Investigating incidents	1
Handling bears	3
Research	8
Training	2

Source: R. Schnoes and E. Starkey, "Bear Management in the National Park System," Oregon State University National Park Service Cooperative Park Studies Unit Report, 1978.

where the bear does not return to the original site and survives in a new area, is often difficult. Yet there are no standardized guidelines for relocations among parks. Many parks do not know how successful their relocations are, and fewer still have good data on the fate of relocated bears. The "squeaking wheel" syndrome also applies well to bear research. Parks like Great Smoky Mountains, Yosemite, and Sequoia Kings Canyon, which have major black bear problems and no grizzlies, have had major black bear research programs. However, in parks such as Yellowstone and Glacier, which have both grizzly and black bears, studies of grizzlies get funding, while almost nothing is known about black bears.

The summary of the problems at Sequoia Kings Canyon is applicable to almost all parks with bear populations:

Problems from the 1930's sound much like the 1980's. . . . Park management has [long] understood that the root of the problem is the incompatibility of bears and the availability of human food. Despite at least 48 years of intending to attack the cause, historically management has had to attack the symptoms to keep incidents under control. . . . Nearly all of the major developments are constructed in or near prime bear habitat. As long as people, their food, and bears coexist and bears find the opportunities to obtain human food, bears will continue to develop destructive and potentially dangerous habits to obtain that food. (Sequoia Kings Canyon, 1987:21)

For all intents, the bear problem in the parks is not being solved. Admittedly, in recent years there have been substantial decreases in confrontations, injuries, and the necessity to kill problem bears, but whether or not this can be attributed to better management or more strict food-storage regulations is not known. This may reflect the effects of recent trends of decreased overnight backpacking in several western parks (Van Wagtendonk 1981). Kendall (1983) noted that backcountry camper nights in Glacier peaked in 1977 and had declined by 47% by 1982. This may also reflect a fewer number of bears.

Bear management is a difficult task. It is complicated by the fact that bears are dangerous, and more than most species, their ecological niche overlaps that of park visitors. Bears and humans have likely interacted as competitors for food and space for thousands of years. In the past two hundred years humans have dominated this competition and won the battle in almost all places. Parks are different; there management policies have allowed bears to dominate the interaction by reducing the human capability to compete (Cliff Martinka, letter to author, June 11, 1987).

Throughout this chapter there have been numerous references to "problem bears." It needs to be recognized that the problem does not originate with the bears. Rather, each occurrence of a problem bear actually reflects some problem or inadequacy with our management. When visitors make mistakes in parks, bears pay the price. With millions of visitors coming to the parks, we can't afford too many mistakes if bears are to survive.[13]

Bears, and the policies in parks that protect them, appear to have broad public support. For example, few people argue that they have a right to carry firearms into areas like Yellowstone or Glacier. As society becomes more urbanized and intolerant of risks in natural systems, one wonders if this will always be the case. Public support is probably the only factor that prevented the grizzly bear from going the way of the wolf in Yellowstone and Glacier. A diminution of support today could still lead to the same fate very quickly.

Likewise, we have no information on whether the well-publicized bear incidents in Yellowstone and Glacier have had an effect on visitation patterns or the way people use the park. The majority of the visitors seem to accept controls that close certain portions of parks to separate grizzly bears and humans. Glacier temporarily closes certain zones to visitor use at critical times of the year. The approach in Yellowstone has been to seasonally close large areas of the park to all use. Over one-third of Yellowstone is now closed seasonally to all visitor use, which has been successful in preventing some interactions. Some visitors, however, chafe at such restrictions, feeling it denies them the opportunity to see certain portions of a park. We cannot be sure that as demands on parks grow, the visiting public will continue to accept such policies. The answers to these and many other issues need to be addressed if bears are to survive in parks.

Bear management in parks has and will remain a controversial issue. There will always be instances where the efficacy of NPS management policy is questioned, sometimes by writers who do not understand the complexity of the situation or who selectively filter the facts in support of a given viewpoint. NPS needs to have the continued scientific knowledge and public support to respond to these challenges to assure the preservation of bears in national parks. Unfortunately the wealth of information accumulated on bear biology alone has not been enough to assure the preservation of bears in parks. NPS also needs to have managers who are not afraid to make controversial decisions and to take imaginative approaches. The combination of these actions will assure that grizzly and black bears will occupy our national parks for generations to come.

NOTES

1. For example, there have been at least 93 graduates theses, 56 journal publications, and 112 technical reports written on bears in the national parks (Wright 1990).

2. The dump controversy was by no means a new issue. As early as 1925 Heller noted that because grizzly bears visited the dumps only after they had been used during the day by black bears, food remaining was minimal. He suggested grizzly bears would benefit by dumping food after sunset and by initiating a spring feeding program between the time when the bears emerged from hibernation and visitor facilities opened. He also felt that special feeding of bears in the late autumn, after the hotels and camps closed, would keep them in the park when they were preparing for hibernation. He suggested that the sudden cut off of the food supply at the dumps when the visitor facilities closed was a "very serious and impractical joke to play on the gentle and confiding bears, who have been led to expect their regular daily rations" (424). He felt that such efforts would prevent depredations to buildings in the park, keep bears in the park, and, likely result in better-behaved bears.

Conversely, other early investigators (e.g., Wright, Dixon, and Thompson 1933; Finley and Finley 1940) suggested that concentrating the bears in the dump areas and feeding them garbage was potentially injurious to the bears, encouraged a lack of fear of humans that could lead to injury and property damages, and was simply unnatural. Finley and Finley argued that "the sight of one bear under natural conditions is more stimulating than a close association with dozens of bears" (1940:347).

3. This disagreement was the culmination of what had been a long-standing animosity between the Craigheads and NPS over conduct of research

in Yellowstone. One point of contention was that the NPS wanted access to the Craigheads' research data. The Craigheads countered that much of the information had already been made available in interim reports and other publications or would be available in future scientific papers. Arguments and counter-arguments over access to the original data continued for several years.

4. Cole's estimate of backcountry grizzly bears was based on observations made during a black bear study by Barnes and Bray (1967). These researchers had, using marked and otherwise identifiable black bears, concluded that there were two separate populations of black bears in the park, one living in the backcountry and a second that frequented the roadsides and developed areas. Cole (1973) felt that the same situation could be applied to grizzly bears, citing personal observations by Barnes that only 1 marked grizzly bear was observed in 113 sightings of grizzlies in backcountry areas at a time when over 50% of the grizzlies using the dumps or developed areas may have had markers.

5. A year later, NAS committee chair Cowen reevaluated the data and concluded that the Craigheads' figures underestimated the backcountry portion of the population. Cowin concluded that an average of 301 grizzlies had occupied the park during the 1959–70 period (Schullery 1986).

6. Martinka (1969a), for example, had found that the cub mortality rate for grizzlies on natural foods in Glacier was only 7%.

7. The NAS committee felt the computer model was unrealistic because it lacked any compensatory mechanisms that could have increased birth rates as the population declined. Lacking these mechanisms, extinction of the grizzly bear was an almost guaranteed outcome of the model when it was run with lowered reproduction rates. The question was whether such mechanisms could come into play quickly enough to increase the population in a species like the grizzly bear, which has a low birth rate and a high age of reproductive maturity (NAS 1974).

8. A threatened species is defined as one likely to become an endangered species within the foreseeable future throughout all or a significant portion of its range.

9. The contrast of Great Smoky Mountains with Yosemite provides some insight. Although the visitation rates at both parks are high, most of the visitors to Yosemite, unlike Great Smoky, stay in the park overnight, mainly in some twenty-five developed campgrounds and numerous backcountry sites. The concentration of food supplies in these areas altered the natural behavior, foraging habits, distribution, and numbers of black bears at a much earlier time than in Great Smoky. Large numbers of bears (over four times larger than under original conditions) were concentrated in Yosemite Valley in the twenties and thirties (Harms 1976). Raids on food, houses, cars, and food-storage areas of the hotels was a constant problem. Throughout the twenties and thirties, bears were regularly fed under large floodlights in an attempt to lure them away from developed areas. This program was only partially successful in protecting visitors' supplies, and it often increased injuries to visi-

tors. Later a feeding program was initiated on the valley rim in an attempt to hold bears on top. Bears continued to cause problems throughout the early seventies, when more rigorous enforcement of food-storage regulations, closure of all open garbage dumps, and other factors began to dramatically reduce incidents in the front country. Since then, the number of personal injuries declined significantly throughout the park. However, there has been no decrease in property damage in the backcountry. There bears have developed sophisticated patterns of depredatory behavior that has become deeply ingrained into the population (Harms 1977). For example, bears have been documented to chew through branches as large as 15 centimeters to obtain food and to jump out of trees, grabbing properly stored food on the way down.

10. Brochures even contain information for women who may be in their menstrual cycle while camping. This factor is raised because of the fatalities of two women in Glacier in 1967, one of whom was in her menstrual period and one who was apparently expecting hers. Although research has been conducted on this and other factors that might initiate an attack, there is no evidence to support the fact that women in their menstrual periods are more susceptible to attack.

11. Though this is being explored as a new technology, this technique is not new. Wasem has described drums placed at Elizabeth Lake, a high-grizzly-use area in Glacier, which were used for secure food storage in the fifties (Robert Wasem, interview with author, North Cascades National Park, Apr. 22, 1987).

12. In Denali, personnel attempt to locate a problem bear at or near the backcountry incident site and test its behavior. If it approaches directly, is not deterred by noisemaking, and fits the description of the bear involved in the incident, it is immobilized and fitted with a radio collar. At intervals through the summer, the bear is located and a test setup simulating a backpacker's camp is placed in a location where the bear will notice it. If the bear approaches within 30 meters of the camp it is hit with a slug. Personnel remain quiet inside the tent so that the bear will hopefully associate the unpleasant experience with the camp rather than people, since bears often raid camps at night or when hikers are away during the day. To date, this experiment has been limited to only five bears and the results are inconclusive (Dalle-Molle and Van Horn 1987).

13. Some people might interpret NPS experience in bear management as indicating that the agencies management policies produce "problem bears." In fact, other land-management agencies experience similar rates of visitor incidents, but they have fewer visitors. They also tend to place less emphasis on recordkeeping than does NPS.

8

Wolf Reintroduction

One of the most dramatic reversals in attitudes toward predators has been the growing acceptance of the wolf as a natural component of wild ecosystems. This has been exemplified by the vigorous efforts by many conservation groups supporting the reintroduction of wolves back into national parks.

The gray wolf was once one of the most widely distributed land mammals in North America. Since the advent of European settlement on this continent, the range of wolves has steadily declined. Wolves were systematically exterminated in all but the most remote sections of North America. In Montana alone between 1883 and 1918 more than eighty thousand wolves were killed for bounty. Today the wolf survives on less than 1% of its former range in the continental United States, although substantial populations still exist in Canada and Alaska (Mech 1970). The last wolves in national parks in the continental United States were exterminated by the late twenties (see Table 8.1). Since then although periodic sightings continue, with the exception of Isle Royale, Voyageurs, and Glacier National Parks, there are no reproducing wolf packs in any national park in the continental United States. Despite this, they do not seem to be in danger of extinction and are found in all of the Alaskan parks and preserves.

Wolves are surrounded, as few other animals are, by a long history of mythology and folklore. Although Native Americans admired and emulated wolves, Europeans seemed universally to associate wolves with evil. This view of the wolf came to the New World with the first colonists and persisted in generations of Americans. For many years, there was little interest in the study of wolves. Adolph Murie's publication of *The Wolves of Mount McKinley* in 1944 was essentially the first objective ecological study of the species.

Table 8.1 Last Known Occupancy by Timber Wolves

Park	Date	Reference
Crater Lake	1910?	Park Files
Death Valley	1915	Park Files
Glacier	mid-1930s	Singer (1975), Kaley (1976)
Grand Canyon	1900	Park Files
Grand Teton	late 1920s	Grand Teton (1986)
Guadalupe Mts.—Big Bend	1900	Bailey (1905)
Mt. Rainier	1911	Wright, Dixon, and Thompson (1933)
Olympic	1920	Dratch et al. (1975)
Rocky Mountain	1910	Park Files
Sequoia	1900	Park Files
Yellowstone	mid-1930s	Weaver (1978)
Yosemite	1890	Park Files

Much of the recent focus on wolf reintroduction has been in the Rocky Mountain states, where the search for suitable sites has emphasized national parks. The result has been extreme controversy among state and federal resource-management agencies, politicians, and local landowners and frustration among groups sympathetic to reintroduction. Today, other than fire management, there is probably no more controversial resource issue facing the national parks than wolf reintroduction.

The recently completed Northern Rocky Mountain (NRM) Wolf Recovery Plan (Fish and Wildlife Service 1987) provided a clear blueprint for the recovery of the gray wolf in the Rocky Mountains. This plan, mandated by the Endangered Species Act (ESA), outlines steps for the recovery of gray wolf populations in portions of their former range in the Northern Rocky Mountains. The primary goal of the plan is to remove the wolf from the endangered and threatened species lists by securing and maintaining a minimum of ten breeding pairs of wolves in each of three recovery areas for a minimum of three successive years (see Figure 8.1.) The plan emphasizes recovery through natural processes, such as dispersal southward from western Canada for designated recovery areas in northwest Montana (including Glacier) and central Idaho. The plan concludes that the probability of natural reestablishment of wolves in the Yellowstone ecosystem is extremely remote due to its geographic isolation from areas with established wolf populations, and therefore suggests that reintroduction will be necessary.

Returning the wolf to the West will be one of the biggest challenges ever undertaken by wildlife managers and conservationists. To be successful, the task must be approached carefully and it must be carried out with sensitivity to the concerns of all parties. History has already demonstrated that humans can eradicate wolves if they choose to; without adequate planning in a recovery effort, history will likely repeat itself.

For the most part, state wildlife agencies seek three basic assurances before supporting wolf recovery in their respective areas: management flexibility, sufficient funding, and a commitment to delist the species when appropriate (Tilt, Norris, and Eno 1987). Management flexibility has centered on which conditions would allow a threatened or endangered species to be killed. That there will be times when wolves must be killed to protect lawfully present livestock and big-game species is inevitable. Section 10(j) of ESA provides for this by designating reintroduced wolves an "experimental population," which was recognized in the NRM Wolf Recovery Plan.[1]

Adequate funding is vital to wolf recovery. Endangered species programs are generally financed by the federal government under section 6 of the ESA, but funding has failed to keep pace with the number of endangered species in need of support (Tilt, Norris, and Eno 1987). In addition to finding problems, state officials have expressed concern that even if recovery goals are met, the wolf will still not be removed from the threatened and endangered lists. Delisting the species would give the individual states much greater control in managing the wolf. The ESA is specifically designed to achieve that goal, but because it is a recent program, there are few precedents where species have been listed, recovered, and delisted, so no one can be certain what will happen.

The Status of the Wolf in Parks of the Continental United States

Glacier National Park

Because of its proximity to breeding populations in Canada, wolves have been periodically present in Glacier since its establishment. Singer (1975) and Kaley (1976) collected 130 reports of wolf observations in and around the park beginning in 1910. Day (1981) analyzed 279 valid reports of wolves in northwest Montana between 1973 and 1977. Five of these reports were of wolves killed, three of which were verified by taxonomists after examining cleaned skulls. More recent

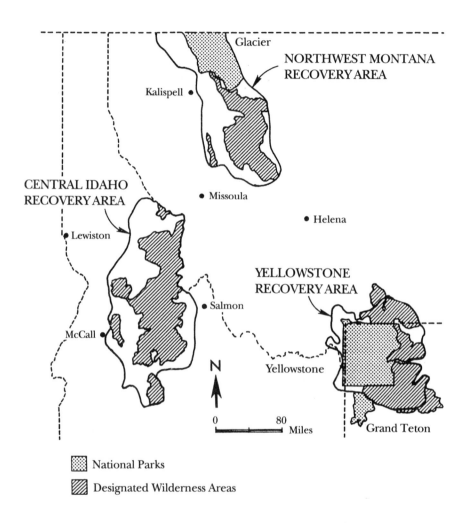

Figure 8.1. Designated wolf recovery areas in the northern Rocky Mountains. (Fish and Wildlife Service, "Northern Rocky Mountain Wolf Recovery Plan," 1987.)

wolf study dates from 1979, when a female was captured and radio-tagged by the University of Montana Wolf Ecology Project in the North Fork Flathead River drainage near the international border (Ream and Mattson 1982; Boyd 1982). During the winter of 1981, a pair of wolves was tracked in the snow in Glacier, and in the spring of 1982, seven pups were observed several miles north of the border. In the winter of 1983–84, an estimated seven to ten wolves were present in the vicinity of the park. Several were radio-collared in 1985. In late 1985, the home range of this pack shifted southward to Glacier. In the spring of 1986, a female from that pack produced a litter of pups, which was the first documented incident in fifty years of gray wolves breeding in the western United States (Ream et al. 1988). In 1987, six wolves, including four pups, were killed near the border during a newly opened wolf hunting season in British Columbia. Criticism of that action forced the provincial government to close the season and to cancel a proposed early winter wolf trapping season.

There are now about twenty-five to thirty wolves in and around the northwestern section of Glacier, and there are probably a few on the east side of the park (Ream et. al. 1988). Of the four prominent sources of wolf mortality, (food stress, disease, interpack strife, and human-induced mortality), at present only human-induced mortality seems to be a factor in their survival. The wolves appear to be healthy, and the prey base consisting of white-tailed deer and elk appears to be adequate and stable (Jenkins and Wright 1987, 1988). Analysis of scats in the park shows no evidence of canine parvovirus. Predictions are for more growth in the numbers of wolves in the park and for dispersal of wolves out of the park. The situation offers a unique opportunity to examine the role of wolf predation in a fairly well controlled situation.

Yellowstone

Like Glacier, wolves have been periodically reported in Yellowstone for many years. Cole (1971) tabulated 126 accepted observations of 214 wolves throughout the park, dating from 1930, and suggested that small numbers of wolves have always been present in the park. Weaver (1978) reported 81 "probable" reports of 109 large canids in the park between 1967 and 1977, with 74% of them occurring from 1968 through 1971.[2] Singles or pairs compromised 91% of the observations. Although up to 10 of these canids may have been present around 1970, no pack activity was detected. Sustained pack activity in

Yellowstone has not been documented for many years (Fish and Wild-life Service 1987). Lemke (1978) gathered five reports of large canids or their sign seen east of the park during 1978. Between 1980 and 1985 nineteen reports of canids were recorded for the Shoshone and Bridger Teton National Forests adjacent to Yellowstone. In the summer of 1988, a mature wolf was killed by an auto on a Yellowstone road. The condition of the wolf led investigators to conclude that it had recently been in captivity and was either purposely released or had escaped from a captive situation.

Isle Royale

The fauna of Isle Royale is distinctly limited compared to the adjacent mainland some 24 kilometers away at its closest point. This factor combined with its isolation and relative freedom from disturbance has made it an ideal ecological laboratory to study predator-prey dynamics. Wolves and their principal prey, moose, have been studied for thirty-three consecutive years, making them one of the best understood populations in existence, and they have provided much insight into the mechanisms of population limitation and regulation.

Moose probably colonized Isle Royale in the early 1900s. At that time there was no effective big-game predator on the island. Moose built up rapidly to a population of about three thousand and practically wiped out the available browse (Allen 1979). The population was drastically reduced in the early thirties by malnutrition and disease (Murie 1934). In 1936 a fire burned about a quarter of the island. This burn supported a regrowth of browse, which allowed the moose population to increase again in the forties. Another decline occurred in the late forties.

A breeding pack of wolves apparently reached Isle Royale in the winter of 1948–49. Because of the numbers of moose and beaver they began to increase in numbers. Ten years later, an intensive program of study on the wolves was initiated by scientists from Purdue University. Since then scientists have accurately tracked the numbers of wolves and moose on the island using intensive winter aerial surveys (see Figure 8.2). Researchers have hypothesized that this predator-prey system is slowly cycling on a very long time scale, with population peaks occurring every three decades (Peterson 1986). However, they are quick to point out that nothing is certain, and every year brings unexpected findings. In 1988, for example, the wolves decreased to their lowest level since the studies began. Researchers were uncertain whether any reproduction at all had taken place. As discussed in chap-

ter 3, there are now serious concerns that the wolf might become extinct on the island—a situation that poses an interesting problem for
the Park Service (Peterson and Krumenaker 1989).

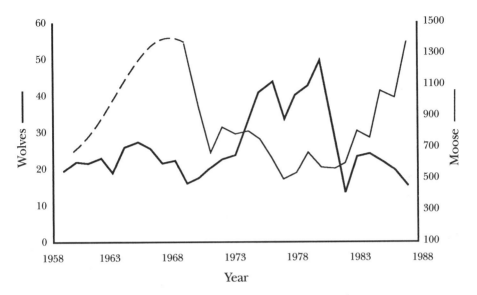

Figure 8.2. Wolf and moose population fluctuations, Isle Royale National Park, 1957-
87. (R. O. Peterson, "Ecological Studies of Wolves on Isle Royale," Michigan
Technical University Cooperative Park Studies Unit Annual Report, 1986.)

Specific Factors to Be Considered in Wolf Reintroduction

Influence on Backcountry Recreation

The natural or artificial reestablishment of wolves in national parks
and adjacent wilderness areas raises the question of how wolves and
humans will interact in backcountry used by large numbers of visitors.
A growing body of research in national parks in Alaska (e.g., Murie
1944), Canada (e.g., Carbyn 1980), and on Isle Royale (Peterson 1979)
documents that far from being a threat to humans, healthy, wild
wolves actually avoid humans. In fact, no case of serious injury of
post–nineteenth-century North Americans by wolves can be documented (Lopez 1978). The challenge, then, is to protect wolves from
humans, rather than humans from wolves. Parks have become a focus
of reintroduction efforts because they offer the best situations for

separating wolves from domestic livestock and protecting them from poachers and various forms of disturbance. Recent surveys have shown that an overwhelming majority of park visitors are aware of the above facts and feel that having wolves in parks would be beneficial.[3] Surveys of public attitudes in Minnesota, where wolves still roam, also show broad support, except among farmers, for protection and conservation of the wolf (Kellert 1985).

The Wolf as a Predator and Competitor

One of the great imponderables in Yellowstone is the effect wolf reintroduction might have on the elk herds. As discussed in chapter 5, Yellowstone has been allowing the elk populations to be limited primarily by available forage. The effect of an additional and efficient predator like the wolf on this situation, while not unprecedented (wolves were numerous in Yellowstone prior to 1900), is now not clear, but could be dramatic. There are some historic data to support the fact that elk were formerly an important prey for wolves in Yellowstone. Skinner (1927) described wolf packs harrying elk during the winter of 1914–15. Bailey (1930) reported that wolf scat collected in 1915 was made entirely of elk hair, and that two recently killed elk were discovered near wolf dens in 1916. The hunting success or predation efficiency of wolves for elk is not known. However, as the elk populations continue to grow and there is renewed concern about overgrazing, the argument that wolves might be an effective control has gained more credence. Peek (1987), a long-time observer of elk in the park, concluded that groups of elk confined to south slopes and adjacent ridgetops in the park in midwinter could be extremely vulnerable to wolf predation. In deep snow conditions, the relative vulnerability of even healthy individuals might be fairly high. He also speculated that the existence of wolves could alter present habitat-use patterns, distributing use to safer, if less productive, areas that are currently little used. Losses of elk to malnutrition might also decrease.

Garton and others (1990) modeled the effect of wolf predation on elk on Yellowstone's northern range. They concluded that the range could support about nine wolf parks, totaling approximately seventy-five animals. The elk population would decrease somewhat in response to this additional mortality, but the decrease would not exceed 10% under the conditions modeled. They further concluded that assuming other factors remained within normal bounds, the relationship between predator and prey would be relatively stable and could therefore continue indefinitely.

Wolf reintroduction in Yellowstone has also raised concern over the impact wolves might have on another endangered species, the grizzly bear. There is concern that competition with wolves would be detrimental to the long-term survival of the bears. In actuality, recent investigations have shown the opposite may be true. Grizzly bears will generally displace wolves from a carcass, and with wolves in Yellowstone, bears should find more ungulate carcasses during a larger portion of the year than are now available (Weaver 1986). The fact that both species were abundant in the park at the turn of the century adds credence to this scenario. Unfortunately, these and many other questions cannot be answered because there are no wolves in Yellowstone.

Potential Reintroductions in Other Parks

Several continental national parks offer the size, isolation, and prey base to support the reintroduction of wolves, including Olympic, North Cascades, Rocky Mountain, Yosemite, Grand Canyon, and Great Smoky Mountains.[4] The potential for reintroduction has been examined only in Olympic. There, estimates indicate that a stable population of between forty to sixty individuals existed in the Olympic National Forest Reserve in the early part of this century (Scheffer 1946). The last documented wolf was killed in the Olympics in 1920.

Mech (1975) suggested that the minimal size of a zone for establishing a well-organized, functioning natural population of wolves would be from 10,000 to 13,000 square kilometers. The area of the entire Olympic Peninsula is just under 10,000 square kilometers, of which 90% to 95% could serve as wolf habitat. Although the area is thus minimal, Dratch and others (1975) evaluated the changes that have occurred in the Olympic ecosystems since the wolf's extermination, and suggested that these altered ecosystems would offer reintroduced wolves a biological advantage. They concluded that Olympic still has the capacity to support at least forty to sixty wolves and that wolf predation would not be a major factor in controlling ungulate numbers in the park.

What Does the Future Portend?

With the natural recolonization of wolves into Glacier continuing, many individuals see the park as the testing ground for future wolf recovery efforts. However, to date there has been little commitment by Montana, the Fish and Wildlife Service, or NPS to study or manage wolves in the park. As Fisher pointed out, "Shunning involvement in wolf management at a time when wolf numbers are rapidly increasing . . . only guarantees that when wolf conflicts arise they will go unresolved" (1987:32). He argued that the Endangered Species Act legally mandates that federal agencies use all methods and procedures appropriate for the conservation of listed species. It does not direct federal agencies to restore endangered wildlife only if it is easy or politically expedient.

Former NPS director Mott (1988) strongly supported wolf reintroduction in Yellowstone and suggested that the responsibility of NPS as stewards of the parks mandated that it support this activity. However, under apparent heavy political pressure, the Park Service has put wolf reintroduction in Yellowstone on hold pending the development of an Environmental Impact Statement on the process. Former Fish and Wildlife Service director Frank Dunkle refused to support his own agency's plan, publicly characterizing any proposal to restore wolves to Yellowstone as "foolhardy" (Fisher 1987), and indicated that if Congress passed a bill forcing wolf reintroduction he would "use every bureaucratic means at his disposal to delay implementation of the law" ("Wildlife Director" 1987).[5]

This and many similar actions make it clear that unlike most species on the endangered list, the chief obstacle to wolf recovery is not biological, but social and political. Numerous hurdles, easily crossed in attempts to recover other species, have proven to be controversial barriers in the case of the wolf. For example, the recently completed NRM wolf recovery plan took over eleven years to write. Thus, it is not clear what the future holds. If wolves in Glacier continue to increase and thrive, it is likely that dispersal will move some of them south toward Yellowstone. This may happen sooner than many anticipate. Ream and others (1988) spoke of one radio-collared wolf from Glacier that dispersed 350 kilometers in a period of a month, but unfortunately it went north. Recent locations of wolves in Montana have placed them south of Glacier National Park in the Swan Mountains. Most biologists now believe that it will only be a matter of time before a reproducing pair naturally reaches Yellowstone.

NOTES

1. An experimental population is defined as a reintroduced population and offspring of a listed species that is geographically isolated from other members of the same species. Such populations can be classified as either "essential" or "nonessential." An essential population is one whose loss would ap-

preciably reduce the likelihood of the species survival in the wild. The experimental population designation was added to the ESA in 1982 to give the secretary of the interior more flexibility in treating listed species introduced outside their current range and to permit animals to be killed when necessary. Populations designated as nonessential "experimental populations" outside national parks or wildlife refuges are treated as if they were a threatened species.

As the NRM recovery plan points out, designating the wolf in the Yellowstone ecosystem as an experimental population would permit the development of special management options:

1. Establishing the authority for livestock owners to take depredating wolves if verified wolf depredations occurred on lawfully present livestock on private lands in certain management zones
2. Delisting of wolves located outside of established recovery zones
3. Reclassifying wolves located outside of established recovery zones
4. Conducting or implementing control actions early on in the recovery effort to reduce or prevent major impacts on prey populations
5. Implementing wolf management or control on those packs that follow ungulate herds outside of national park or wilderness areas

2. The great increase in sightings during this period led to persistent rumors that some wolves were intentionally released in the park. I have not been able to document any cases of this activity. Cole (1971) alternatively suggested that the greater number of observations was due to an established system of reporting wolf sightings and intensified efforts to see the animals.

3. McNaught (1985) surveyed visitor attitudes toward wolf recovery in Yellowstone and found that a large majority of visitors (including residents of affected states) favored the return of the wolf to Yellowstone. Of 1,065 respondents, 82% agreed with the statement "Wolves should still have a place in modern-day Yellowstone." If natural recovery was not feasible, support was expressed for reintroduction by a margin of three to one. About 86% of visitors surveyed indicated that the presence of wolves in the park would improve their park experience, and there was broad support for all aspects of wolf recovery in the park. The great majority of visitors responding did not feel wolves posed a threat to human safety and that they would help maintain balanced wildlife populations in the park.

Minn (1977) undertook a similar study in Rocky Mountain National Park, distributing 502 questionnaires to determine attitudes toward wolf reintroduction. She found that 74% of the respondents would like to have wolves in the park and 76% thought it was a reasonable idea. Only 8% of the respondents thought it would discourage them from coming to the park, and 22% felt they would be discouraged from backpacking in the park. Over 50% of the respondents felt that increased entrance fees should be used to pay for wolf management. Eighty percent felt that wolves would not attack humans.

4. In early 1991 two pairs of red wolves were brought to the Cades Cove area of Great Smoky Mountains and placed in an acclimation compound. Later that year, one pair with possible pups was released in the park and the second pair was held in reserve. These wolves came from a rearing program

established by the Red Wolf Recovery Team in conjunction with the NPS on Horn Island in the Gulf Islands National Seashore.

In the summer of 1991 a pair of gray wolves was known to have occupied a den site in a remote section of North Cascades National Park near the border with British Columbia. This is the second year that wolves have been spotted in this park, although permanent occupancy is still uncertain.

5. Legislation requiring NPS to restore wolves to Yellowstone has been introduced in Congress by Representative Wayne Owens of Utah. The bill, HR 3378, calls for commencing reintroduction steps as expeditiously as practicable and completing them within three years after enactment of the legislation.

9

Human Interactions with Wildlife in National Parks

The opportunity to observe wildlife is a major reason visitors come to national parks, even in those areas originally established to protect scenic or historic sites. The traffic jams that result when even the most common large mammal is spotted along park roads leaves little doubt that park animals are important, and there seems to be a direct correlation between visitor satisfaction and wildlife observed. Hastings (1986) surveyed over four thousand visitors to Cades Cove in Great Smoky Mountains, an area noted for its living-history exhibits and scenery. Even here he found that the expectation of seeing wild animals was a major reason for visiting the area, for 73% of the respondents and over 92% of all visitors reported that actually seeing wildlife was very important to the enjoyment of their trip. He concluded that with its yearly visitation of over 6 million, Cades Cove was one of the more important areas in the southeast for viewing wildlife in a natural setting.

The fascination with park animals is a direct outgrowth of evolving contemporary American attitudes. Today there appears to be a greater spiritual and emotional interest in wildlife among the public than ever before. One survey estimated that over 49 million Americans participated in some form of wildlife observation in 1975, and membership in animal-related organizations has grown tremendously in recent years (Whitter 1977). Along with this interest has been a decreased emphasis on consumptive uses (Scheffer 1976), and there is every indication that this trend will continue (Shafer and Moeller 1974).

Not all animals are equally appreciated, and identifying people's preferences for different species can be difficult. Preferences may vary with viewing situations; the same person may not only respond differently to various species but to the same species in different environments (Moore 1977). Although certain species are clearly more popular with park visitors than others, few quantitative data are available to specifically measure the recreational value of different species of park animals. In general, the aesthetic appeal of an animal derives from a variety of factors, including size, age, color, life history, the habitat it occupies, and its abundance. Most people prefer mammals and birds over reptiles, amphibians, and invertebrates (Kellert and Berry 1980). Large mammals, such as deer, bear, and elk, seem to be more popular than smaller mammals (Shaw and Cooper 1980; Brown, Haus, and Driver 1980). Predatory animals also have a unique appeal. Species that symbolize wilderness values or the wildness of an area have particular appeal to some visitors. Flewelling and Johnson (1981) found that sighting wolves or grizzly bears was important to some backcountry users in Denali National Park. Contor (1978) felt that grizzly bear and bighorn sheep were the most important species in the western parks, at least for serious wildlife observers.

Most surveys have shown that the average visitor generally knows little about park animals and their biological requirements (Sundstrom 1984). Park interpretive programs and management practices typically do too little to alter this fact. Interpretive programs tend to treat park wildlife management problems simplistically, avoiding difficult concepts like natural regulation and alien species control. Whether this is because the public may have little interest in learning about the complexities of park management problems, because certain situations are politically sensitive, or because such programs are difficult to present is not clear. The result is that the potential for naturalists to use park animals and their habits as a means to enhance biological understanding and ecological awareness in the park visitor is largely unrealized (Kellert 1980; Wright 1984a).

Park policies sometimes reduce opportunities for visitors to observe and learn about wildlife. For example, management actions that disperse animals from roadsides, campgrounds, and other visitor-use areas reduce chances of seeing animals. The same is true of road and trail closures designed to protect the habitats of sensitive species. In view of current park policies, one could argue that the Park Service is remiss in not living up to the second part of its mandate, which is to provide for the enjoyment of the wildlife resources of the parks by providing more opportunities for people to observe and learn about wild creatures and their biological relationships. Parks rarely attempt to manage their resources to increase viewing opportunities. They often do the opposite, making habitat alterations designed to provide cover or a buffer to cushion human impact on wildlife.

This separation sometimes imposed between visitors and animals is unfortunate. Interactions with wildlife often provide park visitors with thrills not experienced in daily living. These may range from the exhilaration of seeing a beautiful or unique species to a confrontation, real or imagined, with a formidable species. Hastings (1982) even found that minor damage to camping gear (e.g., a water bottle riddled by bear teeth), not only led to improved respect and understanding of a species, but could serve as a "trophy" and a reminder of an experience worth telling others.

A Brief History of Wildlife Viewing in Parks

As opposed to today's situation, in the early years of NPS park programs were specifically designed to involve visitors with wildlife. In fact, many of the first public programs dealing with wildlife in the United States took place in parks (Albright 1929). A major goal of park managers was to increase visitation, as the more people who enjoyed the parks, the more support the fledgling agency would have. Judged by today's standards, many of the early programs seem misguided or simplistic. The programs often discussed "good" and "bad" animals. Deer, elk, and similar species were considered beneficial, and interpreters would stress that these species needed the safety and protection of the parks to survive. Predators were bad because they killed good species and therefore did not deserve to be protected.

Of all the wildlife programs, the bear shows that developed in several western parks were the most unique and the most popular. Bear feeding shows began in Yellowstone at the Fountain Hotel in the late 1800s when the kitchen garbage was dumped each evening behind the hotel. In the 1920s bleachers were set up at several sites around the dumps in Yellowstone so that the visitors could watch the bears feed and fight (Albright 1929). Organizers sometimes put out choice foods like bacon to encourage fights among bears.

A bear feeding area was also set up in the early twenties in Sequoia National Park. Originally a garbage pit, by 1921 the site had become a popular place to observe bears in the evening. In time, bleachers were erected to facilitate viewing. The site provided a convenient area to view often unusual interactions among bears, such as the time an adult male killed and ate a cub (Sequoia Kings Canyon 1987). The popularity of these shows was startling. Over one thousand people were often in constant attendance at the Sequoia Bear Hill area during feeding hours, compared with ten to twenty visitors at the General Sherman Tree (Sequoia Kings Canyon 1986). The shows were frequently accompanied by talks by ranger-naturalists on various aspects of the park. Similar bear shows were also established at Yosemite and Mt. Rainier, and there was pressure for many years to initiate one at Glacier.

As years passed, there was a gradual recognition in all parks that these shows were harmful and degrading to the animals and dangerous to the public, and efforts were begun to terminate them. In Yellowstone, safety problems became apparent when a bear jumped the fence and ran through a crowd of visitors at the Old Faithful feeding area. From 1931 to 1937 bear feeding at Yellowstone was restricted to Old Faithful and Canyon, and after 1937 only to Canyon, where an elaborate feeding area was built on Otter Creek. Seating was arranged behind a chain-link fence on a hillside overlooking a concrete feeding platform (Haines 1977). In 1939, over 106,000 visitors saw this spectacle. Because of the obvious popularity of these shows, park management recognized that terminating them would not be an easy task. A memo to the director from the Sequoia superintendent suggested that "there is no question but that the bear show despite all the unnatural conditions connected with it is a tourist attraction of the first interest, and we may expect to have many complaints both written and verbal when this attraction is discontinued" (Dixon 1940:2). Controversy over this issue was largely avoided by the advent of World War II. The resulting decrease in visitation and a corresponding decrease in garbage made it a convenient time for the parks to terminate the shows. Sequoia's show was stopped in 1941, and the bear shows in Yellowstone were terminated in 1942.

Bears were not the only animals put on display in the early years of NPS. A popular event in Yellowstone for many years was the annual bison roundup at the Buffalo Ranch. Range riders would dramatically herd the buffalo back to the vicinity of the ranch in a method and setting reminiscent of the old West. The roundups were originally conducted as a management tool to contain and protect the buffalo over the winter months. Later, they were staged deliberately as a display for visitors (Cahalane 1944). The roundups were stopped in the late twenties as a part of a policy to manage the buffalo herd more naturally.

Displays of animals were often established because of the disappointment expressed by visitors who had failed to see wildlife in a park. A small zoo was established by Stephen Mather at Wawona in Yosemite to display the most common animals in the park. This exhibit was discontinued in 1932. Reptiles were put on display at Yosemite, Zion, and Grand Canyon, where they were generally kept during the summer and released in the fall (Bryant and Atwood 1932).

Management of Park Visitors and Wildlife

NPS policy regarding visitor interaction with animals has changed dramatically since the early days. It is now recognized that different species vary widely in their tolerance of humans. Some species are very sensitive to any human activities, and human disturbance can be fatal. Disturbance of other species may trigger an aggressive or hostile response. Other animals tolerate or even benefit from association with humans. In general, animal behavior is not predictable, and species tolerance of humans can be viewed as a continuum from highly tolerant to highly intolerant. In many cases, the reaction of individual mammals to human activities most likely reflects their previous experiences with humans.

The first efforts to minimize contacts between park visitors and animals were regulations adopted in 1938 prohibiting "feeding, touching, teasing, or molesting of bears." This rule was combined with an educational campaign using the press and radio, which stressed the dangers of feeding bears (Cahalane, Presnall, and Beard 1940). This policy was expanded to all animals in 1951. Over the past three decades, some managers have interpreted current policy to mean that all disturbance of wildlife by visitors is unnatural and is to be avoided. The net result has been that over the past twenty-five years there has been a concerted effort to separate visitors and wildlife in parks.

Species Minimally Impacted by Human Disturbance

Many species tolerate nonthreatening human activities with minimal stress. The most common action is for animals to move away from the source of disturbance. Several of the cervid species, which provide the majority of the viewing opportunities in parks, fall into this category. There have been no studies that have explicitly examined the tolerance level of such species to human disturbance in parks, but some generalities can be made based on the observations of different researchers. For example, moose in particular appear to habituate well to the presence of humans (Dale Miquelle, interview with author, Moscow, Id., July 13, 1988). This behavior may be related to its predator defense mechanism, which causes it to stand and fight rather than flee, as do most cervids. Other species in descending order of tolerance are white-tailed deer, mule deer, pronghorn antelope, and, to a lesser extent, Rocky Mountain elk. The latter, which are more commonly found in larger groups, may be more influenced by group dynamics than other species. If one animal turns and flees, others will generally follow.

The degree of tolerance in these species appears to be related to several factors. One is clearly the degree of habituation. For example, elk arriving later in the autumn on the lower elevation meadows in Rocky Mountain apparently tolerate less human disturbance than elk that had arrived on the winter range earlier (Schultz and Bailey 1978). The former group is composed of animals that summer in remote sections of the park where visitors were uncommon. The type of visitor activity is also a determinant. Most observers feel that cervids, and probably other species, are far less disturbed by visitors in autos than those on foot. An exception to this are mountain goats, which in at least some parks are not only tolerant of hikers but are attracted to them by the salt from human sweat and urine (Bansner 1978; Stevens 1983).

Feeding by visitors can be a primary contributor in causing otherwise shy or retiring animals to become highly tolerant of and habituated to human activities. In the early days, it was not unusual for small mammals and birds eliciting such behavior to be shot around campgrounds to curtail this activity. Feeding animals remains one of the most common ways visitors interact with wildlife. Visitors to parks often seem unaware of the reasons for not feeding wildlife or the dangers this can pose for them.[1] This arises in part from experiences in zoos where animals are observed out of the context of their natural environment (Jacobsen and Kushlan 1986). Short visits to parks that result in little contact with park officials probably also contribute to the tendency to ignore feeding restrictions.

Another problem is that regulations prohibiting feeding animals are generally not enforced uniformly either among parks or species. Most rangers are reluctant to fine or hassle a visitor "innocently" feeding a chipmunk but will probably fine a person feeding a bear. Generally parks have viewed the feeding of small mammals and birds as relatively innocuous, causing only minor behavioral aberrations or higher-than-normal densities in certain areas,[2] but there is evidence that feeding some animals might have long-term effects on ecosystem processes.[3]

Animals such as black bears may become a danger to visitors when they become habituated by feeding. Park employees may deliberately harass such species to separate them from visitors. Park management may also endeavor to encourage a characteristic behavior. This is true in Glacier, where management seeks to protect grizzly bears by encouraging shyness and avoidance of humans as a behavioral trait. This policy recognizes that shyness may not be a completely natural behavior but the result of selective pressures against bears with aggressive traits. This selective pressure is maintained by removing individuals with tendencies toward aggressive conflict with humans.

Species Sensitive to Disturbance

Many of the species that are the most sensitive to disturbance are those most interesting to visitors. The most common management action to protect such species from disturbance is to close specific areas either temporarily or permanently to visitor use. Closures may be seasonal or permanent, and may vary in size from a few acres (such as around an eagle nest) to an entire watershed to protect wolf dens. To date the public has generally shown a great willingness to go along with such restrictions when it is given an adequate explanation and is probably more willing to yield rights to benefit wildlife than most managers realize.[4] However, such actions often separate visitors from the very wildlife they are most interested in seeing, and in the long run this can erode support for parks.

Wolves

Management on Isle Royale is committed to protect the eastern timber wolf from human disturbance (Peterson and Morehead 1980). Although in some areas wolves with little or no contact with humans may exhibit no outright fear, on Isle Royale they continue to show pronounced avoidance of humans despite a forty-year history of protection. Researchers feel that a fear of humans seems to be acquired early in the life of a wolf on Isle Royale, and this fear has probably been transmitted from the islands' first wolves to the present generation. The management goal is to perpetuate this fear because it enhances the public perception of wolves as elusive, wilderness creatures and prevents the spectacle of wolves foraging for food in campgrounds or running off with backpacks (Peterson and Morehead 1980). To assist in this isolation, trails have purposely been made to avoid known denning areas or critical habitat, and a winter closure of the park was put into effect in 1975. No research involving handling of the animals (e.g., attaching radio-transmitters) or closely approaching the denning areas was permitted until last year.

This policy results in few wolf sightings (an average of twelve to twenty-four per year) by visitors. That most visitors are denied one of the few opportunities in the continental United States to view this unique species in a natural setting probably makes their visit less satisfactory. Some might argue that the average park visitor does not possess the experience or skills needed to find and see such elusive species in parks even if given the opportunity. Others argue that visitors to Isle Royale are a different breed. They are seeking a wilderness experience with the hope of seeing wolves, and they often possess the prerequisite skills. In either case it is likely that though the policy at the park protects the wolves, it does not teach the visitor much about the species and could adversely influence support for their survival elsewhere. On the other hand, learning that few visitors ever see a wolf and none are attacked by wolves on Isle Royale might help efforts to protect the wolf.

Bighorn Sheep

The sensitivity of Rocky Mountain and desert bighorn sheep to disturbance by humans has long been recognized. As early as 1939, Packard described bighorn sheep leaving the Sheep Lakes area in Rocky Mountain because they were "annoyed by camera enthusiasts" (1946:12). Rocky Mountain bighorn sheep are susceptible to a lungworm infection resulting in pneumonia, which greatly depleted the population in most parks in the early thirties (Potts 1938). Since then, lungworm and pneumonia have been associated with most populations of Rocky Mountain bighorn sheep, and they have limited population growth. Post (1976) and Stevens (1982) postulated that stress may be a major factor in aggravating the influences of such infections, and that disturbance by human activities could place sheep under such stress.

Desert bighorn sheep also appear to be highly susceptible to stress. Again, human disturbance has been implicated. Space seems to be a necessary prerequisite for bighorn. Human displacement has become particularly acute in several southwestern parks and monuments such as Joshua Tree, which have experienced dramatic increases in backcountry visitation (Douglas 1976). Joshua Tree National Monument has been bisected by roads, trails, campgrounds, and parking areas, which have expanded visitor use. In addition, important habitat was removed in the fifties for mineral development. As in most southwestern parks, peak visitation occurs between February and May during the lambing season, which is already a period of stress. Visitors tend to use the same habitats as bighorn sheep, e.g., the higher elevations and areas with shade and water, thus increasing resource competition. As a result, several zones in these parks have been closed or restricted to human use to prevent displacement of sheep.

Species That Pose a Threat to Visitors

Some observers contend that parks devote too much of their effort toward species that may threaten or endanger visitors (Kellert 1980). As early as 1922, Adams wrote, "Generally speaking, I fear that too many of our park administrators think of wildlife mainly when it *conflicts* with their visiting public, that is, when an animal disturbs or injures the park visitors"(129).

The emphasis on conflict resolution has resulted in the death of many animals through control activities, particularly bears (see chapter 7). Problems with animals with the capability to injure or kill park visitors often arise because visitors do not perceive some animals to be dangerous and they do not understand animal behavioral patterns (Bryan and Janssan 1973; Marsh 1970).[5] These inaccurate perceptions can result in visitors separating a cow moose and calf or getting too close to a buffalo. Either case can result in serious injury or death.

Park managers realize that efforts to assure the safety of visitors can only go so far (Bell 1963), but they also recognize that in almost all situations in which a visitor is injured by an animal, no matter where the blame lies, the animal usually suffers. Clearly, NPS is mandated to provide for the safety of park visitors, however, this should not mean that the visitor should not assume any risks or responsibilities (Giles 1963). NPS needs to be less concerned about problem animals and spend more effort developing effective management programs for visitors. This approach has been tried successfully at Everglades, where alligators pose a potential threat. Management of problem alligators is directed toward the management of visitors by anticipating and preventing potential conflicts. This program has combined the use of signs, barriers, education, increased law enforcement, and research (Jacobsen and Kushlan 1986).

Winter Use of Parks

The growing winter use of parks, particularly by cross-country skiers and snowmobile users (where permitted) is causing a new set of problems for park wildlife and managers alike. Traditionally a time of quiet, many parks in northern climes are experiencing explosive growth in winter use. In Yellowstone, for example, winter use has increased 995% since 1966, and now exceeds seventy thousand visitors a year. Over thirty thousand privately owned snowmobiles enter the park each year, and on heavy-use days, as many as one thousand will travel from West Yellowstone to Old Faithful.

'During the winter months, animals are often under physiological stress from cold and marginal food supplies. The added trauma of visitor disturbance may force animals out of preferred habitats, and in extreme cases may result in death to individual animals. In most cases, the animals react simply to the presence of humans in the occupied habitat or to the noise of their machines. There are, however, several accounts in the northern parks of wildlife being deliberately chased or hit by snowmobiles.

Aune (1981) studied the impact of cross-country skiing, snowshoeing, and snowmobile use on wildlife in the Geyser Basin region of Yellowstone (see Table 9.1). Although he concluded that winter rec-

Table 9.1 Snowmobile-Wildlife Encounters for the Winters of 1978–79 and 1979–80 in Yellowstone

Species	Encounters	Percentage Responding	Percentage Fleeing
		Early Winter	
Bison	14	35	63
Coyote	4	100	100
Elk	56	47	40
Mule deer	8	87	45
		Mid-Winter	
Bison	32	5	86
Coyote	6	89	75
Elk	87	12	16
Mule deer	2	23	67
		Late Winter	
Bison	68	5	82
Coyote	8	83	80
Elk	92	4	17
Mule deer	4	20	50

Source: Adapted from K. E. Aune, "Impacts of Winter Recreationists on Wildlife in a Portion of Yellowstone National Park," M.S. Thesis, Montana State University, 1981.

reation activity in the region was not a major factor in influencing wildlife distribution, population, or movement, he did identify several conflicts. Animals were not distributed randomly throughout the study area but were concentrated in the geothermally active basins and along the rivers. Recreation activity was also concentrated in these areas, and as a result the ski and snowmobile trails crossed critical wildlife habitat. Many of the encounters between snowmobiles and wildlife occurred because animals tended to use the snowmobile trails as travel lanes, particularly in times of deep snow. There is some indication that elk, mule deer, and bison can habituate to snowmobile noise over the course of the winter. The number of encounters and the proportion of animals fleeing encounters with humans was greater for cross-country skiers than for snowmobiles, probably because snowmobile traffic in the park was more predictable and not as localized. Encounters were particularly severe in areas where skiers were not restricted to trails, and thus less predictable (Francis Casseres, interview with author, Moscow, Id., May 13, 1989).

Harassment of Animals

Little is known about how much intentional harassment of wildlife by visitors occurs in national parks. Given that violence and criminal activity appear to be increasing in our society and in the parks, one is tempted to conclude that aggressive harassment is also increasing. Common forms of aggressive harassment include purposely frightening or chasing an animal or pelting it with rocks or other debris to elicit some response. This behavior can be separated from other forms of harassment, such as when visitors get too close to an animal or attempt to feed it, because these actions are not purposely done to harass the animal, but usually occur out of ignorance. Both types of aggression may result in displacement of wildlife. Aggressive harassment may also result in reduced reproductive rates and increased mortality (Geist 1970). More study is needed to know the extent of this activity, and more intense enforcement is needed to curb it.

Another form of intentional harassment is through the actions of researchers. Although most wildlife researchers do not like to admit it, their activities are often the most stressful that animals encounter. Of particular note is when animals are chased by vehicle or plane to a new location or a trap, disturbed by aerial censuses, and shot with immobilizing drugs. Animals are sometimes killed by the improper application or dosage of such drugs. Most animals are immobilized to place radio transmitters on them that facilitate future relocation. An immense amount of information has been gained from such studies, which have been invaluable in protecting and saving many species, but the use of radio-collared animals has also become a crutch, and at times it seems as if no wildlife study can be undertaken without them.

Needed Innovative Management and Interpretive Techniques

Shrinking wildlife habitat and space for humans to recreate continues to place growing pressure on our national parks. Effectively dealing with this issue is one of the greatest challenges confronting the Park Service. Unfortunately, this is a challenge NPS is ill-prepared to face. Little is known about the viewing habits and interests of visitors or of the tolerances of the various animals to different levels of human disturbance. Closure of specific areas within parks to protect wildlife is a common management action. More restrictions on use will undoubtedly occur in the future that are bound to be controversial and not readily accepted. The use of closures is often necessary and the easiest course of action, but it is also too frequent. One reason is that many park managers adhere to traditional values. They question whether the Park Service should be in the business of showing wildlife to visitors. They also believe that if visitors want to see a particular species, they need to put out the effort, e.g., hike several miles (Stan Schelgel, interview with author, Mt. Rainier, Jan. 13, 1988).

Innovative techniques are needed that would allow visitors the opportunity to view wildlife without disturbing them. This is an exciting and challenging field that has received little attention. It requires the biologist or planner to walk a fine line between providing for visitor enjoyment and avoiding making parks artificial environments. For although visitors often come to the parks to see animals, national parks are not intended to be zoos without cages. Visitors must be made aware that parks were established as sanctuaries for all animals; they are areas where animals must have a natural existence and not be placed on display.[6]

Examples of ways in which the requirements of the animals and the desires of the visitors can both be accommodated are not common. In Glacier National Park mountain goats have traditionally used a mineral lick on the southeast corner of the park that necessitated their crossing a major highway. Visitors aware of this crossing point often congregated to observe the goats. In 1975 a decision was made to widen and upgrade the highway. An environmental impact analysis revealed that the resulting high-speed traffic would not only threaten the goats but also endanger the visitors who stopped to watch them. To mitigate these effects, fencing was placed along the highway to restrict goat movement and two tunnels were constructed under the highway to allow the mountain goats to safely cross the highway to reach the lick. At the same time, the park constructed a special observation platform to allow visitors to unobtrusively observe mountain goats on the lick. These modifications were completed in 1981. Pedevillano and Wright (1987) examined how well the mountain goats adjusted to these new crossing devices and how much disturbance visitors on the observation platform caused mountain goats on the lick. Both the crossing tunnels and observation platform were very successful. Almost 100% of the goats used the tunnels, eliminating all highway mortality, and visitors on the observation platform did not appear to disturb mountain goats on the lick. Although expensive, this project did show that with proper planning, it is possible to develop methods that provide for both the safety and well-being of the animal while enhancing visitor experience.

Another approach to minimizing wildlife-visitor interactions occurs at Horseshoe Park in Rocky Mountain, where bighorn sheep cross the main park road to get to a mineral lick. Two 100-meter-long crossing zones were established in 1976 and signs were added to prohibit stopping, standing, or walking within the zone. In 1980 a visitor contact station was established adjacent to the zones and attended during the summer by a uniformed park interpreter. Stevens (1982) reported that in 1965, before any visitor control was implemented, sheep used the licks an average of fifteen days each year during the summer season. By 1981 use had increased to forty-six days. He felt that reducing the disturbance, particularly with an interpreter enforcing the rules, played a substantial role in this increase.

NOTES

1. Regulations are established not only to protect the visitor but also to prevent animals from becoming dependent on artificial food sources and from eating dangerous foods. There have been no in-depth studies to examine why visitors insist on feeding park animals. Probably one of the most common reasons is the misguided belief that their food will help an animal survive.

2. For example, in campgrounds at Rocky Mountain, Friedrichsen (1977) measured some of the highest densities of chipmunks and golden-mantled ground squirrel populations ever recorded.

3. A study done on Clark's nutcrackers at road turnouts in Rocky Mountain National Park by Tomback (1985) suggested that many of these birds become dependent on visitor handouts and that this trait is transmitted to their young. Food from visitors may sustain unusually high densities of nutcrackers in the park during the summer months. Clark's nutcrackers play a major role in maintaining the subalpine ecosystem by caching seeds from whitebark, pinyon, and limber pines. Since the nutcracker will also feed on seed at this time, higher-than-normal densities of birds may deplete most of the seed supply before they are ripe. This would prevent the buildup of seed caches, thus influencing the bird's survival in winter, and it would make fewer seeds available for pine germination. The long-term impact might be a decrease in pine regeneration in the forests of the park.

4. Factual support for this judgment is limited. Rocky Mountain closed a popular trail to the top of Specimen Mountain in 1971 during the spring lambing period to eliminate stress on bighorn sheep. Further study indicated that sheep use of the area was extended when temporarily closed to visitors. During the temporary closure, the park explained its reasoning and sought public opinion on the issue. Public input was supportive, so the trail closure was made permanent in 1978 (Stevens 1982).

5. Current management policies in Yellowstone have had the effect of moving bears away from the roadsides where they had panhandled for years. The lack of opportunities to see bears has resulted in great dissatisfation among many visitors, particularly those accustomed to viewing them in the past. Several visitors told me they would not go back to the park unless things changed.

6. An exception to the policy of not displaying animals are those cases where a population of a domesticated or feral species is maintained in the park for interpretive reasons. For example, a small population of feral horses inhabits the South Unit of Theodore Roosevelt National Monument. These animals are descendants of domestic horses that escaped or were released from neighboring ranches in the late forties and midfifties. They are managed as a livestock display, signifying the presence of feral horses in the area during Theodore Roosevelt's time. A small herd of single-sex longhorn cattle is also maintained for the same purpose in the North Unit of the park.

Aesthetics plays an important role in the management of the horses. The park, for example, desires to minimize inbreeding to maintain a healthy, aesthetically pleasing herd. Accordingly, when necessary, a strong effort is made to locate mares or studs to introduce into the park herd to maintain genetic vigor. The herd is also managed to maintain a herd size large enough to display representative sex and age classes (Theodore Roosevelt 1978).

10

The National Preserve
Land-Management Classification

National preserves are one of several land-management classifications administered by the NPS, though they have no strict legislative
definition. Unlike national lakeshores or national seashores, the national preserve designation has not been applied to a specific type of
landscape, and unlike national recreation areas, it has not been used
to manage diverse forms of recreation. This new classification is an
important issue for wildlife management because of its recent widespread use in a variety of landscapes and its potential for accommo-
dating sport hunting in parks.

The national preserve concept was first applied as a land classification in 1974 to the Big Cypress area adjacent to Everglades and to
the Big Thicket region of southeast Texas. Its underlying philosophy
is outlined in a U.S. senate report:

> National preserves will be areas . . . which possess within their bound-
> aries exceptional values or qualities illustrating the natural heritage of
> the Nation. Such areas would be characterized by significant scientific
> values, including . . . ecological communities, habitat supporting a rare
> or restricted species, a relic . . . fauna . . . or large concentrations of
> wildlife species . . . The principal thrust of these areas should be the
> preservation of the natural values which they contain. They might dif-
> fer, in some respect, from national parks . . . insofar as administrative
> policies are concerned. Hunting, for example, subject to reasonable
> regulation by the Secretary, could be permitted to the extent compati-
> ble with the purposes for which the area is established. (Senate Report
> 1979:138)

In both Big Cypress and Big Thicket, sport hunting and trapping
were considered compatible uses and were permitted. In fact, hunting
has long been the primary use of both areas (Schmidly and Burnette

1980).[1] The laws establishing both areas allowed NPS to designate zones and times when hunting and trapping would be prohibited for public safety and wildlife protection and management. Classifying Big Cypress and Big Thicket as national preserves was supported by environmental groups as a politically feasible way to extend NPS protection to lands previously not under federal control. In addition, the inaccessibility of these lands would limit large numbers of visitors and thus conflict with some of the consumptive resource uses.

The next application of the national preserve classification was in many of the new NPS areas established in Alaska. Of the thirteen new areas established in 1980, three are classified solely as national preserves, and portions of seven other units have national preserve lands within them. Unlike the first application in Big Thicket and Big Cypress, all of the new areas in Alaska were considered to fit all of the criteria for national park classification. The national preserve was used primarily as a compromise management classification to accommodate sport hunters. As a result, its application was closely monitored and its use was highly controversial.

The Creation of the New Alaskan Parks

The Alaska Native Claims Settlement Act (ANCSA) of 1971 was the basis for efforts to establish new parks in the state. The act was passed primarily because of conflicts over native and state land claims, and its aim was to provide a fair and just settlement of native claims based on aboriginal title (Hopkins 1979).[2] It did much more. Recognizing the significant impact of massive state and native land selections made from the public domain, Congress inserted a section in ANCSA to address the national interest in the Alaskan lands. This section allowed the secretary of the interior to withdraw from all forms of appropriation up to 32.4 million hectares throughout the state to determine their suitability for national parks, wildlife refuges, forests, and scenic rivers.

The debates over this provision were lengthy and politically charged. Most of the arguments centered on how much land should be placed in national parks, the most restrictive of the land-management categories. The similarity of these arguments to those surrounding the establishment of earlier national parks was striking. Comments such as "why do we need to protect these remote areas as no one will ever go there" were nearly identical to those made during the hearings for the establishment of Yellowstone in 1872.

Between 1972 and 1980 (the deadline imposed for a settlement by ANCSA), many proposals were developed by NPS, conservation groups, and the state. Between 1975 and 1978, at least eight recognized proposals were submitted for congressional consideration. These proposals differed significantly in the land area set aside for parks. For example, in the Wrangell St. Elias area, one proposal advocated by conservation groups recommended a 7.31-million-hectare park, while another advanced by prodevelopment groups proposed a 1.5-million-hectare park consisting mostly of high mountain peaks and glaciers (Wright 1984b).

Use of the National Preserve Classification

Since sport hunting would be prohibited in all new national parks in Alaska, the impact of establishing a large number of new parks on this activity dominated the debate over park establishment. The new parks had a large variety of game species and also provided livelihood for over one hundred full and part-time guides. A compromise to resolve the sport-hunting conflict was to classify a certain portion of the lands under study as national preserves (Roseburg 1984). National preserve lands would be subject to all NPS policies except that sport hunting would be permitted under state regulation.

Many individuals, both within and outside the NPS, were opposed to national preserves in Alaska, viewing them as an abrogation of the national park concept of total resource protection. Others viewed this concession to a special-interest group (hunters) as a dangerous precedent that might have important repercussions in the fight to establish future parks elsewhere. Those who agreed with the national preserve classification saw this compromise as the only way to establish park areas large enough to provide resource protection. They also felt that these classifications could possibly be changed at some future time. Political realities eventually dictated that the national preserve concept be adopted. From that point on, the main debate then shifted to determining which and how much land would be designated as national preserves.

The lack of data on wildlife for all areas, and the fact that the rugged terrain and remoteness of most potential parks made research expensive and difficult, dictated that a qualitative approach be taken in planning preserve boundaries. A data base consisting of sport-harvest data for four major species, mountain goat, Dall sheep, moose, and caribou, was assembled. However, because of their relatively large

Table 10.1 Past Hunter Harvests on the Lands Contained within the Established Wrangell St. Elias National Park and National Preserve (WRST) and Harvests Occurring on Competing Land-Use Plans for the Region (percent)

Species	Proportion of total harvest in Alaska	(WRST) park	preserve	Proposal 1[a] park	preserve	Proposal 2[b] park	preserve
Caribou	7	53	47	100	0	20	80
Dall sheep	29	46	54	100	0	38	62
Mountain goat	7	50	50	100	0	15	85
Moose	2	49	51	100	0	12	88

[a]Proposal represents HR 2063
[b]Proposal made by the state; lands in the preserve include Alaska resource and Forest Service lands.
Source: R. G. Wright, "Wildlife Resources in Creating the New Alaskan Parks and Preserves," *Environmental Management* 8 (1984):123.

numbers in many parks and importance to the guiding industry as a trophy species, Dall sheep were accorded most weight in the decision-making process (Wright 1985).

The procedure used to define the areas designated as national park and national preserve in the Wrangell St. Elias region, one of the most controversial of all proposed park units, illustrates how these harvest data were used. The Wrangell and St. Elias Mountains have one of the largest populations of Dall sheep in North America, and in the past accounted for 29% of the total Alaskan harvest. The data base included the number of hunters and the number of animals killed between 1970 and 1976 for twelve distinct units in the park, based on natural physiographic divides and river drainages.[3] Once this data base was assembled, planning became a numbers game, as planners and legislators could use these subdivisions to identify park and preserve configurations that would theoretically permit a given harvest level. The final compromise resulted in a nearly equal balance between the numbers of Dall sheep available for harvest in the preserve and those protected in the park (see Table 10.1).

An interesting sidenote to the battle over the Alaska lands occurred late in 1978 when President Carter used the Antiquities Act to designate all of the lands under consideration for park status as national monuments. This action was identical to the action taken by President Roosevelt in 1943 for the Grand Tetons and was done for a similar reason: concerns that a compromise bill could not be achieved by 1980, at which time ANCSA would expire. The action also evoked a similar response: an immediate legal challenge by the state of Alaska.

The action made all sport hunting illegal on national monument lands, which inspired tremendous local outrage and severely taxed the limited NPS personnel available to patrol the new monuments.

Just as the state of Wyoming had done in 1943 (see next section), Alaska claimed that the purpose of the Antiquities Act was to reserve only as much land as was absolutely necessary to protect a given site and that it was being illegally used to protect large land areas. These legal arguments were rejected, primarily because the courts determined that such challenges must clearly show that there was no factual basis for the president's proclamation, a difficult feat to accomplish. The main result of the national monument proclamation was to spur both sides to reach a compromise.

Statewide Classification of National Preserve Areas

Approximately 43%, or almost 7.5 million hectares, of the total NPS-managed lands in Alaska were eventually classified as national preserves in the Alaska National Interest Lands Conservation Act (ANILCA) of 1980. In retrospect, the use of the preserve classification was probably a necessary compromise, although at the time both park supporters and opponents each felt they had lost. For example, one Alaska Department of Fish and Game employee expressed this feeling: "Ironically the concerns of those environmentally oriented groups have placed Dall sheep in a more precarious position throughout Alaska than they occupied before the battle" (Heimer 1982:1). He argued that the new parks lost the support of sheep hunters and therefore lost the protective mantle such groups place over favored species like Dall sheep. He felt this loss was regrettable and "an unnecessary displacement of one segment of the sheep interested public. Interest in public hunting must be kept at a high level if sheep are to fare well in Alaska amid conflicting activities such as mineral extraction and agricultural development. . . . Sport hunters are the only reliable source of revenue and support for continued land use practices which ensure the integrity of mountain sheep habitat" (6–7). Park supporters, citing instances of unethical conduct by guides and sport hunters and the fact that over 50% of the Dall sheep hunters were foreigners with little lasting interest in the long-term conservation of U.S. lands, maintained that only national park status offered real protection for Dall sheep.

Although the passage of ANILCA settled the immediate battle over new park and preserve lands in Alaska, the war between opposing groups was not over. In 1983, Alaskan Senator Stevens introduced

Senate bill S 49, which called for the reclassification of an additional 5 million hectares of national park lands to national preserve. Included in these lands were important areas in the Wrangell St. Elias Park with large numbers of trophy-caliber Dall sheep. The Senate Committee on Energy and Natural Resources amended the bill to consider only 2 million hectares and stipulated that it would not apply to other parks. However, nothing precludes Congress from taking similar actions elsewhere. Though S 49 did not pass, such actions remain a continued threat to national park lands in Alaska.

The Role of Sport Hunting in the Establishment of Grand Teton National Park

The fight to preserve the Jackson Hole area of Wyoming as a national park more than any other situation exemplifies the role that sport-hunting interests can play in influencing national park policy. This was one of the longest-running conservation battles in history, with the struggle focusing on the management and control of the Jackson Hole elk herd. It set a unique precedent for sport hunting in national parks that is often raised today. It is likely, however, that had the battles been fought in recent times a portion of Grand Teton would have been designated as a national preserve.

The Jackson Hole Elk Herd

The Jackson Hole area is an integral part of an ecosystem that includes the southern portion of Yellowstone, the Bridger-Teton National Forest, and the National Elk Refuge. Elk migrate between the high-elevation summer ranges in Yellowstone and adjacent national forests to winter ranges around Jackson Hole. During the late 1800s and early 1900s there was growing concern for the long-term survival of this herd. New ranches established in Jackson Hole and in the Green River Valley to the south blocked traditional migration routes, concentrating larger numbers of wintering elk in Jackson Hole where space and forage was limited, and during severe winters starvation was a threat.

The plight of starving elk drew national attention in the severe winter of 1908–9. Both Wyoming and Congress appropriated money to buy hay, thereby starting what was to become a continuing feeding program. In an attempt to reduce conflicts between elk and cattle ranches in the valley, Congress in 1912 authorized the purchase of 700 hectares to form the nucleus of the National Elk Refuge. In subsequent years, congressional land withdrawals combined with private land donations extended the refuge to its present 9,200 hectares.

Two of the three main segments of the Jackson Hole herd summer in national parks, one in the southern portion of Yellowstone and the other in Grand Teton (Cole 1969). Both segments winter primarily on the National Elk Refuge or on one of three state feedgrounds in the upper Gros Ventre River valley. Most of the hunter harvest occurs during the migration period. Understanding the distribution and movements of migrating elk is thus important if a desired distribution of the harvest is to be achieved among various herd segments. Of particular concern is the segment that summers in Yellowstone and moves through Grand Teton to the Elk Refuge.

Along with the Park Service, three other agencies are responsible for managing the Jackson Hole herd and the lands it occupies. The Wyoming Game and Fish Commission (WGFC) sets hunting seasons, monitors harvests, licenses hunters, and enforces regulations. The National Forest Service administers the Bridger-Teton National Forest, which encompasses most of the elk habitat in the ecosystem. The Fish and Wildlife Service administers the National Elk Refuge, whose primary objective is to provide winter habitat and supplemental feeding for a major portion of the Jackson Hole herd. In 1959, the four agencies formed the Jackson Hole Cooperative Elk Studies Group to coordinate studies on the Jackson Hole herd. The group has since functioned as a clearinghouse and sounding board for all issues affecting the herd (Grand Teton 1986).

The Establishment of Grand Teton National Park

The idea that lands south of Yellowstone should be set aside to protect wildlife was first suggested by General Philip Sheridan in 1882 (Haines 1977). Five years later, Colonel Young, Acting Superintendent of Yellowstone, also recommended that park authority be extended into Jackson Hole to protect elk migration routes and to curtail poaching (Saylor 1970). Young felt it was incongruous for the government to protect elk on their Yellowstone summer range while exposing them to slaughter during the winter. He had little faith that the state of Wyoming or the existing Teton Forest Reserve could provide the necessary protection.

Over the next half century, there were many failed attempts to act on these and other similar recommendations. Finally, in 1929 Grand Teton National Park was established, which contained only the Teton

Mountains. It omitted the valley to the east and was of little value in protecting wildlife and thus did not solve any of the original problems. As a result, extensive debate continued throughout the thirties on the need to expand the park to include lowlands of the Snake River drainage. Proposals for expanding the park, however, met with tremendous local and state opposition. Reasons for this opposition included loss of local property-tax revenue, loss of grazing privileges, loss of hunting areas, and general antagonism to any form of federal control. Throughout this period, John D. Rockefeller, Jr., who became very concerned about conservation of the valley and its elk, was secretly buying up and consolidating private lands in the valley to preserve them from further development.[4]

Throughout the thirties park supporters stymied by local and state politicians made little progress in their efforts to promote a larger park. They were also becoming frightened by rumors that Rockefeller, because of this lack of progress, might begin to dispose of his lands. Finally, in 1943 President Roosevelt was persuaded to use the Antiquities Act to proclaim the Jackson Hole National Monument (JHNM), which included an additional 19,644 hectares of private lands east of Grand Teton National Park, 65% of which were owned by Rockefeller (Righter 1982).

The proclamation caused an immediate fire storm of controversy. The state of Wyoming sought a court injunction, maintaining that the president had no authority under the act to establish the monument. Wyoming attempted to show that the lands within JHNM contained no objects of particular scientific or historical interest (Righter 1982). Federal government witnesses effectively countered these claims, with biologist Olaus Murie's testimony on the importance of the elk populations being particularly effective (Righter 1982). The judge did not rule on the merits of the case, considering only that the court had no jurisdiction in the controversy, and therefore let the proclamation stand. The court ruling did little to settle the intense local hostility that existed toward the Park Service. In the interim, pressure by the Wyoming delegation resulted in congressional action that prevented NPS from spending appropriated funds to administer the monument. A stalemate thus existed: NPS controlled the lands but could not effectively administer their resources.

Changes in Elk Management Philosophies

The fight over the legitimacy of the national monument occurred simultaneously with changes in the way biologists believed the elk herd should be managed. The early preservationist attitude had given way to the belief that more intensive management and hunting was needed to manage the herd and limit it to a desirable size. This concept played a prominent role in the fight to abolish JHNM (Grand Teton 1986). The state was concerned that retaining a national monument in Jackson Hole where hunting was prohibited would jeopardize the proper management of elk that summered in Yellowstone and Bridger-Teton National Forest and migrated through them. In addition, the state had a considerable financial interest in feeding elk on the national refuge and in state feedgrounds and feared that elk protected by the JHNM would increase and dominate these feeding areas. Conversely, the Park Service was caught between its opposition to sport hunting on park lands and its interest in seeing the park expanded.

A compromise was finally achieved, formalized in Public Law 81-787 signed in September 1950, which abolished JHNM and expanded the national park. The law provided that the management of the elk herd in the park would become the joint responsibility of the federal government and the state of Wyoming. It provided that about 57,875 hectares, or about 47% of the enlarged park, could be opened to public hunting of elk as needed to conserve and control park elk. The law provided that the WGFC and the NPS jointly recommend to the secretary of the interior and the governor of Wyoming a program to insure the permanent conservation of elk within Grand Teton. This program was to include

> the controlled reduction of elk in such park, by hunters licensed by the State of Wyoming and deputized as rangers by the Secretary of the Interior, when it is found necessary for the purpose of the proper management and protection of the elk. At least once a year . . . the Wyoming Game and Fish Commission and the National Park Service shall submit to the Secretary of the Interior their joint recommendations for the management, protection, and control of the elk for that year. The yearly plan . . . shall include a provision for controlled and managed reduction by qualified and experienced hunters licensed by the State . . . and deputized as rangers by the Secretary of the Interior, if and when a reduction in the number of elk by this method within the Grand Teton National Park established by this act is required. . . . Such orders . . . shall apply only to the lands within the park which lie east of the Snake River. (NPS 1985:52–53)

No one was enthusiastic over this compromise. Director Drury admitted that he accepted it with great reluctance (Righter 1982:149). Ise termed the compromise "a most unfortunate concession to the selfish demands of Wyoming sportsmen . . . [and] an insult to the National Park Service and ordinary decency (1961:507). In the years immediately following its passage, the NPS and WGFC differed sharply in their interpretations of the legislative provisions of the act. The state believed that opening the park to sport hunting was the main objective of the legislation, maintaining that it allowed the harvest of all elk (i.e., those elk that migrated from Yellowstone through the park as well as those that summered there) (Cole 1969). The Park Service, however, felt that hunting in the park was a transitory issue that soon could be phased out (Murie 1952). It felt that hunting would be permitted in the park only when a reduction of the elk summering in the park was needed. Since elk numbers were small and Grand Teton had no range problem, the Park Service saw no necessity for hunting in the park (Murie 1951).

The state's viewpoint persisted and NPS acquiesced. Hunting took place throughout the fifties although the harvest was small. The number of elk killed in the park declined from a mean of 1,324 between 1942 and 1950 to 157 between 1951 and 1962 (Grand Teton 1986).[5]

From the beginning, many NPS personnel were highly critical of the park hunt. McIntire, Chief Naturalist at Yellowstone, noted that throughout the fifties hunter success averaged 27%, or about 14% of the total animal reduction desired by managers, and suggested that hunter participation was a poor tool for park wildlife management. Arguing against proponents of a similar program in Yellowstone, he noted that if these hunters were equal in ability to those at Grand Teton, then "nearly 18,000 sports hunters, theoretically, would have killed the 5,000 legal elk needed for reduction purposes, plus 196 illegal moose, 410 illegal elk, and 17.8 men along with an undetermined number of bears, coyotes, bighorn sheep, antelope, bison, mule deer and horses which moved in front of their gun sights" (1962:17).

Cole (1969) calculated that known illegal kills of elk and other wildlife in Grand Teton areas open to hunting totaled 64 elk, 24 moose, 1 mule deer, and 1 antelope over the 1957–66 period. A total of 118 elk, 5 moose, 3 mule deer, and 2 coyotes were known to have been killed in park areas closed to hunting during the same period. Arrest records showed that most illegal kills were made by holders of park elk permits.

In the early sixties as elk numbers began to increase on the summer range, NPS was persuaded by the fear of potential habitat damage by increasing numbers of elk to accept the broader interpretation of the law held by the state of Wyoming. Reasons for this change in philosophy are not clear, but beginning in 1963, increased emphasis was given to harvesting elk to (1) reduce the early migration onto the National Elk Refuge of elk that summered in the park; (2) reduce the numbers of late migrating elk that summered in Yellowstone; and (3) reduce the hunting pressure on elk that migrated through areas east of the park or that summered on the more accessible national forest lands between the two national parks. This increased emphasis on hunting elk that summered in the park has continued to the present time. The mean number of elk killed increased from 157 per year for the first eleven years to 598 per year from 1963 to 1983 (see Figure 10.1). This increase has been due to the issuance of more hunting permits and higher hunting success, primarily because of the opening of the Hayfields area of the park.

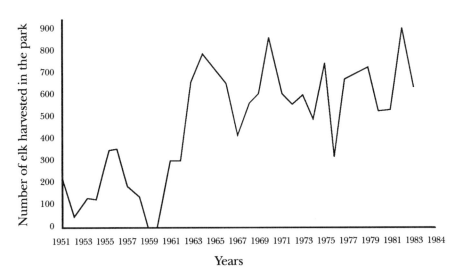

Figure 10.1. Number of elk killed in Grand Teton National Park 1951-84. (Grand Teton National Park, "Natural Resource Management Plan and Environmental Assessment, Grand Teton National Park," 1986.)

The amount of the park actually opened to elk hunting has varied over the years but has usually been about one-half of the legal maximum (about 22% of the park). The 19,300-hectare Berry Creek–Moose Basin area in the north end, representing 33% of the area that could be opened to hunting, has been open only eight years between 1950 and 1983 and has been closed since 1967. Elk harvests in this area were low, averaging only fifteen per year.

Is the Hunt Necessary?

Prior to 1950 indications were that few elk summered in the central valley of Jackson Hole because they had been displaced by agricultural activities (Cole 1969). Thus, elk killed were primarily those migrating to the winter range from other areas. However, after the expansion of the park in 1950, the termination of hunting west of the Snake River, and the termination of much of the cattle grazing in the valley after 1957 elk numbers on the summer range increased substantially. These numbers appeared to stabilize in the midsixties, and data from Barmore (1984) and Boyce (1989) indicate that elk numbers in the central valley of the park have changed little between 1963 and 1985. Because of the numbers of elk now using the summer range of the park, the park hunt is now viewed by WFGC as an important means of keeping elk numbers wintering on the National Elk Refuge within acceptable limits. The park harvest is particularly important in years when the harvests on other herd segments are not adequate to check population growth.

In 1964 the agencies responsible for managing the herd agreed that the long-range objective should be to reduce the need to kill large numbers of elk within Grand Teton National Park. This objective poses a dilemma for WGFC because it believes it cannot secure an adequate harvest on this herd segment elsewhere. It feels that without the park harvest the park herd segment would become a larger proportion of the elk wintering on the refuge. Increasing the fraction of park elk on the refuge might reduce state support for feeding operations (Dexter 1984). Boyce (1989) suggested that stopping the park hunt would increase the summer population in the park's central valley by 30% to 50% to an estimated two thousand elk.

Aside from NPS policy, there are several arguments against the park hunt. One is that it is not a quality experience. Most of the elk are taken on sagebrush flats where they have little escape cover.[6] In the early years of the hunt, regardless of the number of permits issued, only about 50% of the permittees actually arrived in the park to hunt. Because of the desire to increase the harvest, the number of permits was increased to three thousand in 1965. Hunter success continues to be low, averaging only 37% between 1974 and 1983. Over the entire period, the harvest success rate reaches 50% only when climatic conditions are optimal.

In the beginning, the public interest in participating in the park's elk management program was low. Bendt (1962) felt that many hunters participated only when they were unsuccessful in killing an elk elsewhere during the regular season. He also felt that the restrictions placed on the hunters, e.g., they had to check in and out if they were successful, were restricted to road and established camping areas, and were required to clean up campsites and remove tent frames and corrals, detracted from a desire to hunt in the park. In an effort to increase hunter interest, an either-sex season was initiated in the park in 1976. Since then, hunter success has been higher.

Public reactions to the elk hunt in the park today are mixed and difficult to measure. Thomas and others (1984) considered the hunt to be an excellent example of interagency cooperation to ensure proper wildlife management. Boyce (1989) reported that the hunt was generally popular among hunters and that there was no shortage of hunters willing to participate because success was usually high and the area relatively accessible.

Pressures to reduce or eliminate hunting in the park coming from traditional antihunting groups and park visitors continue (Robert Wood, interview with author, Grand Teton National Park, Jan. 16, 1987). Disturbances from hunting and killing animals often cause elk to leave areas where they would otherwise provide exceptional viewing and photographic opportunities for park visitors. Although park visitation is low during the time of the hunt (about 8% of the total visitation), hunters, particularly on the sagebrush flats, are often highly visible. Since park brochures contain no information regarding the hunt, the activity often shocks visitors. In recent years, in an effort to minimize some of these conflicts, visitor's visibility of the hunters in the Hayfields area had been reduced by closing a zone .25 mile on either side of Highway 26.

The long-term objective of the park is to reduce the need to kill large numbers of elk within the park. The preferred action in the park's 1986 Resource Management Plan calls for "an experimental management program to test the hypothesis that the level of elk hunting, which has been about the same for the last 21 years, can be reduced without jeopardizing the Jackson Hole elk herd" (104). If and when an equilibrium level will be reached is, as shown by the Yellowstone experience, uncertain. Certainly the state would be very cautious in agreeing to even a temporary termination of the hunt because public sentiment could make it an irreversible decision.

NOTES

1. Traditionally, hunting has been a primary use of the Big Cypress National Preserve. The Calusa, Seminole, and Miccosukee tribes have always hunted in the area. In the fifties and sixties, with improved access, there has

been a tremendous increase in sport hunting. Preserve estimates suggest that between 2,500 and 4,000 hunters may be present in the preserve at peak times (weekends) during the hunting season. The majority of hunters use off-road vehicles and permanent camps throughout the area. The Florida white-tailed deer, wild turkey, feral hog, and bob-white quail are the most common species hunted, but in the past several species that have become threatened or endangered, such as the mangrove fox squirrel, black bear, and panther, were hunted.

Sport hunting in the area poses major management problems. The wilderness quality of Big Cypress promotes a feeling of freedom in hunters. NPS presence and rules are seen as a burden to hunters' pleasure. Because of this, illegal activities, including poaching game and protected species; collecting plants, animals, and artifacts; arson; and vandalism are common. "Nightlighting," or "fire hunting," has also been a major illegal activity in Big Cypress. In the past, hunters have acknowledged that the illegal game harvest in Big Cypress is as great or greater than the legal harvest and that a lack of law enforcement was the main reason for it. Today, the situation is improving, although enforcement remains a problem. Few state wildlife officers are assigned to the area, and NPS staffing is also inadequate (Duever et al. 1979).

2. At the time the act was passed, the federal government owned most of the lands in the state. Although the statehood act had granted 40 million hectares to the state of Alaska in 1958, the state had actually taken title to only a small amount of land.

3. Ironically, the Alaska Department of Fish and Game, the agency that collected and administered the data and one of the principle opponents of new parks, repeatedly argued that this use of the data was inappropriate. However, when pressed by Congress, they had no better information to use in making land-classification decisions.

4. The purchases were made through several intermediaries. Rockefeller's role in these purchases was known to NPS but not to local residents. The plan was to turn these lands over to the federal government when a larger park was approved.

5. The earlier harvests took place in the monument because there were no funds to prevent it. There was no hunting in 1959 and 1960 at the request of the Wyoming Game and Fish Commission.

6. This situation was detailed in an unflattering account of the hunt broadcast in 1983 on a CBS-TV "60 Minutes" program entitled "A Sporting Chance."

11

Scientific Research in the National Parks: Concluding Thoughts

Over the years, the role scientific study has played in the development of NPS management programs has not been inconsequential but is nowhere near the level most scientists would have preferred. Until 1930, the Park Service employed only a few scientists and lacked a program of scientific research. Not until the sixties did staff and budget permit the development of a national science program, and even this program was severely limited. Today, expenditures for scientific study remain small and lag far behind other land-management agencies. Research funding of all types has averaged less than 1.5% of the total NPS budget (Elfring 1985). Today the science program lacks cohesiveness, and Park Service scientists often feel isolated and frustrated because their research is either ignored or has little impact on agency management decisions.

There are many reasons why science in the NPS has struggled and research has been ignored. Administrative or organizational problems are often cited as the chief culprit, and they certainly play a role. However, a more important problem derives from a fundamental dichotomy over what parks represent: dynamic systems whose components can be naturally altered by ecological processes or static entities where any disruption of the status quo is a concern. This causes different reactions to phenomena such as natural fire, floods, "overpopulations" of animals, disease, winter mortality, or the control of alien species. Scientists generally view these phenomena as natural processes or as the result of an imbalance in the ecosystem.[1] Administrators often tend to view these processes as "problems" that should not have occurred in the first place and need to be corrected. They often define research as the mechanism to solve these "problems."

This latter viewpoint not only ignores the role of research as a knowledge-generating process but undermines scientists' abilities to engage in long-term programs. Considering each "problem" as a distinct entity encourages a "quick-and-dirty" approach to problem solving that has long been typical of the Park Service. In this approach, funding and personnel are allocated only to solve a given problem rather than to provide an understanding of its underlying causes. Once a problem is "solved" focus quickly shifts to another "more critical" problem.

The shifting emphasis given to the major resource problems at Yellowstone over the past thirty years (shown schematically in Figure 11.1), provides a simplistic picture of this situation. Figure 11.1 points out two factors. One is the tendency to focus on only one problem at a time. Thus, although the growth of the elk population continued throughout the period, it ceased to be a resource concern in 1968 when a new management approach was adopted. Likewise, concern over grizzly bears was replaced by that for wolf reintroduction. Recently, with both renewed concern for elk and fire management (following the summer of 1988), the park is faced with the interesting conundrum of dealing with two equally important problems. Since money and support is closely tied to the perceived importance of a

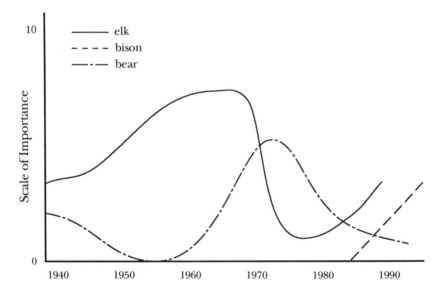

Figure 11.1. Wildlife resource management emphasis at Yellowstone over time.

problem, Figure 11.1 also reflects research efforts that were associated with the various problems. Clearly continuity of effort was limited, which is not unusual since continuity in resource study is the single biggest failing of the NPS science program.[2] The chief casualty of this deficiency has been a lack of basic research and long-term monitoring efforts. While the need for basic research and resource monitoring has long been recognized, the ramifications of its neglect are only now becoming apparent.[3]

Improving the Park Service Science Program

When ways to improve the NPS science and research program are discussed, the emphasis is typically directed toward structural changes in the organization. Virtually every independent analysis of the Park Service science program over the past twenty-five years (e.g., Robbins et al. 1963, NPCA 1988) has come to the same conclusion—the creation of an independent science organization with adequate funding and staff distinct from management and operations. However, since these evaluations were conducted by persons outside the agency, the difficulties in making such profound changes in the administrative structure were not recognized. Even if funding were increased and organizational changes were to occur, the hope that they alone could bring about reform is probably unrealistic.

Real reform in the NPS science program can only occur by changing the ways the agency thinks about the role of science. This implies a long-term evolving process requiring the placement of more individuals trained in the sciences in key management positions.[4] This would create a novel situation. A natural scientist has never been in charge of the agency, and few have been regional directors or even superintendents. Whereas most federal agency land managers have degrees in a natural-resouce field, more NPS managers are trained in liberal arts, education, or even police science than in natural-resource management (Shanks 1984).

There must also be a concerted effort to attract existing scientists and resource managers into program administration. Many such individuals are now reluctant to make this move because of the economic and social "sacrifices" of moving to the urban environment associated with these offices and because they question the ability of these positions to change the status quo. The result is that many of the talented people stay at lower grades. Shanks described this phenomenon as follows: "A type of selective promotion takes place, creating an agency schizophrenia. Top bureaucrats often have little field experience and minimal affection for wild areas. Lower-level field personnel hold the most cherished values of the agency but are overruled for political expediency. Park administration at regional or national levels is notably unimpressive" (1984:224). A management cadre with scientific literacy would have several benefits. Most important, it would help assure that science was placed on par with visitor services, maintenance, and other NPS operations. It would also create a better working environment, helping to eliminate the adversarial relationship that has long existed between scientists and superintendents.

Improve Communication

The decentralized nature of the science program has always complicated communication between professional personnel within the agency. Opportunities for consultation with other scientists have traditionally been minimal. Many of the problems and management questions confronting parks demand a multidisplinary approach, but the opportunity to develop such teams has been rare. Opportunities for consultation with academic scientists (except for CPSU personnel) is even more difficult. Attendance at professional meetings has often been restricted and the concept of a sabbatical is nonexistent.

In parks, communication between scientists and other divisions has historically been a problem. Greater efforts are needed to overcome the psychological and physical isolation scientists face in some parks. Parks like Great Smoky Mountains (Uplands Field Research Lab), Everglades (Daniel Beard Research Center), and Yosemite have placed scientists in facilities widely separated from park headquarters. Unfortunately, while these research centers often have good facilities, the personnel are denied the day-to-day contacts with other park personnel essential in achieving a smooth-running program.

Altering the Resource Management Decision-Making Process

The process by which most major resource-management decisions are currently made is ambiguous. The organizational level with the authority to make a given decision often varies with the political sensitivity of the problem under consideration and the relative rank and experience of the personnel.[5] Problems are solved on a case-by-case basis, and there tends to be a strong reluctance to rely on precedents and uniform procedures. Proponents of this practice assert that this flexibility in decision making permits tailoring the policies to different parks, encourages innovation, and eliminates bureaucratic rigidity (Kitchell and Nichols 1987). It also makes it extremely difficult to undertake controversial management programs. Political factors rather than formalized rules and procedures are generally the key elements considered before a specific management action is implemented (Clarke and McCool 1986). In the final analysis, the process contributes to a strong desire to avoid situations that might cause problems.[6]

The lack of reliance on precedents and procedures also contributes to inconsistencies in policy and management between parks, making legal challenges to administrative actions possible. For example, one park may shoot alien animals to restore the natural environment, another may have only a limited control program, and a third may tolerate them because local politics prevents their removal. Such practices can result in individual park decisions becoming precedents for the entire system.

What Can Scientists Do?

Recognize the Importance of Adaptability

NPS has always been too small an agency to have sufficient personnel to deal with all the problems it encounters or to employ all the disciplines needed to solve those problems. As a result, from the earliest days NPS scientists and resource managers have had to work on problems well beyond their disciplines. For example, in Yellowstone wildlife biologists had to deal with fisheries problems and ungulate biologists worked with pelicans. In Glacier the fisheries biologist worked with elk and bear transplants. Because there is limited opportunity (and often limited tolerance) for specialists, the successful career scientists that stay in the Park Service are those who are capable of becoming generalists with the ability to cope with changing agency demands and idiosyncrasies. This is a fact of life that needs to be recognized by many scientists in the agency.

Increasing Publications by Scientific Personnel

Scientists often subject themselves to criticism because they typically fail to publish the results of their studies. Reviews of scientific literature have shown that only a small portion of the research done by NPS scientists appears in professional journals or other published outlets (Wright and Hayward 1985). Most reasons given for not publishing have little validity. Some scientists argue that there are strong institutional disincentives to publish research results. Although there have been accusations (e.g., Chase 1986) that NPS has purposely suppressed the publication of a study to prevent embarrassment or controversy, these are difficult to document. A more common situation appears to be that scientists lack the motivation or desire or discipline to publish. Admittedly in the past there was little incentive for having a good publication record. Only recently has a good publication record been one of the criteria by which the competence of a research scientist is judged.

Other scientists have argued that the nature of their studies, i.e., applied rather than basic research, makes them less acceptable to scientific journals. Some journals do typically reject applied-science articles, but there is a large and growing number of journals oriented toward management applications. Peer reviews of one's research are valuable in that they not only improve one's own ability but also, when positive, provide support for what might be controversial management recommendations. Publications also provide a proven way to enhance communication among otherwise isolated scientists.

Incorporating Park Research into Interpretive Programs

NPS scientists in general do a poor job in communicating the results of their studies in a manner that can be understood and used by park naturalists in their public information programs. This is unfortunate, because the interpretive programs of the parks are one of the best ways of alerting the visiting public to the research being done in the national parks and the problems and the needs that exist. The small amount of extra effort that is needed to communicate research findings in a clear and understandable manner so that they can be used by park naturalists can pay great dividends. To develop a credible science program and to be effective in its management programs, NPS will be forced to rely to an ever-greater extent on public understanding of its problems and public acceptance of the methods that need to be used. This is particularly true when controversial management actions, such as population reductions, are contemplated.

Directions for the Future

There are many resources and processes in parks that require much more study than is presently being devoted to them. Every park has a resource-management plan that is, in essence, a prioritized list of all projects that should be undertaken if the park is to properly manage its resources. Obviously, because of funding limitations, most of these are never accomplished. Even a partial listing of these studies would make for rather lengthy (and boring) reading. Instead, in this concluding section I will focus briefly on two broad categories of scientific endeavor required in parks: the need for more extensive resource inventories and the need for ecosystemwide studies.

Resource Inventories

As seen in the preceding chapters, the unique environments and management policies of parks have provided great opportunities to study animal life and have historically attracted researchers of wide renown. As a consequence parks have witnessed an impressive amount of research on many species on a variety of subjects. Unfortunately, despite this legacy of scientific study little is known about the numbers or habits of most animals that inhabit parks. The best information and most extensive study has been confined to those species that historically have been of greatest management concern or visitor interest: ungulates and bears. Likewise, studies of park wildlife are primarily limited to those times when the parks are fully staffed and travel is easiest. Thus, in most northern parks there is little knowledge about conditions in winter, and the extent of winter mortality in many parks is often unknown except when an animal dies by the road. All parks need better inventories of their resources not only because this knowledge is of intrinsic value but because it can serve as a valuable baseline to monitor environmental change.

One of the greatest scientific benefits of national parks is that they provide an undisturbed long-term baseline to monitor changes in the environment. Unfortunately, over the years no area of resource management has been given more lip service and so little support as programs to collect baseline data or to monitor resource status. In any budget shortfall, these are usually the first programs to be cut and the last to be initiated in times of surplus.

In almost every park one can find reference to programs that were established to monitor a given resource. In most cases these were usually discontinued when personnel changed, policies altered, or funds were cut. As a result data from these efforts were generally lost, plots cannot be relocated, and, in some cases, plots have been destroyed. In Rocky Mountain, for example, Stevens (1980) reported that in 1964, four of the original exclosures that were established between 1933 and 1935 to monitor ungulate browsing were removed as they were considered to be of no further value. This is not an unusual occurrence. The result is that we know very little about what exists in parks and how current conditions differ from the past. Even the fourteen parks classed as Biosphere Reserves, the most studied natural areas in the system, have a poor record (see Table 11.1). Only the collection of climatic data has received any emphasis at all. When looked at on a park-by-park basis (see Table 11.2), the effort committed to baseline inventory and long-term environmental monitoring has been very low but was still twice that devoted to long-term ecological research.

There are several reasons why monitoring programs are not supported. First, there is no glamour in collecting most baseline data: it is repetitive and systematic work. As a result, it is often relegated to seasonal employees who by the nature of their positions lack the perspective to see its value. Administrators see little payoff from these programs since they do not solve immediate "problems." In addition, payoffs that do accrue are often poorly documented or not brought to management's attention, thus reinforcing the idea that monitoring programs produce limited benefits. Finally, it is often difficult to convince researchers to include the establishment of a monitoring program in their studies or to be involved in setting up monitoring efforts. Studies that include observation and baseline data collection seem to have a low esteem in scientific disciplines because it is often difficult, if not impossible, to obtain funds to collect routine data as opposed to conducting basic research involving new environmental information.

Table 11.1. The Amount of Long-term Monitoring Effort Devoted to Resource Categories in Biosphere Reserves (depending on the completeness of a given activity, scale can vary between 0 and 100)

Resource Monitored	Effort Devoted
Vegetation, Recovery from Disturbance	47
Macroclimate	38
Disturbances Caused by Exotic Species	34
Chemical Parameters in Aquatic Systems	31
Anthropogenic Disturbances	25
Natural Disturbances	22
Physical Parameters in Aquatic Systems	15
Biological Parameters in Aquatic Systems	7

Source: Adapted from A. Mack, et al., "A Survey of Ecological Inventory, Monitoring, and Research in U.S. National Park Biosphere Reserves," *Biological Conservation* 26 (1983).

Table 11.2. Numerical Rating of the Major Scientific Activities in National Park Biosphere Reserves (depending on the completeness of a given activity, dimensionless scale can vary between 0 and 100)

Park	Baseline Inventory	Long-term Environmental Monitoring	Long-term Ecological Research
Big Bend	23	11	0
Channel Is.	37	14	9
Denali	32	21	5
Everglades	61	38	30
Glacier	35	14	10
Great Smokies	62	63	35
Hawaiian Parks	40	13	8
Isle Royale	34	20	29
Olympic	41	21	12
Organ Pipe	35	8	9
Rocky Mountain	48	25	15
Sequoia KC	47	23	10
Virgin Is.	33	7	0
Yellowstone	53	15	20
Average	41	21	14

Source: Adapted from A. Mack, et al., "A Survey of Ecological Inventory, Monitoring, and Research in U.S. National Park Biosphere Reserves," *Biological Conservation* 26 (1983).

Regional Ecosystem Studies

At the other extreme, greater focus needs to be placed on systems-level research, including the use of ecosystem models that may extend beyond park boundaries and encompass complete regional ecosystems. There is considerable interest in finding ways to design parks that can optimize the protection of wildlife and other natural resources within them. Unfortunately the debates on the merits of this approach have been largely theoretical, and there has been little practical application to actual park design. In the United States, as in most of the world, park design has been defined primarily by political and economic rather than ecological considerations and likely will remain so.

For some species parks do, as is shown in Table 11.3, provide a relatively complete ecosystem. However, for most species, including large carnivores, this is not the case. The issue of whether parks are capable of protecting their wildlife becomes more volatile as more and more lands external to parks are converted to consumptive uses. For many

Table 11.3 Parks Estimated to Provide Complete Ecological Units for
Naturally Limited Populations of Large Mammals

Species	Degree Population Is Limited	Approximate Population	Reference
	Big Bend		
Mule deer	completely	2,000–3,000	Krausman and Ables (1976)
White-tailed deer	completely	500–800	Krausman and Ables (1976)
	Big Cypress		
Black bear	almost completely	20–100	Duever et al. (1979)
White-tailed deer	completely	unknown	Duever et al. (1979)
	Canyonlands		
Desert bighorn	almost totally	~20	Ravey and Schmidt (1981)
	Death Valley		
Desert bighorn	almost totally	~100	Welles and Weles (1961)
	Everglades		
Black bear	almost totally	<100	Duever et al. (1979)
	Glacier		
Bighorn sheep	completey	<100	Hayward, Wright, and Krumpe (1984)
Black bear	completely	~500	Jope (1981)
Elk (west side)	almost totally	300–600	Hayward, Wright, and Krumpe (1984)
Grizzly bear	completely	175–230	Martinka (pers. comm.)
Moose	completely	~100	Hayward, Wright, and Krumpe (1984)
Mountain goats	completely	1,800–2,000	Chadwick (1977)
Mule deer (west side)	completely	400–600	Hayward, Wright, and Krumpe (1984)

Table 11.3 Parks Estimated to Provide Complete Ecological Units for
Naturally Limited Populations of Large Mammals (continued)

Species	Degree Population Is Limited	Approximate Population	Reference
	Grand Canyon		
Desert bighorn	completely	unknown	
	Grand Teton		
Bighorn sheep	completely	~125	Whitfield (1983)
Moose	almost totally	~250	Grand Teton (1986)
	Great Smoky Mountains		
Black bear	complete	500–600	Walthem (pers. comm.)
White-tailed deer	probably	1,700–5,000	Park Files
	Isle Royale		
Moose	completely	1,175–1,585	Peterson (1986)
	Joshua Tree		
Desert bighorn	almost totally	~150	Hekkers (1979)
	Mesa Verde		
Mule deer	probably	~1200	Mierau and Schmidt (1981)
	Mt. Rainier		
Black bear	completely	~100	Schnoes and Starkey (1978)
Mountain goats	completely	500–800	Schelgel (pers. comm.)
	North Cascades		
Black bear	completely	300–550	Schnoes and Starkey (1978)
Mule deer	completely	unknown	
	Olympic		
Black bear	completely	200–300	Schnoes and Starkey (1978)

Table 11.3 Parks Estimated to Provide Complete Ecological Units for Naturally Limited Populations of Large Mammals (continued)

Species	Degree Population Is Limited	Approximate Population	Reference
Black-tailed deer (west side)	completely	~5,000	Moorhead (pers. comm.)
Elk (west side)	completely	~4,000	Houston, (pers. comm.)
Mountain goats	completely	~1,000	Houston, Moorhead, and Olson (1986)
Organ Pipe Cactus			
Desert bighorn	almost completely	70–100	Coss (1964)
Rocky Mountain			
Bighorn sheep	completely	~500	Goodsen (pers. comm.)
Saguaro			
Desert bighorn	completely	unknown	
Sequoia Kings Canyon			
Black bear	completely	~350	Schnoes and Starkey (1978)
Mule deer	completely	>2,000	Sequoia (1983)
Voyageurs			
Moose	almost totally	~25	Cole (1982)
Black bear	completely	100–200	Schnoes and Starkey (1978)
Yellowstone			
Bighorn sheep	partially	200–250	Whitfield (1983)
Bison (Pelican and Firehole herds)	completely	200–300	Meagher (pers. comm.)
Black bear	completely	500–650	Park Files
Elk (Northern herd)	almost totally	~18,000	Singer (pers. comm.)

Table 11.3 Parks Estimated to Provide Complete Ecological Units for
Naturally Limited Populations of Large Mammals (continued)

Species	Degree Population Is Limited	Approximate Population	Reference
Grizzly bear	almost totally	200–300	Knight and Eberhart (1985)
Moose	completely	200	Despain et al. (1986)
		Yosemite	
Black bear	completely	220–350	Harms (1977)
Mule deer	completely	>5,000	Park Files

parks, the issue of land uses and management techniques on lands surrounding the park will be the next battle.[7] This is not a fight the Park Service is currently prepared to fight. NPS managers have traditionally concluded that their jurisdiction ends at the park boundary. Continued pursuance of this tactic will only mean that a given park will have no influence on the decisions made on surrounding lands that ultimately will determine the park's destiny. This need not and should not be the case. Managers and scientists need to become more concerned with regional resource management. Scientists need to be concerned about how factors external to the parks influence park resources and vice versa. Regional land-use planning organizations, such as the Greater Yellowstone Coalition and the Man and the Biosphere Program, can serve as models in this regard. In lieu of mutual cooperation, activist managers will find that there is considerable existing legal authority allowing them to regulate or at least effectively control activities or developments occurring on lands outside park boundaries that may threaten park resources (Sax and Keiter 1987).

Conclusions

The first seven decades of the Park Service have seen tremendous changes in the ways animals are viewed, managed, and studied in national parks. Predicting what the next few decades will bring is risky at best. Public support for the NPS is high and is likely to remain so. The economic (and ecological?) benefit of national parks is slowly being recognized even in areas that have for the most part staunchly resisted the establishment of parks. It is almost certain that in the future more lands will be protected in parks.[8]

Whether the scientific mission of the NPS will be able to meet its future obligations is less certain. Some of the scientific programs of the past fifteen years, including barrier island research, fire research, and management of the effects of alien species control are encouraging. Whether the enthusiasm for recent service-wide initiatives for inventory and monitoring and wildlife population regulation are maintained remains to be seen. The scientific staff of the agency has grown in recent years, although this increase has been offset by the increases in new areas and responsibilities. Likewise, funding increases have not kept pace with expansion, more complex environmental problems, and inflation.

Perhaps change must be incremental to deal with the tremendous inertia an established bureaucracy develops. However, in an era of fast-paced environmental change, this may be a tactic doomed to failure. The last thing we want in the future is a marvelous assemblage of parks about which we know even less than we do today. Certainly, the resources of the parks demand differently. Peek (1986) has written that the ultimate value of national parks is in the story their resources can tell and the lessons we can learn. Without sufficient scientific study we won't be able to read the story and surely will fail to learn the lessons.

NOTES

1. For example, the great size of the fires in Yellowstone in the summer of 1988 can be attributed in part as a natural consequence of severe drought and hot weather, but also to a history of fire suppression and fuel build up.

2. To reach a consensus on some of the factors that might enhance research and the role of science in NPS, a questionnaire was developed and sent to virtually all (n = 45) NPS research wildlife biologists (Wright 1987). The results of that questionnaire combined with insights obtained from interviews with present and retired NPS personnel were used in developing parts of this chapter.

3. A good example of a situation where basic research could have made a significant impact concerns the purposeful alterations of the hydrologic regime of Everglades. The problems resulting from this activity have been extensively documented by James Kushlan and are only now being dealt with as the result of threatened legal action.

4. This is a long-recognized problem. Adams first suggested that "the chief problem of national parks is that they are not being run by technical people"

nical people" (1922:143). Sumner (interview with author, Glenwood, N. Mex., May 9, 1987) concluded that throughout his thirty-year career ending in 1965, most administrators had no understanding about what research should provide or how a research program should be structured and supervised. Cole (telephone conversation with author, Aug. 28, 1986), retiring in 1989, reached the same conclusion.

5. For example, a decision to reintroduce peregrine falcons in an area might be made at the park level while a decision to reintroduce wolves would probably be made by the secretary of the interior.

6. This situation has been prevalent for many years. For example, when biologist Coleman Newman reported for duty in Olympic in 1957 to investigate the elk situation, the superintendent's only comment to him was "don't get me in trouble" (Coleman Newman, letter to author, Apr. 11, 1986). Similar stories have been put forth by many contemporary scientists.

7. In essence, things have changed little in the fifty-five years since Wright and others (1933) ranked the inability of parks to function as complete biological units as the most important wildlife problem in parks.

8. Witness the recent establishment of Great Basin, Nevada's first national park, and the new national monument and reserve in Idaho.

Appendix

Common and Scientific Names of Animals

Common Name	Scientific Name
Mammals	
Bear, black	*Ursus americanus*
Bear, grizzly	*Ursus arctos*
Beaver	*Castor canadensis*
Bison	*Bison bison*
Boar, European wild	*Sus scrofa*
Bobcat	*Felis rufus*
Burro	*Equus asinus*
Cattle, domestic	*Bos taurus*
Caribou	*Rangifer tarandus*
Chipmunk, yellow pine	*Eutamias amoenus*
Cougar	*Felis concolor*
Coyote	*Canus latrans*
Deer, axis	*Axis axis*
Deer, black-tailed	*Odocoileus heminonus columbianus*
Deer, European fallow	*Dama dama dama*
Deer, mule	*Odocoileus hemionus*
Deer, white-tailed	*Odocoileus virginianus*
Elk, Rocky Mountain	*Cervis elaphus*
Elk, Roosevelt	*Cervis elaphus roosevelti*
Fisher	*Martes pennanti*
Fox, gray	*Urocyon cinereoargentus*
Fox, red	*Vulpes fulva*
Fox, swift	*Vulpes velox*
Gemsbok	*Oryx gazella*
Goat, domestic	*Capra hircus*

Common and Scientific Names of Animals

Common Name	Scientific Name
Goat, Rocky Mountain	*Oreamnos americanus*
Ground squirrel, golden mantled	*Spermophilus lateralis*
Horse, domestic	*Equus caballus*
Lynx	*Felis lynx*
Marmot, yellow-bellied	*Marmota flaviventris*
Martin	*Martes martes*
Mink	*Mustela vison*
Mongoose, small Indian	*Herpestes auropanetatus*
Moose	*Alces alces*
Mouse, white-footed	*Peromyscus leucopus*
Otter, river	*Lutra canadensis*
Pig, wild	*Sus scrofa domesticus*
Porcupine	*Erethizon dorsatum*
Pronghorn	*Antilocapra americana*
Rat, black	*Rattus rattus*
Rat, Norway	*Rattus norvegicus*
Raccoon	*Procyon lotor*
Sheep, bighorn	*Ovis canadensis*
Sheep, California bighorn	*Ovis canadensis californicus*
Sheep, Dall	*Ovis dalli*
Sheep, desert bighorn	*Ovis canadensis nelsoni*
Sheep, domestic	*Ovis musimon*
Skunk, striped	*Mephitis mephitus*
Squirrel, fox	*Sciurus niger*
Weasel, least	*Mustela nivalis*
Wolf, gray	*Canus lupis*
Wolf, red	*Canus rufus*
Wolverine	*Gulo gulo*

Birds

Eagle, bald	*Haliacetus leucocephalus*
Kingfisher, belted	*Megaceryle alcyon*
Nene	*Nesochen sandvicensis*
Nutcracker, Clark's	*Nucifraga columbiana*
Owl, great horned	*Bubu virginianus*
Pelican, white	*Pelecanus erythrorhynchos*
Po'ouli	*Melamprosops phaeosoma*
Quail, bobwhite	*Colinus virginianus*
Starling, European	*Sturnus vulgaris*
Stork, North American wood	*Mycteria americana*
Swan, trumpeter	*Cygnus buccinator*
Turkey, wild	*Meleagris gallopavo*

Common and Scientific Names of Animals

Common Name	Scientific Name
Fish	
Trout, cutthroat	*Salmo clarki*
Grayling, American	*Thymallus arcticus*
Reptiles	
Alligator, American	*Alligator mississippiensis*
Invertebrates	
Deer tick, northern	*Ixodes dammini*

Bibliography

Adams, C. 1922. "The Relation of Wildlife to the Public in National and State Parks." *Proceedings of the Second Conference of State Parks,* 129–47.

Agee, J. K., D. R. Field, and E. S. Starkey. 1983. "Cooperative Park Studies Units: University-based Science Program in the National Park Service." *Journal of Environmental Education* 14(2):24–28.

Aiton, J. F. 1938. "Relationship of Predators to Whitetail Deer in Glacier National Park." *Transactions of the North American Wildlife Conference* 3:302–4.

Albright, H. M. 1933. "Research in the National Parks." *Scientific Monthly* 24:483–501.

———.1931. "National Parks Predator Policy." *Journal of Mammalogy* 12:185–86.

———.1929. "Our National Parks as Wildlife Sanctuaries." *American Forests and Forest Life* 35:505–7.

———. 1920. "Annual Report of the Superintendent." Yellowstone National Park.

Aldous, S. E., and L. W. Krefting. 1946. "The Present Status of Moose on Isle Royale." *Transactions of the North American Wildlife Conference* 11:296–308.

Allard, W. A. 1967. "Yellowstone Wildlife in Winter." *National Geographic* 132:637–61.

Allen, D. L. 1979. *Wolves of Minong: Their Vital Role in a Wild Community.* Boston: Houghton Mifflin.

Allen, D. L., et al. 1981. "A Review and Recommendations on Animal Problems and Related Management Needs in Units of the National Park System: A Report to the Secretary of Interior." Reprinted in *George Wright Forum* 1(2):11–22.

American Association for the Advancement of Science. 1922. "Resolution on the Maintenance of Natural Conditions in National and State Parks." *Science* 55:63.

Ames, D. B., and C. P. Stone. 1985. "Problem Species in Hawaii Volcanoes National Park Biosphere Reserve." In *Proceedings of the Conference on the*

Management of Biosphere Reserves, ed. J. D. Peine. Great Smoky Mountains National Park, Uplands Field Lab, Nov. 27–29, 1984.

Aune, K. E. 1981. "Impacts of Winter Recreationists on Wildlife in a Portion of Yellowstone National Park." Master's Thesis, Montana State University.

Bailey, V. 1905. "Biological Survey of Texas." *North American Fauna* 25:1–222.

———. 1930. *Animal Life of Yellowstone National Park.* Springfield, Ill.: C. E. Thomas.

Baker, J. K. 1979. "The Feral Pig in Hawaii Volcanoes National Park." In vol. 5 of *Proceedings of the First Conference on Scientific Research in the National Parks.*

Baldwin, S. B., et al. 1985. "Habitat Mapping in the Two-Medicine Area of Glacier National Park Combining Information Gathering Techniques." University of Idaho Cooperative Park Studies Unit Report no. SB–85–2.

Bansner, U. 1978. "Mountain Goat–Human Interactions in the Sperry Gunsight Area of Glacier National Park." Final Report, Glacier National Park.

Barmore, W. J. 1984. "A Synthesis of Information on Elk That Summer in or Migrate through Grand Teton National Park." Unpublished report, Grand Teton National Park.

Barnes, V. G., and O. E. Bray. 1967. "Population Characteristics and Activities of Black Bears in Yellowstone National Park." Final Report, Colorado Cooperative Wildlife Research Unit, Colorado State University.

Baron, J. S. 1979. "Vegetation Damage by Feral Hogs on Horn Island, Gulf Island National Seashore, Mississippi." Master's Thesis, University of Wisconsin.

Barrett, R. H., and C. P. Stone. 1983. "Hunting as a Control Method for Wild Pigs in Hawaii Volcanoes National Park." Unpublished report, Hawaii Volcanoes National Park.

Beeman, L. E. 1975. "Population Characteristics, Movements, and Activities of the Black Bear in the Great Smoky Mountains National Park." Ph.D. diss., University of Tennessee.

———. 1971. "Seasonal Food Habits of the Black Bear in the Smoky Mountains of Tennessee and North Carolina." Master's Thesis, University of Tennessee.

Beetle, A. A. 1974. "The Zootic Disclimax Concept." *Journal of Range Management* 27:30–32.

Bell, J. N. 1963. "Wild Animals Are Wild." *National Wildlife* 1(5):34–36.

Bendt, R. H. 1962. "The Jackson Hole Elk Herd in Yellowstone and Grand Teton National Parks." *Transactions of the North American Wildlife and Natural Resources Conference* 27:191–201.

———. 1957. "Status of Bighorn Sheep in Grand Canyon National Park and Monument." *Transactions of the Desert Bighorn Council* 1:16–19.

Bennett, P. S., et al. 1980. "Effects of Burro Foraging in Four Types of Grand Canyon Vegetation." In vol. 8 of *Proceedings of the Second Conference on Scientific Research in the National Parks.*

Blong, B., and W. Pollard. 1968. "Summer Water Requirements of Desert Bighorn Sheep in Santa Rosa Mountains, California in 1965." *California Fish and Game* 54(4):289–96.

Boyce, M. S. 1989. *The Jackson Hole Elk Herd.* Cambridge: Cambridge University Press.

Boyd, D. 1982. "Food Habits and Spatial Relationships of Coyotes and a Lone Wolf in the Rocky Mountains." Master's Thesis, University of Montana.

Bratton, S. P. 1986. "Feral Horses, Grazing Impacts and Genetics and Birth Control." *Park Science* 7(1):23–24.

———. 1980. "Impacts of White-tailed Deer on the Vegetation of Cades Cove, Great Smoky Mountains National Park." Unpublished report, Uplands Field Research Lab, Great Smoky Mountains National Park.

———. 1975. "The Effect of the European Wild Boar, *Sus scrofa,* on Grey Beech Forest in the Great Smoky Mountains." *Ecology* 56:1356–66.

———. 1974. "The Effect of the European Wild Boar in High Elevation Vernal Flora of the Great Smoky Mountains National Park." *Bulletin of the Torrey Botanical Club* 101:198–206.

Brower, K. 1985. "The Pig War." *Atlantic Monthly,* Aug., 44–58.

Brown, P. J., G. E. Haus, and B. L. Driver. 1980. "Value of Wildlife to Wilderness Users." In vol. 6 of *Proceedings of the Second Conference on Scientific Research in the National Parks.*

Bryan, R., and M. Janssan. 1973. "Perception of Wildlife Hazard in National Parks." *Transactions of the North American Wildlife and Natural Resources Conference* 38:281–95.

Bryant, H. C., and W. W. Atwood. 1932. "Research and Education in the National Parks." Washington, D.C.: GPO.

Burst, T. L., and M. R. Pelton. 1973. "Observations of a White-tailed Deer Die-off in the Great Smoky Mountains National Park." *Proceedings of the Annual Conference of the Southern Association of Game and Fish Commissioners* 27:297–301.

Buttery, R. F. 1955. "Range Conditions and Trends Resulting from Concentration of Elk in Rocky Mountain National Park." Master's Thesis, Colorado State University.

Cahalane, V. H. 1961. "Public Hunting in the National Parks?" *Atlantic Naturalist* 16(3):191–92.

———. 1948a. "Conserving Wildlife in the National Parks." *Proceedings of the Seventh Pacific Science Congress* 4:646–52.

———. 1948b. "Predators and People." *National Parks Magazine* 22:5–12.

———. 1947. "Wildlife and the National Park Land-use Concept." *Transactions of the North American Wildlife Conference* 12:431–36.

———. 1946. "Shall We Save the Larger Carnivores." *Living Wilderness,* June.

———. 1944. "Restoration of Wild Bison." *Transactions of the North American Wildlife Conference* 9:135–43.

———. 1943. "Elk Management and Herd Regulation—Yellowstone National Park." *Transactions of the North American Wildlife Conference* 8:95–101.

———. 1941. "Wildlife Surpluses in the National Parks." *Transactions of the North American Wildlife Conference* 6:355–61.

———. 1939. "The Evolution of Predator Control in the National Parks." *Journal of Wildlife Management* 3:229–37.

Cahalane, V. H., C. Presnall, and D. B. Beard. 1940. "Wildlife Conservation in Areas Administered by the National Park Service, 1930–1939: A Report to the Special Committee of the U.S. Senate on the Conservation of Wildlife Resources." In *The Status of Wildlife in the United States.* Washington, D.C.: GPO.

Cameron, J. 1922. *The NPS: Its History, Activities, and Organization.* Service Monograph of the U.S. Government, no. 11. New York: D. Appleton.

Carbyn, L. N. 1980. "Ecology and Management of Wolves in Riding Mountain National Park, Manitoba." Canadian Wildlife Service Report.

Carhart, A. H. 1961. "Shall We Hunt in National Parks?" *Sports Afield,* Dec.

Carothers, S. W., M. E. Stitt, and R. R. Johnson. 1976. "Feral Asses on Public Lands: An Analysis of Biotic Impact, Legal Considerations, and Management Alternatives." *Transactions of the North American Wildlife and Natural Resources Conference* 41:396–405.

Cart, T. W. 1973. "A New Deal for Wildlife." *Pacific Northwest Quarterly* 63(July):113–20.

Caughley, G. 1970. "Eruption of Ungulate Populations with Emphasis on Himalayan Thar in New Zealand." *Ecology* 51:53–71.

Cella, W. B., and J. A. Keay. 1980. "Annual Bear Management and Incident Report." Unpublished report, Yosemite National Park.

Chadwick, D. H. 1977. "Ecology of the Rocky Mountain Goat in Glacier National Park and the Swan Mountains, Montana." Final Report, Glacier National Park.

Chase, A. 1986. *Playing God in Yellowstone.* Boston: Atlantic Monthly Press Books.

———. 1983. "The Last Bears of Yellowstone." *Atlantic Monthly,* Feb., 63–73.

Christensen, N. L., et al. 1989a. "Interpreting the Yellowstone Fires of 1988." *Bioscience* 39:678–85.

———. 1989b. "Report of the Greater Yellowstone Ecological Assessment Panel on the Ecological Impact of the 1988 Yellowstone Fires." Unpublished report, Greater Yellowstone Coordinating Committee.

Clarke, J. N., and D. McCool. 1986. *Staking Out the Terrain: Power Differentials among Natural Resource Agencies.* Albany: State University of New York Press.

Cole, G. F. 1982. "Restoring Natural Conditions in a Boreal Forest Park." *Transactions of the North American Wildlife and Natural Resources Conference* 47:411–20.

———. 1973. "Management Involving Grizzly Bears in Yellowstone National Park 1970–72." Natural Resource Report no. 7.

———. 1972. "Grizzly Bear–Elk Relationships in Yellowstone National Park." *Journal of Wildlife Management* 36:556–61.

———. 1971. "An Ecological Rationale for the Natural or Artificial Regulation of Native Ungulates in Parks." *Transactions of the North American Wildlife and Natural Resources Conference* 36:417–25.

———. 1969. "The Elk of Grand Teton and Southern Yellowstone National Parks." Research Report no. GRTE–N–1, Grand Teton National Park.

Coleman, S. 1984. "Control Efforts in Great Smoky Mountains National Park Since 1978." In *Techniques for Controlling Wild Hogs in Great Smoky Mountains National Park: Proceedings of a Workshop,* ed. J. Tate. National Park Service Research/Resource Management Report no. SER–78.

Condon, D. D. 1944. "Elk-Deer Management Program 1943–44." Unpublished Report, Rocky Mountain National Park.

Contor, R. 1978. "Illustrative Wilderness-Wildlife-Management Approaches." In *Wildlife Management in Wilderness,* ed. C. Schoenfeld and J. Hendee. Pacific Grove, Calif.: Boxwood.

Coss, H. T. 1964. "Status of the Bighorn Sheep in Organ Pipe Cactus National Monument." *Transactions of the Desert Bighorn Council* 8:117–21.

Craighead, F. C. 1973. "They're Killing Yellowstone's Grizzlies." *National Wildlife* 11(6).

Craighead, J. J., and F. C. Craighead. 1971. "Grizzly Bear–Man Relationships in Yellowstone National Park." Unpublished report, Yellowstone National Park.

———. 1967. "Management of Bears in Yellowstone National Park." Unpublished report, Yellowstone National Park.

Craighead, J. J., J. R. Varney, and F. C. Craighead. 1974. "A Population Analysis of the Yellowstone Grizzly Bears." Montana Forest and Conservation Experiment Station Bulletin no. 40, Montana State University.

Culler, M. 1931. Letter to Guy Edwards, Acting Superintendent, Yellowstone. Nov. 27.

Cypher, B. L., and E. A. Cypher. 1988. "Ecology and Management of White-tailed Deer in Northeastern Coastal Habitats." U.S. Fish and Wildlife Service Biological Report no. 88(15).

Cypher, B. L., R. H. Yahner, and E. A. Cypher. 1985. "Ecology and Management of White-tailed Deer at Valley Forage National Historical Park." National Park Service Mid-Atlantic Research/Resource Management Report no. MAR–15.

Dalle-Molle, J. L., M. A. Coffey, and H. W. Werner. 1986. "Evaluation of Bear Resistant Food Containers for Backpackers." In *Proceedings of the National Wilderness Research Conference,* ed. R. Lucas. U.S. Forest Service General Technical Report no. INT–212.

Dalle-Molle, J. L., and J. C. Van Horn. 1987. "Successful Bear-People Conflict Management in Denali National Park, Alaska." In *Proceedings of the Bear-People Conflicts Symposium,* ed. M. Bromley. Northwest Territories Department of Renewable Resources.

Darling, F. F., and N. D. Eichhorn. 1967. *Man and Nature in the National Parks.* Washington, D.C.: Conservation Foundation.

Day, G. L. 1981. "The Status and Distribution of Wolves in the Northern Rocky Mountains of the United States." Master's Thesis, University of Montana.

Despain, D., et al. 1986. *Wildlife in Transition.* Boulder: Roberts Rinehart.

Dexter, D. 1984. "*Sixty Minutes* and the Teton Elk." *Wyoming Wildlife* 48 (5):3.

Dixon, J. S. 1940. "Special Report on the Bear Situation at Giant Forest, Sequoia National Park California." Unpublished report, National Park Service.

————. 1938. *Birds and Mammals of Mount McKinley National Park.* National Park Service Fauna Series, no. 3. Washington, D.C.: GPO.

————. 1935. "Report on the Control of Coyotes and Cougars in and Adjacent to the Four National Parks of California." Paper presented at the Annual Meeting of the California Wool Growers Association, Nov. 21.

————. 1931. "Report on Needed Winter Range for Big Game in Rocky Mountain." Unpublished report, Rocky Mountain National Park.

Dixon, J. S., and E. L. Sumner. 1939. "The Deer Problem, Deer Trapping and Deer Removal at Zion Canyon, Utah." *Transactions of the North American Wildlife Conference* 4:231–35.

Douglas, C. L. 1976. "Coordination of Bighorn Research and Management in Joshua Tree National Monument." *Transactions of the North American Wild Sheep Conference* 2:1–14.

Douglas, C. L., and D. M. Leslie. 1984. "Simulated Effect of Transplant Removal from the River Mountains Bighorn Herd II." *Transactions of the Desert Bighorn Council* 28:26–29.

Dratch, P., et al. 1975. "A Case Study for Species Reintroduction: The Wolf in Olympic National Park." A National Science Foundation Student Study, Evergreen State College.

Drury, N. 1946. "The Wolf Problem in Mt. McKinley National Park." National Park Service memo.

Duever, M. J., et al. 1979. "Resource Inventory and Analysis of Big Cypress National Preserve." Final Report, Contract no. CX–5000–70–899.

Duncan, R. W. 1974. "Reproductive Biology of the European Wild Hog in the Great Smoky Mountains National Park." Master's Thesis, University of Tennessee.

Dunn, W. C. 1984. "Ecological Relationships between Desert Bighorn and Feral Burros in Death Valley National Monument, California." University of Nevada Cooperative Park Studies Unit Contribution no. 006/32.

Eagar, J. T., and M. R. Pelton. 1979. "Panhandler Bears in the Great Smoky Mountains National Park." Unpublished report, Great Smoky Mountains National Park.

Elfring, C. 1985. "Wildlife and the National Park Service." In *Audubon Wildlife Report,* ed. W. Chandler. New York: National Audubon Society.

Emergency Conservation Commission. 1933. "Disaster to the Yellowstone Park Elk Herds." Final Report, U.S. Department of the Interior.

Erickson, G. L. 1981. "The Northern Yellowstone Elk Herd: A Conflict of Policies." *Proceedings of the Western Association of Fish and Wildlife Agencies.* 61:92–108.

Evison, S. H. 1964. "The National Park Service—Conservator of America's Scenic and Historic Heritage." Unpublished report, National Park Service.

Finley, M. 1985. "Structure of the Feral Horse Population 1985, Cumberland Island National Seashore." University of Georgia Cooperative Park Studies Unit Technical Report no. 17.

Finley, W. L., and I. Finley. 1940. "To Feed or Not to Feed, That Is the Bear Question." *American Forests* 46(8).

Fish and Wildlife Service. 1987. "Northern Rocky Mountain Wolf Recovery Plan." Denver: United States Fish and Wildlife Service.

———. 1982. "Grizzly Bear Recovery Plan." Denver: United States Fish and Wildlife Service.

Fisher, H. 1987. "Deep Freeze for Wolf Recovery?" *Defenders of Wildlife*, Nov-Dec., 29–33.

Flewelling, B., and D. Johnson. 1981. "Wildlife Experiences and Trip Satisfaction in the Backcountry: A Preliminary Summary of the McKinley Backcountry Survey Data." University of Washington Cooperative Park Studies Unit Report.

Fox, J. R. 1972. "An Evaluation of Control Techniques for the European Wild Hog in the Great Smoky Mountains National Park of Tennessee." Master's Thesis, University of Tennessee.

Fox, J. R., and M. R. Pelton. 1973. "Observations of a White-tailed Deer Die-off in the Great Smoky Mountains National Park." *Proceedings of the Annual Conference Southeast Association of Game and Fish Commissioners* 27:297–301.

Friedrichsen, T. T. 1977. "Responses of Rodent Population to Visitors in a National Park." Master's Thesis, Colorado State University.

Garton, E. O., et al. 1990. "The Potential Impact of a Reintroduced Wolf Population on the Northern Yellowstone Elk Herd." In *Wolves for Yellowstone? A Report to the U.S. Congress.* Yellowstone National Park.

Geist. V. 1970. "A Behavioral Approach to the Management of Wild Ungulates." In *Scientific Management of Animal and Plant Communities for Conservation,* ed. E. Duffy and A. S. Watt. London: British Ecological Society.

Gennett, T. F. 1982. "Comparative Feeding Ecology of Feral Burros and Desert Bighorn Sheep in Death Valley National Monument." University of Nevada Cooperative Park Studies Unit Contribution no. 26.

Genoways, H. H., and R. J. Baker, eds. 1979. *Biological Investigations in the Guadalupe Mountains National Park, Texas.* National Park Service Proceedings and Transactions Series, no. 4. Washington, D.C.: GPO.

Giles, J. W. 1963. "Bear Facts." *American Forests* 69(7):26.

Goigel, M., and S. P. Bratton. 1983. "Exotics in Parks." *National Parks Magazine* 57(1):24–29.

Graber, D. M. 1986. "Backpackers, Backcountry Bears: The Sierra Nevada Experience." *Park Science* 7(1):12–13.

Grand Canyon National Park. 1980. "Proposed Feral Burro Management and Ecosystem Restoration Plan and Final Environmental Statement." Final Report, Grand Canyon National Park.

Grand Teton National Park. 1986. "Natural Resource Management Plan and Environmental Assessment, Grand Teton National Park." Final Report, Grand Teton National Park.

Grater, R. K. 1945. "Report of the Elk-Deer Reduction Program of 1944–45, Rocky Mountain National Park." Unpublished report, Rocky Mountain National Park.

Gray, E. M. 1943. "Elk Food Requirements in Rocky Mountain." Final Report, Colorado Department of Fish and Game Pittman-Robertson Project 4R.

Grinnell, J. B., and T. Storer. 1916. "Animal Life as an Asset of National Parks." *Science* 44:375–80.

Gruell, G. E. 1973. "An Ecological Evaluation of Big Game Ridge." Final Report, United States Forest Service Intermountain Region.

Guse, N. G. 1966. "An Administrative History of an Elk Herd." Master's Thesis, Colorado State University.

Hague, A. 1893. "The Yellowstone Park as a Game Reservation." In *American Big Game Hunting: The Book of the Boone and Crockett Club*, ed. T. Roosevelt and G. Grinnell. New York: Forest and Stream.

Haines, A. L. 1977. *The Yellowstone Story.* 2 vols. Boulder: Colorado Associated University Press.

Hall, P. 1970. "Yellowstone Elk Slaughter." *National Sportsman's Digest* 1(2):3–7.

Hampton, H. D. 1971. *How the U.S. Cavalry Saved Our National Parks.* Bloomington: Indiana University Press.

Harbour, D. 1963. "Who Should Do the Shooting? Can Public Hunting Solve the Elk Problem? Yes." *Shooting Times* 4(10).

Harms, D. R. 1977. "Black Bear Management in Yosemite." *Western State Game and Fish Commissioners Proceedings* 57:159–81.

———. 1976. "The 1975 Human-Bear Management Program, Yosemite National Park." National Park Service mimeo.

Hastings, B. C. 1986. "Wildlife-related Perceptions of Visitors in Cades Cove, Great Smoky Mountains National Park." Ph.D. diss., University of Tennessee.

———. 1982. "Human-Bear Interactions in the Backcountry of Yosemite National Park." Master's Thesis, Utah State University.

Hastings, B. C., B. K. Gilbert, and D. L. Turner. 1981. "Black Bear Behavior and Human Bear Relationships in Yosemite." University of California, Davis Cooperative Park Studies Unit Technical Report no. 2.

Hawaii Volcanoes National Park. 1986. "Natural Resources Management Plan and Environmental Assessment." Unpublished report, Hawaii Volcanoes National Park.

Hayward, P., R. G. Wright, and E. E. Krumpe. 1984. "Glacier National Park Biosphere Reserve: A History of Scientific Studies." U.S. Man in the Biosphere Report no. 9, University of Idaho.

Heimer, W. E. 1982. "Dall Sheep Management in Alaska Following Congressional Settlement of the Alaska Lands Issue." *Biennial Symposium of the Northern Wild Sheep and Goat Council* 3:1–8.

Hekkers, J. 1979. "Mountain Devil." *Colorado Outdoors,* July-Aug.

Heller, E. 1925, "The Big Game Animals of Yellowstone National Park." *Roosevelt Wildlife Bulletin* 2(4):405–67.

Henneberger, J. W. 1965. "To Protect and Preserve—A History of the National Park Ranger." Unpublished report, National Park Service.

Henning, D. H. 1965. "National Park Wildlife Management Policy: A Field Administration and Political Study at Rocky Mountain National Park." Ph.D. diss., Syracuse University.

Henry, M. 1963. *Brighty of the Grand Canyon.* New York: Rand McNally.

Herrero, S. 1974. "Conflicts between Man and Grizzly Bear in National Parks of North America." In *Bears: Their Biology and Management,* ed. M. R. Pelton, J. W. Lentfer, and G. E. Folk. IUCN Publication New Series no. 40.

———. 1970. "Human Injury Inflicted by Grizzly Bears." *Science* 170:593–98.

Hoffman, R., and R. G. Wright. 1990. "Fertility Control in a Non-native Population of Mountain Goats." *Northwest Science* 64:1–5.

Holt, H. B. 1986. "Can Indians Hunt in National Parks?" *Environmental Law* 16:207–54.

Hone, C., and C. P. Stone. 1989. "A Comparison and Evaluation of Management of Feral Pigs in Two National Parks." *Wildlife Society Bulletin,* forthcoming.

Hopkins, R. M. 1979. "The Alaskan National Monuments of 1978: Another Chapter in the Great Alaskan Land War." *Boston College Environmental Affairs Law Review* 8:59–87.

Hornaday, W. T. 1913. *Our Vanishing Wild Life.* New York: New York Zoological Society.

Hough, E. 1874. "*Forest and Stream*'s Yellowstone Park Game Exploration." *Forest and Stream,* May 5 and June 16.

Houston, D. B. 1982. *The Northern Yellowstone Elk.* New York: MacMillan.

———. 1968. "Shiras Moose in Jackson Hole, Wyoming." Grand Teton Natural History Association Technical Bulletin no. 1.

Houston, D. B., B. B. Moorhead, and R. W. Olsen. 1986. "An Aerial Census of Mountain Goats in the Olympic Mountain Range, Washington." *Northwest Science* 60:131–36.

Howe, R. 1963. "Long Range Management Plan for Northern Yellowstone Wildlife and Range." Unpublished report, Yellowstone National Park.

Hydrick, R. 1984. "The Genesis of National Park Management: John Roberts White and Sequoia National Park, 1920–1947." *Journal of Forest History* 28:68–81.

Ise, J. 1961. *Our National Park Policy: A Critical History.* Baltimore: John Hopkins University Press.

Jacobsen, T., and J. A. Kushlan. 1986. "Alligators in Natural Areas: Choosing Conservation Policies Consistent with Local Objectives." *Biological Conservation* 36:181–96.

Jenkins, K. J., and R. G. Wright. 1988. "Resource Partitioning and Competition among Cervids in the Northern Rocky Mountains." *Journal of Applied Ecology* 25:11–24.

———. 1987. "Dietary Niche Relationships among Cervids Relative to Winter Snowpack in Northwest Montana." *Canadian Journal of Zoology* 65:1397–1401.

Joffe, J. 1941. "Reminiscences." Joffe file, Yellowstone National Park Archives.

Johnson, A. 1973. "Yellowstone Grizzlies: Endangered or Prospering?" *Defenders of Wildlife News* 48(5):557–68.

Jope, K. L. 1985. "Implications of Grizzly Bear Habituation to Hikers." *Wildlife Society Bulletin* 13:32–37.

———. 1982. "Interactions between Grizzly Bears and Hikers in Glacier National Park, Montana." Oregon State University Cooperative Park Studies Unit Report no. 82–1.

———. 1981. "Factors Contributing to Effectiveness of Black Bear Transplants." *Journal of Wildlife Management* 45:102–10.

———. 1979. "Methods in the Study of Grizzly Bear in Relation to People in Glacier National Park." In vol. 5 of *Proceedings of the Second Conference on Scientific Research in the National Parks*.

Kaley, M R. 1976. "Summary of Wolf Observations since Spring 1975 in Glacier National Park." Unpublished report, Glacier National Park.

Kasten, J. 1966. "Early Wildlife Policy of Yellowstone National Park, 1872–1918." Master's Thesis, East Texas State University.

Katahira, L. K., and C. P. Stone. 1982. "Status of Management of Feral Goats in Hawaii Volcanoes." *Proceedings of the Hawaii Volcanoes Conference on Natural Science* 4:102–8.

Katmai National Park. 1987. "The Use of Interpretation to Prevent Bear Incidents in Katmai National Park." Unpublished report, Katmai National Park.

Keay, J. A. 1990. "Black Bear Population Dynamics in Yosemite National Park." Ph.D. diss., University of Idaho.

Keay, J. A., and N. G. Webb. 1989. "Effectiveness of Human-Bear Management in Protecting Visitors and Property in Yosemite National Park. In *Proceedings of the Bear-People Conflicts Symposium*, ed. M. Bromley. Northwest Territories Department of Reneweable Resources.

Keiper, R. R., M. B. Moss, and S. Zervanos. 1980. "Daily and Seasonal Patterns of Feral Ponies on Assateague Island." In vol. 8 of *Proceedings of the Second Conference on Scientific Research in the National Parks*.

Kellert, S. R. 1985. "The Public and the Timber Wolf in Minnesota." Yale University School of Forestry and Environmental Studies Report.

———. 1980. "Needed Research on People-Animal Interactions in National Parks." In vol. 6 of *Proceedings of the Second Conference on Scientific Research in the National Parks*.

Kellert, S. R., and J. K. Berry. 1980. *Knowledge, Affection, and Basic Attitudes towards Animals in American Society.* Washington, D.C.: GPO.

Kempton, H. B. 1903. "Recommendations of Planting in the Gettysburg National Military Park." Unpublished report, Department of Agriculture, Bureau of Forestry.

Kendeigh, S. C. 1942. "Research Areas in the National Parks." *Ecology* 23:236–38.

Kendall, K. C. 1986. "Grizzly and Black Bear Feeding Ecology in Glacier National Park." Unpublished progress report, Glacier National Park.

———. 1983. "Trends in Grizzly Bear/Human Interactions in Glacier National Park, Montana." Paper presented at the Sixth International Conference on Bear Research and Management, Grand Canyon National Park.

Kilgore, B. 1962. "Too Many Elk." *Sierra Club Bulletin*, Nov.

King, W. 1935. Letter to Victor H. Cahalane. July 24. Great Smoky Mountains National Park files.

Kiningham, M. J. 1980. "Density and Distribution of White-tailed Deer in Cades Cove, Great Smoky Mountains National Park, Tennessee." Master's Thesis, University of Tennessee.

Kitchell, K. P., and R. Nichols. 1987. "Scientists, Superintendents Differ on Researchers' Role in RM Region." *Park Science* 6(2):4–5.

Kituta, A. H., and C. P. Stone. 1986. "Food Preferences of Captive Feral Pigs: A Preliminary Report." In *Proceedings of the Hawaii Volcanoes Conference on Natural Science* 6:27–38.

Knight, R. R., and L. L. Eberhardt. 1985. "Population Dynamics of Yellowstone Grizzly Bears." *Ecology* 66:323–34.

———. 1984. "Projected Future Abundance of the Yellowstone Grizzly Bear." *Journal of Wildlife Management* 48:1434–38.

Krausman, P. R., and E. D. Ables. 1976. *Ecology of the Carmean Mountains White-tailed Deer, Big Bend National Park, Texas.* National Park Service Science Monograph Series, no. 15. Washington, D.C.: GPO.

Krefting, L. W. 1951. "What Is the Future of the Isle Royale Moose Herd." *Transactions of the North American Wildlife Conference* 16:461–72.

Lamb, S. H. 1938. "Wildlife Problems in Hawaii National Park." *Transactions of the North America Wildlife Conference* 3:597–602.

Laycock, G. 1974. "Dilemma in the Desert: Bighorns or Burros?" *Audubon* 76(5):116–17.

Lee, R. F. 1972. *Family Tree of the National Park System.* Philadelphia: Eastern National Parks and Monument Association.

Lemke, T. 1978. "Final Report on 1978 Wolf Survey." Worland District Office Bureau of Land Management Report no. Wyoming–019–PH8.

Leopold, A. S. 1963. "Wildlife Management in the Future." Presentation made to the superintendent's meeting, Yosemite National Park. Oct. 12.

———. 1927. Letter to Charles J. Kraebel, Superintendent, Glacier National Park. Jan. 18.

Leopold, A. S., et al. 1963. "Wildlife Management in the National Parks." *Transactions of the North American Wildlife and Natural Resources Conference* 28:28–45.

Lick, H. 1932. Letter to George W. Miller, Asst. Chief Ranger, Yellowstone National Park. Jan. 22.

Lopez, B. H. 1978. *Of Wolves and Men.* New York: Charles Scribners Sons.

McCollum, M. T. 1974. "Research and Management of Black Bears in Crater Lake National Park." Unpublished report, National Park Service.

McCullough, D. R. 1982. "Behavior, Bears, and Humans." *Wildlife Society Bulletin* 10:27–33.

McIntire, R. N. 1962. "The Threat of Public Sport Hunting in Yellowstone and Other National Parks." National Park Service mimeo.

Mack, A., et al. 1983. "A Survey of Ecological Inventory, Monitoring, and Research in the U.S. National Park Service Biosphere Reserves." *Biological Conservation* 26:33–45.

McKnight, T. L. 1958. "The Feral Burro in the United States: Distribution and Problems." *Journal of Wildlife Management* 22:163–79.

McNaught, D. 1985. "Park Visitor Attitudes toward Wolf Recovery in Yellowstone National Park." Master's Thesis, University of Montana.

Marcum, L. C. 1974. "An Evaluation of Radioactive Feces-Tagging as a Technique for Determining Population Densities of the Black Bear in the Great Smoky Mountains National Park." Master's Thesis, University of Tennessee.

Margart, J. R., and R. D. Ohmart. 1976. "Observations on the Biology of Burros on Bandalier National Monument." Unpublished report, National Park Service.

Marquis, D. A. 1983. "Regeneration of Black Cherry in the Alleghenies." In *The Hardwood Resource and Its Utilization: Where Are We Going?* Proceedings of the Hardwood Symposium of the Hardwood Research Council, U.S. Forest Service, New Orleans.

———. 1981. "Effect of Deer Browsing on Timber Production in Allegheny Hardwood Forests of Northwestern Pennsylvania." U.S. Forest Service Research Paper NE–475.

Marquis, D. A., and R. Brenneman. 1981. "The Impact of Deer on Forest Vegetation in Pennsylvania." U.S. Forest Service General Technical Report no. NE–65.

Marsh, J. 1970. "Bears and the Public in Our National Parks." *Canadian Audubon* 32:43–45.

Martinka, C. J. 1982. "Rationale and Options for Management in Grizzly Bear Sanctuaries." *Transactions of the North American Wildlife and Natural Resources Conference* 47:470–75.

———. 1969a. "Grizzly Ecology Studies, Glacier National Park." Unpublished progress report, Glacier National Park.

———. 1969b. "Ungulate Winter Ecological Studies, Glacier National Park." National Park Service Progress Report no. Glac–N–17.

Mather, S. 1928. "Remarks to the 10th Superintendents Conference, Washington, D.C." Yellowstone Library, mimeo.

Matschke, G. H. 1980. "Efficacy of Steroid Implants in Preventing Pregnancy in White-tailed Deer." *Journal of Wildlife Management* 43:756–58.

Mattson, D., B. Blanchard, and R. Knight. 1986. "Food Habits of the Yellowstone Grizzly Bear." Paper presented at the Seventh International Conference on Bear Research and Management, Williamsburg, Va.

Meagher, M. 1989. "Evaluation of Boundary Control for Bison of Yellowstone National Park." *Wildlife Society Bulletin* 17:15–19.

———. 1973. *The Bison of Yellowstone National Park.* National Park Service Scientific Monograph, no. 1. Washington, D.C.: GPO.

————. 1971. "Snow as a Factor Influencing Bison Distribution and Numbers in the Pelican Valley, Yellowstone National Park." Paper presented at the Snow and Ice Symposium, Ames, Iowa.

Mech, L. D. 1975. "Transplant and Reintroduction of Wolves in the Wild." Paper presented at the Symposium on Behavior and Ecology of Wolves, Wilmington, N.C., May 24.

————. 1970. *The Wolves of Isle Royale*. National Park Service Fauna Series, no. 7. Washington, D.C.: GPO.

Metherell, R. D. 1966. "Progress Report on the Deer Reduction Program Yosemite Deer Herd." Unpublished report, Yosemite National Park.

Mierau, G. W., and J. L. Schmidt. 1981. "The Mule Deer of Mesa Verde National Park." Mesa Verde Research Series Paper no. 2.

Minn, B. P. 1977. "Attitudes towards Wolf Reintroduction in Rocky Mountain National Park." Master's Thesis, Colorado State University.

Moehlman, P. D. 1972. "Getting to Know the Wild Burros of Death Valley." *National Geographic* 141(4):502–17.

Moment, G. 1969. "Bears and Conservation: Realities and Recommendations." *Bioscience* 19:1019–20.

Moore, B. 1925. "Nature in the National Parks." In *Hunting and Conservation*, ed. G. B. Grinnell and C. Sheldon. New Haven: Yale University Press.

Moore, T. A. 1977. "The Formation of Wildlife Perceptions." *Transactions of the Northeast Fish and Wildlife Conference* 14:81–85.

Mott, W. P. 1988. "Bringing Back the Wolf." *Courier* 33(4):1.

Murie, A. 1945. "A Review of the Mountain Sheep Situation in Mount McKinley National Park, Alaska." Unpublished mimeo.

————. 1944. *The Wolves of Mt. McKinley*. National Park Service Fauna Series, no. 5. Washington, D.C.: GPO.

————. 1940. *Ecology of the Coyote in Yellowstone*. National Park Service Fauna Series, no. 4. Washington, D.C.: GPO.

————. 1934. "The Moose of Isle Royale." University of Michigan Museum of Zoology Miscellaneous Publication no. 25.

Murie, O. J. 1952. "Elk Shooting in Grand Teton Again." *National Parks* 26(110):118.

————. 1951. "Grand Teton and Its Elk." *National Parks* 25(107).

————. 1944. "Progress Report on the Yellowstone Bear Study." Unpublished special research report, Yellowstone National Park.

Musselman, L. K. 1971. *Rocky Mountain National Park, Administrative History, 1915–1965*. Washington, D.C.: Office of History and Historic Architecture, Eastern Service Center, National Park Service.

National Academy of Science. 1974. "Report of the Committee on the Yellowstone Grizzlies." Washington, D.C.: Division of Biological Sciences, National Research Council.

National Parks and Conservation Association. 1988. *Investing in Park Futures: The National Park System Plan*. 9 vols. Washington, D.C.: National Parks and Conservation Association.

National Park Service. 1989. "Draft Statement for Management, Gettysburg National Military Park." Unpublished report, National Park Service.
———. 1988. "Management Policies." Washington, D.C.: GPO.
———. 1985. "Statement for Management, Grand Teton National Park." Final Report, National Park Service, Rocky Mountain Regional Office.
———. 1980. "State of the Parks-1980. A Report to Congress." Washington, D.C.: GPO.
———. 1963. "Wildlife Management in the National Parks." Washington, D.C.: United States Department of the Interior.
———. 1962. "Wildlife Management in the National Parks." Washington, D.C.: United States Department of the Interior.
———. 1950. "Wildlife Resources of the National Park System: A Report on Wildlife Conditions in 1950." Washington, D.C.: United States Department of the Interior.
———. 1949. "Wildlife Resources of the National Park System: A Report on Wildlife Conditions in 1949." Washington, D.C.: United States Department of the Interior.
———. 1948. "Wildlife Resources of the National Park System: A Report on Wildlife Conditions in 1948." Washington, D.C.: United States Department of the Interior.
———. 1947. "Wildlife Resources of the National Park System: A Report on Wildlife Conditions in 1947." Washington, D.C.: United States Department of the Interior.
———. 1920. "Director's Annual Report." Washington, D.C.: United States Department of the Interior.
National Wool Growers Association. 1980. Letter to the regional director, U.S. Fish and Wildlife Service. Nov. 14.
New Mexico Game Commission v. Udall. 1969. (410 F 2nd 1197, 1201). 10 Circuit Court.
Norris, P. W. 1881. "Annual Report of the Superintendent of Yellowstone National Park to the Secretary of the Interior for the Year 1880." Washington, D.C.: GPO.
Ohasi, T. J., and C. P. Stone. 1987. "Feral Goat Trend Count and Census Procedures in Haleakala National Park." Unpublished report, Haleakala National Park.
Olmsted, C. E. 1979. "The Ecology of Aspen with Reference to Utilization by Large Herbivores in Rocky Mountain." In *North American Elk: Ecology, Behavior and Management,* ed. M. Boyce and L. Hayden-Wing. Laramie: University of Wyoming Press.
Olsen, G. C. 1986. "A History of Natural Resource Management within the National Park Service." Master's Thesis, Slippery Rock University.
Packard, F. M. 1947. "A Study of the Deer and Elk Herds of Rocky Mountain National Park Colorado." *Journal of Mammalogy* 28:4–12.
———. 1946. "An Ecological Study of the Bighorn Sheep in Rocky Mountain National Park, Colorado." *Journal of Mammalogy* 27:3–28.

Paige, J. C. 1985. *The Civilian Conservation Corps and the National Park Service 1933–1942: An Administrative History.* Washington, D.C.: National Park Service.

Palmer, T. S. 1912. "National Reservations for the Protection of Wildlife." USDA Circular no. 87.

Pavlov, P. M. 1981. "Feral Pigs—Ungulate Predators." *New Zealand Journal of Ecology* 4:132–33.

Pedevillano, C., and R. G. Wright. 1987. "Mountain Goat–Visitor Interactions in Glacier National Park." *Biological Conservation* 39:1–11.

Peek, J. M. 1987. "A Case for the Wolf in Yellowstone." Unpublished report, University of Idaho.

———. 1986. *A Review of Wildlife Management.* Englewood Cliffs, N.J.: Prentice-Hall.

Peek, J. M., D. G. Miquelle, and R. G. Wright. 1987. "Are Bison Exotic in the Wrangell St. Elias National Park and Preserve?" *Environmental Management* 11:149–53.

Pelton, M. R. 1976. "Summary of Black Bear Research in the Great Smoky Mountains National Park." In *Proceedings of the Third Eastern Workshop on Black Bear Management and Research,* Hershey, Penn.

Peterson, R. O. 1986. "Ecological Studies of Wolves on Isle Royale." Michigan Technological University Cooperative Park Studies Unit Annual Report, 1985–86.

———. 1979. "The Role of Wolf Predation in a Moose Population Decline." In vol. 5 of *Proceedings of the First Conference on Scientific Research in the National Parks.*

Peterson, R. O., and J. M. Morehead. 1980. "Isle Royale Wolves and National Park Management." In vol. 7 of *Proceedings of the Second Conference on Scientific Research in the National Parks.*

Peterson, R. O., and R. J. Krumenaker. 1989. "Wolves Approach Extinction at Isle Royale: A Biological and Policy Conundrum." *George Wright Forum* 6(4):10–16.

Picton, H. D. 1978. "Climate and Reproduction of Grizzly Bears in Yellowstone National Park." *Nature* 274:888–89.

Picton, H. D., et al. 1986. "Climate, Carrying Capacity and the Yellowstone Grizzly Bear." In *Proceedings of the Grizzly Bear Habitat Symposium,* Missoula, Mt., Apr. 30–May 2. U.S. Forest Service Report no. INT 205.

Pitt, K. P. 1985. "The Wild Free-ranging Horses and Burros Act: A Western Melodrama." *Environmental Law* 15:503–31.

Post, G. 1976. "Diagnostics and Diseases of Wild Sheep." *Transactions of the Second North American Wild Sheep Conference,* Denver, Apr. 22–23.

Potts, M. K. 1938. "Observations on Diseases of Bighorn in Rocky Mountain National Park." *Transactions of the North American Wildlife Conference* 3:893–97.

Powell, R. D. 1977. "Reduction and Disposal of Surplus Wildlife." Paper presented at the Chief Rangers Conference, Jackson, Wyoming, Nov. 21–24.

Rary, J. M., et al. 1969. "The Cytogenetics of Swine in the Tellico Wildlife Management Area. *Tennessee Journal of Heredity* 59:210–14.

Ratcliff, H. M. 1941. "Winter Range Conditions in Rocky Mountain National Park." *Transactions of the North American Wildlife Conference* 6:136–40.

Ravey, R. R., and J. Schmidt. 1981. "Reintroduction of Desert Bighorn Sheep into Colorado National Monument." *Transactions of the North American Desert Bighorn Council* 25:38–42.

Ream, R. R., and U. Mattson. 1982. "Wolf Studies in the Northern Rockies." In *Wolves of the World: Perspectives of Behavior, Ecology, and Conservation*, ed. F. H. Harrington and P. C. Pacquet. Park Ridge, N.J.: Noyes Publishers.

Ream, R. R., et al. 1988. "Wolf Populations in and near Glacier National Park." Paper presented at the Annual Meeting of the Northwest Section of the Wildlife Society, Cour de Alene, Id., Apr. 18–20.

Reich, C. A. 1962. *Bureaucracy and the Forests.* Santa Clara, Calif.: Fund for the Republic.

Reid, N. J. 1968. "Ecosystem Management in the National Parks." *Transactions of the North American Wildlife and Natural Resources Conference* 33:160–68.

Reid, W. H., and G. R. Patrick. 1983. "Gemsbok in White Sands National Monument." *Southwestern Naturalist* 28:99–100.

Reiger, J. F. 1975. *American Sportsmen and the Origins of Conservation.* New York: Winchester.

Riggs, R. A., and C. Armour. 1981. "A Hypothesis for Predicting Grizzly Bear Habitat Use in Spring Floodplain Habitat Mosaics with Special Reference to Reducing Human-Bear Contact Rates." Completion Report no. 1–43, Glacier National Park.

Righter, R. W. 1982. *Crucible for Conservation: The Creation of Grand Teton National Park.* Boulder: Colorado Associated University Press.

Robbins, W. J., et al. 1963. "A Report by the Advisory Committee to the National Park Service on Research." Washington, D.C.: National Academy of Sciences.

Roseburg, D. M. 1984. "The Concept of National Preserves in Senate Bill 49: A Dangerous Precedent." *Harvard Journal of Legislation* 21:549–57.

Ruffner, G. A., G. M. Phillips, and G. W. Goldberg, eds. 1977. "Biology and Ecology of Feral Burros at Grand Canyon." Final Research Report, National Park Service.

Rush, W. 1929. "What Is to Become of Our Northern Elk Herd?" *American Forests and Forest Life* 35.

Russell, C. P. 1937. "Opportunities of the Wildlife Technician in National Parks." *Transactions of the North American Wildlife Conference* 2:68–77.

Russo, J. P. 1964. "The Kaibab North Deer Herd: Its History, Problems, and Management." Arizona Game and Fish Department Wildlife Bulletin no. 7.

Saylor, D. J. 1970. *Jackson Hole, Wyoming.* Norman: University of Oklahoma Press.

Sax, J. L., and R. B. Keiter. 1987. "Glacier National Park and Its Neighbors: A Study of Federal Inter-agency Relationships." *Ecology Law Quarterly* 14:207–63.

Schaller, G. B. 1964. "Breeding Behavior of the White Pelican at Yellowstone Lake, Wyoming." *The Condor* 66:3–23.

Scheffer, V. B. 1976. "The Future Management of Wildlife." *Wildlife Society Bulletin* 4:51–54.

———. 1946. "Mammals of the Olympic Park, Washington." Unpublished report, U.S. Fish and Wildlife Service.

Schmidly, D. J., and B. Burnette. 1980. "The Mammals of Big Thicket National Preserve." In vol. 12 of *Proceedings of the Second Conference on Scientific Research in the National Parks.*

Schnoes, R., and E. E. Starkey. 1978. "Bear Management in the National Park System." Oregon State University Cooperative Park Studies Unit Report.

Schullery, P. 1989a. "Feral Fish and Kayak Tracks: Thoughts on the Writing of a New Leopold Report." *George Wright Forum* 6(4):41–47.

———. 1989b. "Yellowstone Grizzlies: The New Breed." *National Parks and Conservation,* Nov.–Dec., 25–29.

———. 1986. *The Bears of Yellowstone.* Boulder: Roberts Rinehart.

———, ed. 1979. *Old Yellowstone Days.* Boulder: Colorado Associated University Press.

Schultz, R. D., and J. A. Bailey. 1978. "Responses of National Park Elk to Human Activity." *Journal of Wildlife Management* 42:91–100.

Scott, J. M., C. B. Kepler, and J. L. Sincock. 1985. "Distribution and Abundance of Hawaii's Endemic Land Birds: Conservation and Management Strategies." In *Hawaii's Terrestrial Ecosystems: Preservation and Management,* ed. C. P. Stone and J. M. Scott. Honolulu: University of Hawaii Press.

Senate Report. 1979. "Alaska National Interest Lands." Report no. 96–413 of the Committee on Energy and Natural Resources, U.S. Senate. Washington, D.C.: GPO.

Sequoia Kings Canyon National Park. 1987. "Wildlife Management Plan." Unpublished report, Sequoia Kings Canyon National Park.

———. 1986. "Bear Management Plan." Unpublished report, Sequoia Kings Canyon National Park.

———. 1983. "Natural Resource Management Plan." Unpublished report, Sequoia Kings Canyon National Park.

Sequoia Kings Canyon Superintendent's Annual Report. 1939. Sequoia Kings Canyon National Park files.

Servheen, C. 1986. "Habitat Research Needs for Grizzly Bear Recovery." In *Proceedings of the Grizzly Bear Habitat Symposium,* Missoula, Mt., Apr. 30–May 2. U.S. Forest Service Report no. INT 207.

Shafer, E., and G. Moeller. 1974. "Wildlife Priorities and Benefits Now, 2000 and Beyond." *Transactions of the North American Wildlife and Natural Resources Conference* 39:208–20.

Shankland, R. 1970. *Steve Mather of the National Parks.* New York: Alfred A. Knopf.

Shanks, B. 1984. *This Land Is Your Land.* San Francisco: Sierra Club Books.

Shaw, W. 1974. "Meanings of Wildlife for Americans: Contemporary Attitudes and Social Trends." *Transactions of the North American Wildlife and Natural Resources Conference* 39:151–55.

Shaw, W., and T. Cooper. 1980. "Managing Wildlife in National Parks for Human Benefits." In vol. 6 of *Proceedings of the Second Conference on Scientific Research in the National Parks.*

Shelford, V. E. 1933. "Preservation of Natural Biotic Communities." *Ecology* 14:240–45.

Sherfy, M. M. 1978. "The National Park Service and the First World War." *Journal of Forest History* 22:203–5.

Simmons, I. G. 1974. "National Parks in Developed Countries." In *Conservation in Practice,* ed. A. Warren and F. Goldsmith. New York: Wiley.

Singer, F. J. 1989. "Yellowstone Northern Range Revisited." *Park Science* 9(5):18–19.

———. 1986. "History of Caribou and Wolves in Denali National Park and Preserve—Appendices." Alaska Regional Office, National Park Service Research/Resource Management Report no. AR–11.

———. 1981. "Wild Pig Populations in the National Parks." *Environmental Management* 5:263–70.

———. 1975. "Status and History of Timber Wolves in Glacier National Park, Montana." Scientific Paper no. 1, Glacier National Park.

Singer, F. J., and S. P. Bratton. 1977. "Black Bear Human Conflicts in Great Smoky Mountains National Park." In *Bears—Their Biology and Management,* ed. C. J. Martinka and K. L. McArthur. *Proceedings of the Fourth International Conference on Bear Research and Management.*

Singer, F. J., and S. Coleman. 1980. "Ecology and Management of European Wild Boar in Great Smoky Mountain National Park. In vol. 8 of *Proceedings of the Second Conference on Scientific Research in the National Parks.*

Singer, F. J., and P. Schullery. 1989. "Yellowstone Wildlife: Populations in Process." *Western Wildlife* 15(2):18–22.

Singer, F. J., et al. 1989. "Drought, Fires, and Large Mammals." *Bioscience* 39:716–22.

Skibby, E. J. 1960. "Big Game Hunting in National Parks." *Proceedings of the Western Association of State Game and Fish Commissioners* 40:91–93.

Skinner, M. P. 1928. "The Elk Situation." *Journal of Mammalogy* 9:309–17.

———. 1927. "The Predatory and Fur Bearing Animals of the Yellowstone National Park." *Roosevelt Wildlife Bulletin* 4:163–281.

Smathers, G., and E. L. Sumner. 1975. "History of Resources Management Planning in the NPS." Unpublished report, National Park Service.

Smith, C. W. 1985. "Impact of Alien Plants on Hawaii's Native Biota." In *Hawaii's Terrestrial Ecosystems: Preservation and Management,* ed. C. P. Stone and J. M. Scott. Honolulu: University of Hawaii Press.

Stagner, H. C. 1962. "Get the Facts and Put Them to Work: A Comprehensive Natural History Research Program for the National Parks." Mimeo. Reprinted in *George Wright Forum* 1983. 3(4):28–38.

Stegeman, L. C. 1938. "The European Wild Boar in the Cherokee National Forest, Tennessee." *Journal of Mammalogy* 19:279–90.

Stevens, D. R. 1982. "Bighorn Sheep Management in Rocky Mountain National Park." *Biennial Symposium of the Northern Wild Sheep and Goat Council* 3:244–53.

———. 1980. "Elk and Mule Deer of Rocky Mountain National Park." National Park Service Report no. ROMO–N–13.

Stevens, V. 1983. "The Dynamics of Dispersal in an Introduced Mountain Goat Population." Ph.D. diss., University of Washington.

Stokes, A. J. 1970. "An Ethologist's Views on Managing Grizzly Bears." *Bioscience* 20:1154–57.

Stone, C. P. 1985. "Feral Pig Research and Management in Hawaii." Unpublished report, Hawaii Volcanoes National Park.

Stone, C. P., and J. O. Keith. 1987. "Control of Feral Ungulates and Small Mammals in Hawaii's National Parks: Research and Management Strategies." In *Control of Mammal Pests*, ed. C. G. J. Richards and J. Y. Ku. London: Taylor and Francis.

Stone, C. P., and D. B. Taylor. 1984. "Status of Feral Pig Management and Research in Hawaii Volcanoes." *Proceedings of the Fifth Conference on Natural Sciences, Hawaii Volcanoes National Park.* 5:106–17.

Storm, G. L., et al. 1989. "Population Status, Movements, Habitat Use, and Impact of White-tailed Deer at Gettysburg National Military Park and Eisenhower National Historic Site, Pennsylvania." National Park Service Technical Report no. NPS/MAR/NRTR–89/043.

Strong, W. E. 1875. *A Trip to the Yellowstone National Park in July, August and September, 1875.* Norman: University of Oklahoma Press.

Stuart, T. W. 1978. "Management Models for Human Use of Grizzly Bear Habitat." *Transactions of the North American Wildlife and Natural Resources Conference* 38:434–41.

Stupka, A. 1950. "Bears in the Great Smoky Mountains." Unpublished report, Great Smoky Mountains National Park.

Sumner, E. L. 1968. "A History of the Office of Natural Science Studies." In *Proceedings of the Meeting of Research Scientists and Management Biologists of the National Park Service,* Grand Canyon National Park, Apr. 6–8. National Park Service Office of Natural Science Studies.

———. 1967. "Biological Research and Management in the National Park Service: A History." Unpublished report, National Park Service.

———. 1959. "Effects of Wild Burros on Bighorn in Death Valley National Monument." *Transactions of the Desert Bighorn Council* 3:4–9.

Sundstrom, T. C. 1984. "An Analysis of Denali National Park Management Program to Educate Visitors Regarding Behavior while in Bear Country." Master's Thesis, University of Wyoming.

Superintendent's Annual Report. 1931. Rocky Mountain National Park Archives.

Swain, D. C., ed. 1969. "The National Parks—Six Chapters in the History of an American Idea." *American West* 6(5):4–72.

Taylor, D., and L. Katahira. 1988. "Radio Telemetry as an Aid in Eradicating Remnant Feral Goats." *Wildlife Society Bulletin* 16:297–99.

Teague, R. D. 1972. "Elk Management Problems Associated with Rocky Mountain National Park with Specific Impact on the 1963 Special Elk Season." In *Proceedings of the National Extension Wildlife Workshop,* ed. J. L. Schmidt. Estes Park, Colo., Dec. 12–14.

Theodore Roosevelt National Park. 1978. "Environmental Assessment: Proposed Feral Horse Reduction Program." Final Report, National Park Service.

Thomas, E., D. Crowe, and L. L. Kruckenberg. 1984. "Managing Teton Elk." *Wyoming Wildlife* 48(5):18–21.

Tilghman, N. G. 1989. "Impacts of White-tailed Deer on Forest Regeneration in Northwestern Pennsylvania." *Journal of Wildlife Management* 53:524–32.

Tilt, W., R. Norris, and A. S. Eno. 1987. "Wolf Recovery in the Northern Rocky Mountains." Washington, D.C.: National Audubon Society.

Titus, H. 1962. "Park Service Rebuked for Snubbing States." *Field and Stream,* Mar.

Tolson, H. A. 1944. "Is Hunting a Remedy." National Park Service memo.

———. 1933. *Laws Relating to the National Park Service.* Washington, D.C.: GPO.

Tomback, D. F. 1985. "Effect of Artificial Feeding on the Behavior and Ecology of Clark's Nutcracker in Rocky Mountain National Park." Colorado State University Cooperative Park Studies Unit Report.

Turner, M. G. 1986. "Effects of Feral Horse Grazing, Clipping, Trampling and a Late Winter Burn on a Salt Marsh, Cumberland Island National Seashore, Georgia." University of Georgia Cooperative Park Studies Unit Report no. 23.

Udall, S. 1962. Letter to D. W. Bronk, President of the National Academy of Sciences. Mar. 16.

Underwood, H. B., et al. 1989. "Deer and Vegetation Interactions on Saratoga National Historic Park." Final Report, National Park Service.

Unrau, H. D., and C. F. Williss. 1983. "Administrative History: Expansion of the National Park Service in the 1930s." Unpublished report, National Park Service.

USA v. Arch A. Moore et al. 1986. Civil Action no. 2. 86–0724.

U.S. Department of the Interior. 1962. Press release, Office of the Secretary. May 23.

U.S. Senate. 1967. "Hearings before a Subcommittee on Appropriations, U.S. Senate: First Session on Control of Elk Populations in Yellowstone National Park." Washington, D.C.: GPO.

Van Wagtendonk, J. W. 1981. "The Effect of Use Limits on Back Country Visitation Trends in Yosemite National Park." *Leisure Science* 4:311–23.

Wasem, R. 1963. "The History of Elk and Elk Management in Glacier National Park." Unpublished report, Glacier National Park.

Wauer, R. H., and J. G. Dennis. 1980. "Impacts of Feral Burros upon the Breeding Avifauna of a Pinyon Juniper Woodland in Bandelier National

Monument New Mexico." In vol. 8 of *Proceedings of the Second Conference on Scientific Research in the National Parks.*

Wauer, R. H., and W. Supernaugh. 1983. "Wildlife Management in the National Parks." *National Parks and Conservation* 57(7–9):12–16.

Weaver, J. 1978. "The Wolves of Yellowstone." Natural Resources Report no. 14, Yellowstone National Park. Washington, D.C.: GPO.

———. 1986. "Of Wolves and Grizzly Bears." *Western Wildlands* 12(3):27–29.

Welles, R. E., and F. B. Welles. 1961. *The Bighorn of Death Valley.* National Park Service Fauna Series, no. 6. Washington, D.C.: GPO.

Whitfield, M. B. 1983. "Bighorn Sheep History, Distribution, and Habitat Relationship in the Teton Mountains." Master's Thesis, Idaho State University.

Whitter, D. J. 1977. "Attitudes toward Animals and Their Users: Literature Citations and Animal Welfare Organization Data." USDA Economic Research Service Paper no. 16.

Wirth, C. L. 1980. *Parks, Politics and the People.* Norman: University of Oklahoma Press.

———. 1962. "Wildlife Conservation and Management." *National Parks Magazine* 36(172):15–17.

"Wildlife Director Rolls Over for Sheep." 1987. *Casper Wyoming, Star Tribune,* Nov. 23.

Wright, G. M., J. Dixon, and B. Thompson. 1933. "A Preliminary Survey of Faunal Relations in National Parks." National Park Service Fauna Series, no. 1. Washington, D.C.: GPO.

Wright, G. M., and B. H. Thompson. 1935. "Fauna of the National Parks of the United States." National Park Service Fauna Series, no. 2. Washington, D.C.: GPO.

Wright, R. G. 1990a. "Deer Management Alternatives for Gettysburg National Military Park and an Associated Environmental Analysis." University of Idaho Cooperative Park Studies Unit Draft Report.

———. 1990b. "An Index Bibliography of Wildlife Research in the U.S. National Parks." National Park Service Technical Report no. NPS/NRUI/NRTR–90/05.

———. 1987. "Improving the Science Program in the National Park Service: A Rejoinder." *Park Science* 6(2):14–15.

———. 1985. "Principles of New Park Area Planning as Applied to the Wrangell St. Elias Region of Alaska." *Environmental Conservation* 12:59–66.

———. 1984a. "The Challenges for Interpretation in the New Alaskan Parks." *Journal of Interpretation* 9:39–46.

———. 1984b. "Wildlife Resources in Creating the New Alaskan Parks and Preserves." *Environmental Management* 8:121–24.

Wright, R. G., and P. Hayward. 1985. "National Parks as Research Areas, with a Focus on Glacier National Park, Montana." *Bulletin of the Ecological Society of America* 66:354–57.

Yosemite National Park. 1965. "Progress Report: Deer Reduction Program." Unpublished report, Yosemite National Park.

Index